American Heretics

Catholics, Jews, Muslims, and the History of Religious Intolerance

PETER GOTTSCHALK

FOREWORD BY MARTIN E. MARTY

palgrave
macmillan

First published in 2013 by PALGRAVE MACMILLAN® in the U.S.—a division
of St. Martin's Press LLC, 175 Fifth Avenue, New York, NY 10010.

Where this book is distributed in the UK, Europe and the rest of the world, this
is by Palgrave Macmillan, a division of Macmillan Publishers Limited, registered
in England, company number 785998, of Houndmills, Basingstoke, Hampshire
RG21 6XS.

Palgrave Macmillan is the global academic imprint of the above companies and
has companies and representatives throughout the world.

Palgrave® and Macmillan® are registered trademarks in the United States, the
United Kingdom, Europe and other countries.

ISBN: 978-1-137-27829-6

Library of Congress Cataloging-in-Publication Data
Gottschalk, Peter, 1963-
    American heretics: Catholics, Jews, Muslims, and the history of religious
intolerance / Peter Gottschalk.
        pages   cm
    1. United States—Religion—History. 2. Religious discrimination—United
States—History. 3. Religious tolerance—United States—History. 4. Religions—
Relations. I. Title.
BL2525.G687   2013
    305.60973—dc23
                                                                2013019003

A catalogue record of the book is available from the British Library.

Design by Letra Libre

First edition: November 2013

10 9 8 7 6 5 4 3 2 1

Printed in the United States of America.

This book is dedicated to all the generations of my family

especially my parents

Rudolf and Babette Gottschalk

who taught me

to question

and care

MORMONS AND INDIANS.

The reported alliance between the Mormons and Indians, which forms the subject of Mr. Nast's cartoon, creates great uneasiness in Arizona and New Mexico. Scouts and other well-informed persons assert that the Mormons are furnishing the Indians with arms, ammunition, provisions, and whiskey, and that there is a prospect of a general uprising in the spring. Secretary Kirkwood has instructed the United States Indian agents to exercise the utmost diligence to ascertain the exact truth of these charges, and to promptly report any evidence of interference with the tribes under their control.

EXILES FROM RUSSIA.

The Jewish exodus from Russia, to which we referred last week, promises to assume great importance. There appears to be no prospect of any abatement in the cruel persecutions to which they are subjected by their ignorant and barbarous foes, and they are looking toward the West for a new land of promise. A company of three hundred of these refugees from the rage of fanaticism sailed from Liverpool on the 10th inst., and a pastoral of the chief rabbi in London affirms that tens of thousands of his co-religionists will probably seek new homes and freedom from persecution within the present year. He says that enormous sums will be necessary to assist them in migrating to happier lands, and in providing for their immediate wants.

A large number of these unfortunate people, driven from home by the most cruel and relentless hatred, have already found refuge in this country. They have been kindly received by their co-religionists here, who have manifested the greatest hospitality in relieving their necessities, and aiding them to reach their destination in the West.

THE WATER-COLOR ARTISTS.

The landscape artists are particularly well represented in the present Water-color Exhibition, and their work is of unusual interest. With the better knowledge that has been gained of the technical limitations of water-color painting, its scope and best uses, there has been manifested a great improvement in the general direction and purpose of the work. The qualities of water-color that constitute its principal charm are tenderness and freshness of tint, delicacy of tone, and the finer gradations and variety of atmosphere that are conveyed by the use of transparent color. These qualities are attained only by the most faithful reference to nature herself; they are not the exploits of the studio or of mere dexterity, they are the results of the most conscientious study in the presence of the objects in nature that it is sought to represent, and in the fullest sympathy with and feeling for the conditions under which nature happens to reveal them. The most simple sketches made in the open air, where the expression of a single but distinct effect has been faithfully sought, possess a far greater value than the most elaborate efforts of the self-reliant colorist, however much the latter may delight the eye by their decorative charm, or by the beauty of composition that they may contain.

With the knowledge acquired of what they could not or ought not to do, our artists naturally have become less pretentious in their choice of subjects, seeking the picturesque rather than the scenic, and contenting themselves with materials susceptible of more intimate study. Once turned in this direction, they have speedily become aware of the picturesque value of the material at their very doors, in association with which they have grown up, but of which they had before remained wholly unconscious. There had been exceptions, of course—American artists working faithfully at home, unsuspected of any particular ambition, and in the annual displays observed to their merits by pretentious Venices, Italian lakes, echoes of French art from Brittany, and color-explosions from the Orient. These were feeble reflections of no effect and purpose, imitative instead of original, and in no sense American. After a weary procession of them, it is a relief to find that the wharves, the home-tops, the streets, and the bay of even a place so near to us as New York, the woods, meadows, and common places of the country hard by us—that all such as these have a beauty and picturesque interest that are all their own, and that are as valuable for the uses of the artist as anything contained in the older continent. The best landscapes in our present exhibition, which contains the best showing of art that this country has yet made, are those that are the most simple in their subjects and the most restricted in their themes. It needs no exhaustive scrutiny to determine this, but it is interesting and instructive to look into the evidence of it that is afforded by the work of A. H. Wyant, J. F. Murphy, J. M. Shurtleff, R. M. Hunkin, C. Waggons, F. H. Smith, J. Smillie, C. Van Borneck, A. Quartley, G. H. Smillie, C. M. Dewey, B. Crane, and others. Among the most assiduous, vigorous, and effective

"WHEN THE SPRING-TIME COMES, GENTLE"—INDIAN!

POLYGAMOUS BARBARIAN. "Much guns, much ammunition, much whiskey, and much kill pale-face."

Mormons, Indians, and Jews, as depicted in Harper's Weekly *(February 18, 1882). Courtesy of Library of Congress, LC-USZ62-105116.*

Contents

List of Illustrations

*The wording of an illustration label given in quotes derives
from the original artist, photographer, or publisher.*

Foreword

Since "heresy" derives from the Greek word for "choosing" or "choice," we may think of heretics as choosers. Americans in this sense are all choosy, since, however they got to where they are, be it religiously or anti-religiously, they are free to be something else, and millions put that freedom to work. On those terms, every American, even one who chooses to stay put with an inherited, established faith or converts to a new faith community or a non-faith, can be a heretic in the eyes and minds of those who have made other choices.

That word "other" is what gets us heretics into trouble. In this book that other may be a witch or a Quaker, a Sioux who dances the Ghost Dance or the Irish Catholic, who dances to her own tunes. Jews have been the other to American Christians for more than three centuries, so, in Gottschalk's observation and analysis, they were long victims because they had made the wrong choice of parents. To complete his mini-roll-call of choosers—the author chose his examples well—he focuses on those who *really* upset neighbors who were settled into what they had considered to be sameness. The upsetters *were* different, often apart in their "sects" or "cults"—now politically classified as NRMs, members of New Religious Movements.

To majorities who feared them, wished they would go away, or victimized them, it was usually the intensity of the faith of the other that agitated them. So they were labeled fanatics. Peter Finley Dunne, an Irish-American humorist, defined "a fanatic is a man that does what he thinks the Lord would do if He knew the facts of the case."[1] Often those who opposed such fanatics took up the weapons of fanaticism themselves.

With myriad examples for a religion-scholar like Gottschalk to choose from, we who read him will judge the book in part by the choices he made and his explanation of why all this matters. His stories are attractive, but the author has a serious purpose and little time to call readers' attention to it. We re-learn that there is trouble whenever we as citizens are prejudiced and intolerant, especially when we put our prejudices to work at the expense of others. Ignorance and hatred of others are dangerous in our crowded, weapon-filled world.

Just when readers are ready to ask how can we do better? Gottschalk accommodates them with a capital-lettered version of that question: "How Can We Do Better?" It heads the last chapter which the author and many others of us hope can become the impetus to find new ways to move beyond the suspicion and hatred that plague the republic time and again. To reinforce his point, let's try italics: *We Can Do Better.* And that chapter suggests how.

Martin E. Marty
Fairfax M. Cone Distinguished Professor Emeritus,
The University of Chicago

Acknowledgments

I am first and foremost indebted to Marissa Napolitano and Kayla Reiman, whose persistent and insightful work as research assistants provided many of the materials and insights that inform this book. During my research, the staff of Wesleyan University's library system and the Library of Congress proved invaluable, especially Eric Frazier in Rare Books and Jeff Bridgers in Prints and Photographs. I also thank my daughter, Ariadne Skoufos, for her contributions in editing parts of the manuscript.

A number of colleagues offered crucial, critical readings of chapters of this book, including Sumbul Ali-Karamali, J. Spencer Fluhman, Eugene Gallagher, Anne Greene, Bruce Lawrence, Edward T. O'Donnell, Annalise Glauz-Todrank, David Walker, and—most especially—Jeremy Zwelling. Others provided feedback on various elements of the argument, including Mathew N. Schmalz, Elizabeth McAlister, John Esposito, Winnifred Fallers Sullivan, and Raymond J. DeMallie. As always, my gratitude also goes to my students, whose comments in our seminars help shape my thinking and introduce new perspectives.

The administration at Wesleyan University have been responsible for the financial and sabbatical assistance that made this volume possible. I especially appreciate the support of Dean Gary Shaw and Provost Rob Rosenthal.

I thank all of the staff at Palgrave Macmillan who helped steer this project from idea to manuscript to book. Special appreciation goes to

Laura Lancaster, Katherine Haigler, and Georgia Maas, for their detailed editing and Burke Gerstenschlager for his continued support.

Parts of chapters six and seven appeared in "Religion Out of Place: Islam and Cults as Perceived Threats in the United States," published in *From Moral Panic to Permanent War: Lessons and Legacies of the War on Terror,* edited by Gershon Shafir, Everard Meade, and William Aceves. The material is used with the permission of Routledge Press.

Finally, as ever, I am always in the debt of my family and friends, who saw less of me as I wrote this book yet continued to show unselfish support despite my absence. Beginning with my daughter and radiating outward across the bonds of love, I assure you that your presence, support, and affection run as lifeblood through these words.

Introduction

I was raised an Islamophobe.

I was brought up to be scared of Muslims and of Islam. When I imagined Muslims, I pictured men with beards, wearing flowing white garments, sometimes with guns in their hands.

When I write that I was raised this way, I don't mean that my parents instilled these lessons in my head (in fact, they would be responsible for important experiences that undermined my stereotypes). Children are not only brought up by their parents and immediate family, but by larger society as well. The society in which I was raised in the 1960s and '70s saw Muslims through the lens of a series of conflicts: the 1973 oil embargo by OPEC, the 1979 Iranian hostage crisis, and the various Arab-Israeli conflicts. It communicated these negative stereotypes about Arabs and Muslims (usually and incorrectly depicting one as necessarily the other) through entertainment and news media: scimitar-wielding oil ministers in political cartoons, ill-shaven terrorists in television dramas, leering men lusting to add women to their harems in Hollywood films, and perennially violent Muslim-majority countries in newspaper and news reports.

Only by fortuitous circumstances did my views of Muslims gradually change. In my early twenties, opportunities arose both to visit Saudi Arabia, where my parents worked at the time, and to live among Muslims (as well as Hindus, Sikhs, and Christians) for six months during a visit to India. In preparation for these overseas excursions, I took a college course on Islam with John Esposito, one of America's handful of

Islamic scholars at the time. All of this primed me for a signal moment that changed how I viewed Muslims. While sparring good-naturedly with a friend about the characteristics of Islam, Steve said, "Peter, do you hear what you're saying? You're saying that more than a billion Muslims are inherently violent." Having my long-held but never fully elucidated belief spoken back to me and held up to the light of reason, I realized how ridiculous it sounded.

Not long thereafter, a stereotype hit closer to home. While a friend, Luke, and I were sharing a conversation, he suddenly said sharply, "Well, of course you would say that, you're Catholic." Stung by the accusation, bewildered at the connection, I just stared at him dumbly. I knew Luke was Lutheran as well as he knew my religious upbringing, but our topic was wholly unrelated to religion. No one among the solid Protestant majority of my New Jersey suburb in which I had been raised had explicitly directed religious antagonism against me, so this stab of prejudice caught me unaware. Luke came from a part of the Midwest where towns tended to be distinctly Lutheran or Catholic, and stereotypical digs were not uncommon. That he had reduced my views to my Catholic heritage weighed on me, given that our topic was not in any way connected to the Church's teaching, to which—moreover—I was feeling increasingly distant.

This book results from many more moments like these. A great deal has been written and portrayed on film regarding various types of religious persecution. But despite all of these efforts, relatively little is ever said about how oppression has made sense to the people who perpetuated it at the time. Popular representations tend to treat discrimination as though it is some sort of disease that simply requires the inoculation of enlightened education or familiar contact in order to remedy it. In some instances and for some individuals, this may be exactly the right "cure." However, the fact that—as many of the instances demonstrated in the following chapters show—neighbors have often turned against neighbors suggests that matters more complex and difficult to address have often been at play. Some opine that it is the very existence of religion itself that is responsible. They optimistically suggest that if only religions would disappear, discrimination would evaporate. Too many sad moments in American history (and that of other nations) prove this to be naïve and reflect that religion often serves as the flashpoint for conflicts involving many other ingredients.

Religions are seldom solely responsible for conflict. In most of the instances demonstrated in this book, a variety of political, social, economic, and religious factors contribute to outbursts of intolerance. Moreover, underlying sentiments and sensibilities play a crucial role, especially because they are often beyond the level of intellectualization or thought. Finally, the role of nationalism cannot be underestimated. To be a proper American, it has been assumed, is to abide by certain behaviors and beliefs, which include not just membership in the nation, but devotion to it. These notions of nationalism have changed over the centuries and have sometimes favored membership in particular churches: what used to be called "the Protestant establishment."

As an American, I like to imagine myself as an individual who makes up my own mind about the world and the people within it. But as I reflect on the Islamophobia that was for so long ingrained within me, I realize that my decisions are not so simple. Long before I was mature enough to deliberate between arguments and evidence or to explore the wider world, schooling, entertainment, and everyday interactions fashioned in my mind a social world divided into groups, each with particular presumed characteristics. I'm not alone in this experience: many have to actively work backwards from the negative attitudes they considered commonsensical, challenging each assumed presupposition and being willing to buck accepted truths among their family and friends, with possible negative ramifications for doing so.

In the 1960s and '70s, it was common sense that women were worse drivers than men, that blacks committed more crimes that whites, and that all gay men were pedophiles. These received truisms remained widespread even after they were challenged by those they disparaged. Undermining these sorts of sentiments requires more than just people standing up against them; it requires those voices to be broadly heard. Women, blacks, and gays had long protested against their negative stereotypes, but it was not until the media decided to stop perpetuating these baseless portrayals that they could be undermined broadly and effectively.

For years following the 9/11 attacks, non-Muslim Americans repeatedly asked, "Where are the Muslims who protest against these actions?" In fact, Muslim and Islamic organizations like the Islamic Society of North America, the Muslim Student Association, and the Council on American-Islamic Relations routinely have condemned terrorist acts done in the name of Islam on their websites and in press releases. But until news agencies took seriously their responsibility for not only reporting acts of violence done by a few Muslims but also portraying the protests against these acts by the majority of Muslims, these perspectives seldom aired. Meanwhile, various professional Islamophobes have targeted exactly these types of groups, sowing unfounded suspicion to undermine their expressions of positive Islamic sentiment.

In the effort to open a more honest engagement with prejudices such as these, I hope that readers will not only empathize with those who have suffered discrimination but perhaps identify in some small part with those who have been responsible for perpetuating it. A community cannot progress toward greater tolerance as long as it does not grapple realistically with the dynamics of bias and constructively engage individuals struggling with the presence of bigotry in their own thoughts. However, I hasten to add that this attempt to understand belligerent views should not be mistaken for an effort to justify them, just as the endeavor to explain the worldviews and practices of particular religious groups is not an effort to validate them. Understanding is not justification.

This volume does not pretend to be a complete account of religious discrimination in America or to wholly describe the conditions of religious minorities. A comprehensive history of religious persecution would both have more material on the experiences of each group portrayed here and include many other groups, such as enslaved Africans whose religious practices were largely sheared away by the terrible blades of slavery. Moreover, it cannot hope to explore the views of all Americans at any one point in time. The book forefronts the voices of Protestant European Americans not because they are more valuable or most genuinely American, but because the book strives to discuss mainstream opinions held by those allowed the greatest say in American culture. Meanwhile, a broad account of religious pluralism in the country would not focus only on oppression and marginalization as this book does, given that even the traditions depicted here have also met

"Mr. John Rogers, minister of the gospel in London, was the first martyr in Queen MARY'S reign, and was burnt at Smithfield, February 14, 1554." The New-England Primer (1883). Wesleyan University Library, Special Collections & Archives.

acceptance, perhaps for the majority of their history, in North America. The endeavor here is not to overemphasize discrimination but to investigate it so that both its presence in the nation's history—too often celebrated for its successes without conceding its failures—and its social dynamics can be better understood in the hopes of better addressing current instances.

As an American, part of me bridles at this focus on the lapses of religious tolerance. Raised with the national creed—imbued by family and school alike—that the United States is synonymous with religious freedom, I feel like a heretic myself bringing out from under the carpet some unpleasant stories that were swept there. Despite their historical uniqueness, these instances often bear some resemblance to one another and to events today. Living up to one's own ideals is always a perilous process, but one can't start without first accepting the ways in which one has not done so. Fortuitously, these unfortunate narratives also include model moments when some Americans confronted their society's normative inequalities, leading them to publicly hold the line of pluralism and toleration—if not acceptance—despite the dire predictions, loathsome accusations, and provocative actions of their neighbors.

One

Heretics!
Blasphemers!
Witches!

Quakers in Colonial America

Beneath the unfolding blooms and still-tender leaves of New England's spring of 1660, a band of men led Mary Dyer through the streets. As they walked toward Boston Common, some in the party rapped on drums in order to drown out the possibility of their captive's voice being heard. She had walked this path only the year before, then holding the hands of two fellow prisoners similarly sentenced to death by hanging. On that occasion, her husband's request for leniency had brought her a last-minute reprieve. But now she passed where their bodies lay buried beneath the Common as she mounted the gallows stairs to once again have a noose placed around her neck. As before, she neither resisted nor protested the fate decreed when the General Court condemned her to death. Quite the opposite. Describing her time under arrest as she faced the crowd gathered beneath the gallows, she declared, "Yea, I have been in paradise several days now." This time the authorities ignored her husband's pleas, and Mary Dyer dropped to her death.

What had Dyer done that deserved execution in the minds of the court? Had she murdered? Abused? Stolen? No. Instead, her crime stemmed from publicly declaring a theology different from that of the Puritan majority. Her proclamation of Quaker beliefs earned her a death sentence because they diverged from the faith that had driven her judges' Pilgrim predecessors to cross the tempestuous Atlantic in search of—ironically enough—freedom of religion.

The courage of that earlier generation and their resilience in the face of the perils—human and natural—awaiting them in North America have become a core part of an important American national myth: oppression in their homelands led religious groups, including Catholics, Jews, Shakers, Quakers, and Puritans, to become future citizens of the New World. Then, united by their common experiences of persecution and their challenging new lives, they supposedly forged a bond based on religious freedom that became the foundation of the First Amendment in the Bill of Rights. Indeed, every year most Americans play out this ideal of religious freedom as they join their families around the table on Thanksgiving Day. Schoolchildren learn the story of these people in austere dresses and buckle-brimmed hats sharing their harvest with the Native Americans who had made survival possible. However, the image of peaceful pluralism belies the strident theology of the Massachusetts Bay Colony and the reckoning brought upon those like the Quakers who had a different understanding of humanity's relationship with God.

A SHARED STEM

The Puritans and the Quakers represented two dissenting movements of a larger stream of protest collectively called—fittingly enough—the Protestant tradition. After the Roman Catholic monk Martin Luther nailed a list of arguments countering Vatican doctrine on the door of his university's chapel in 1517, he became a symbol of the dissatisfaction European Christians felt toward the Roman Catholic Church. Throughout the Middle Ages, the popes' church had dominated Europe's religious and social life, while playing no small part in political and economic matters. But Luther's rebellion helped unleash pent-up forces that had reached a breaking point, fueling events that would permanently alter the Continent's Christian landscape. While some of the emerging denominations took their names from visionaries whose ideas crystalized into movements—Luther and Lutheranism, John Calvin and Calvinism, Menno Simons and Mennonites—others had titles that reflected defining notions of their communion, such as the Anabaptists, who required all their first adherents to take a second baptism.

A myriad of beliefs were behind the Protestant Reformation, but a democratic and individualistic impulse played a particularly important role in the formation of many of the new religions. The Catholic Church relied on a strict hierarchy of authority that largely controlled both the practice of the liturgy and the reading of the Bible, each of which occurred solely in Latin, a language known almost exclusively by the (church) educated. Protestants tended to favor a "priesthood of all believers" that undermined this hierarchy by allowing laypeople to participate in church services and Bible readings conducted in vernacular languages. One of Luther's first and most revolutionary acts was to translate the Bible into his native language of German, allowing a far greater number of his countrymen to read it, especially when the recently invented Gutenberg press made books substantially less expensive. Many Protestants also began to put more emphasis on preaching and reading the Bible and less on the celebration of the Eucharist so central to the Catholic Mass.

Across the English Channel, King Henry VIII overthrew the Vatican's sway in 1533. Although interest in annulling his marriage to a wife who had not borne him a son played a role, various other concerns drove him to found the Church of England. While sidestepping the more severe theological challenges of some Reformation leaders—such as not requiring priests to be celibate and denying the transubstantiation of the Eucharist—Henry ordered an English translation of the Bible for each church and subordinated the church establishment by declaring himself its head. As on the Continent, however, even these cautious opening moves of reform could not forestall a torrent of change driven by a complex interaction of various forces that overturned the position of the Catholic Church in Britain. By the sixteenth and seventeenth centuries, Catholics in England were becoming more marginalized and their church increasingly demonized.

In this convulsive environment, various English Protestant movements emerged, each finding varying degrees of acceptance and rejection. One of these, the Puritans, initially gained a solid foothold in England and even achieved a certain amount of political power before falling out of favor. Like many other marginalized groups, this community did not choose the name by which it became most readily known. Initially, some in the Church of England used "Puritan" as a derogatory label for those who believed that the reformation of the English church had not gone far enough in purging Catholic elements. The term covered a range of Protestant dissenters within and outside the Church of England. Some, Presbyterians, sought to remove the church's hierarchy of bishops. Others, who came to be known as Congregationalists, wanted to restructure the church so that there was no overarching organization that could dictate the affairs of local churches. At the extreme end of the Puritan spectrum, others sought to exit the Church of England entirely and establish separate congregations. Spanning these divergences, the various branches of Puritanism all shared a commitment to a highly ethical life, the notion of the priesthood of all believers, and the eschewal of any practice unwarranted by a literal interpretation of the Bible (as they understood it). They did away with ornamentation, crosses, and the emphasis on Sunday services, all of which Puritans alleged smacked of Catholicism's idolatry. Finally, most Puritans viewed themselves as responsible for reforming not only the church, but the nation as well.

The early successes of the Puritans at the end of the sixteenth century brought them political and religious influence beyond their numbers, but ultimately more mainstream forces prevailed, and they slipped into a period of persecution. Looking for an escape, a group

of separatists emigrated to the Netherlands before, driven to despera-
tion by oppression there as well, they suffered the two-month-long
passage across the Atlantic's cold, turbulent seas in the claustrophobic
one-hundred-foot-long *Mayflower*. Rejected by their fellow Britons—
and even their church—yet firm in their self-understanding as God's
chosen people, these extreme Puritans sought to redeem the so-called
New World. Confident in their witness to the true faith, they established their first settlement at Plymouth in 1620. Although the separatist Puritans represented a minority of a larger movement—most of the
adherents chose to remain in Britain—significant numbers followed the
Mayflower's example. Within a decade of Plymouth's terrible first winter, in which half its residents died, Puritans in the nearby Massachusetts Bay Colony had built the towns of Salem, Concord, Roxbury, and
Dorchester, alternately using negotiations and aggressiveness toward local Native American nations to obtain land and resources.

Ten years after the first arrival, as he and his fellow passengers prepared to make landfall after their own crossing, leader John Winthrop
expressed Puritan confidence in their community, their god, and their
right to their new land:

> Wee must delight in eache other, make others Condicions our owne
> rejoyce together, mourne together, labour, and suffer together, allwayes
> haveing before our eyes our Commission and Community in the worke,
> our Community as members of the same body, soe shall wee keepe the
> unitie of the spirit in the bond of peace, the Lord will be our God and
> delight to dwell among us.[1]

If successful, "the Lord will be our God and delight to dwell among
us," so that—borrowing a biblical image—theirs would be like a city set
upon a hill, a witness to all humanity. Winthrop pressed his companions
to imagine themselves as the Hebrews just before they set foot in the
Promised Land after their long, dangerous exodus. But God put a condition on this support. Failure would have dire consequences not simply

for individuals, but for the community as a whole. Rephrasing Moses's warning to the Hebrews, Winthrop told the Puritans that if they did not love God, care for one another, and follow God's laws, they would perish in the "wilderness" God had given them (at divinely sanctioned cost to its original inhabitants). Winthrop appeared to have in mind the Exodus incident of the dispirited Hebrews worshipping the golden calf when he warned that without steadfast faith and commitment to one another, "our heartes shall turne away soe that wee will not obey, but shall be seduced and worshipp other Gods our pleasures, and proffitts."[2] Part of the Puritan insistence on living together in settlements arose from the conviction that only with the strength and discipline of the community could individuals resist sinful temptations. The physical and social centrality of the religious meetinghouse in Puritan towns gave concrete expression to this view. While these early Puritans have proven key figures in nationalist narratives of American religious freedom, the same could not be said in regard to liberties of individual conscience, as many colonial Quakers would discover.

SOCIAL DEVIANTS

As its name expresses, the Protestant Reformation arose from protest: protest that God's instrument on Earth—the church—failed to properly teach and practice divine truth. This spirit of splitting from the church as an act of protest meant that the Reformation prompted not only breakaways from the Roman Catholic Church, but also divisions within the subsequent Protestant denominations. While some of these divisions occurred quietly—with one group peacefully drifting away from the majority—others happened loudly, as disaffected members noisily made their disagreements public. There are probably few dynamics among humans as forceful as the confluence of divine injunction and moral righteousness, and some of these splits could unleash fierce energies not only of protest but of reaction as well. Like icebergs floating into warmer waters, Christian denominations—riven with fractures—split and split again. The birth of the Quaker movement from Puritanism represented just one such fissure.

The Society of Friends, as Quakers called themselves, arose at the extreme end of the Protestant spectrum. They took the notion of a priesthood of all believers to such an extent that they eschewed all clergy. Instead of guidance from a minister who read from and preached the Bible, the religious meetings of Friends involved sitting in prayerful silence until a member—woman or man—felt compelled to speak as directed by the "inner light," guided by God. Outside of meeting their behavior could be equally nonconformist, as they refused to show any particular deference to authority, especially if it conflicted with their internal leadings.

In response to the Quaker schism, Puritans alleged blasphemy and heresy, just as the Roman Catholic Church had done for a millennium with many of its theological dissenters. However, the Puritans generally only persecuted those with differing beliefs if they remained in Puritan settlements; those who chose to migrate elsewhere were allowed to go in peace (alleged witches would be an exception, as we shall see). Like most labels used by a majority group to describe a marginalized minority, allegations of heresy reflected more about Puritan beliefs and culture than about those labeled. Puritans relied on these terms because their pursuit of religious freedom was rooted in the effort to realize rigid ideals of community identity and doctrinal cohesion that necessarily came at the cost of the freedom of others to dissent.

The allegation of heresy inherently relies on a notion of orthodoxy (literally, "correct thought").[3] However, not all religions at the time enforced a set of doctrines to which each community member must subscribe or face eviction. For instance, among the Native American nations of colonial New England, travelers often adopted the devotions of their hosts for the length of their stay as they moved from village to village. This flexibility allowed Native Americans to accept without qualms divergent beliefs and practices.[4] Ironically, the early use of the term "heresy" suggests that Christians may have once held similarly flexible attitudes. In the first century, "heresy" could neutrally refer to a school or sect, thus implying that the earliest Christians were less intolerant of differences than they were later, when the term became synonymous with unorthodoxy.[5] The experience of Martin Luther, excommunicated as a heretic in 1521 and forced to flee for his life, offers a potent demonstration of how the Catholic Church had changed its view of heresy. Not all British colonies in America held as strict a line on orthodoxy as did Massachusetts, but even those like Rhode Island that practiced a broader acceptance of dissident theologies did not practice a universally tolerant attitude.

Mary Dyer's life before she joined the Society of Friends reflected the Puritans' emphasis on the continuation of God's providence, which depended upon communal conformity over freedom of individual conscience. When she first arrived in New England in 1634 or 1635, Dyer and her husband attended the Puritan church. Over time, however, they grew close to fellow Boston resident Anne Hutchinson, her family, and Anne's unusual views. Although Hutchinson was the daughter of an Anglican minister, she later committed herself to Puritanism and—fleeing English persecution—landed in Massachusetts with her merchant husband just before the Dyers did. Hutchinson's theological knowledge and insights gained her a growing reputation in Boston until they took a turn considered dangerous by many fellow Puritans. Arguing both that moral behavior did not necessarily signal one's salvation and that each person could engage God's spirit within their soul, Hutchinson found herself at odds with the Puritan insistence on strict moral rectitude and the reliance on reading the Bible (instead of one's heart) for guidance. In other words, Hutchinson promoted a direct association with God that sidestepped prescribed Puritan practices. The colony's General Court leveled charges against her, including those for the impropriety of a woman leading the religious meetings she organized.

By challenging some of the basic tenets of Puritan society, the Hutchinson controversy became more than a theological disagreement. In Puritan America, church, faith, ritual, morality, society, and government were viewed as necessarily influencing one another as colonists sought to create a city of godly light and a bulwark against satanic darkness. The community viewed maintaining a vigilant watch against sin as paramount to its survival. During her spirited and persuasive defense, Hutchinson drew allegations of satanic delusion when she declared that God had revealed to her how she would be persecuted and the colony punished. She left the court with a sentence of banishment, walking hand in hand with a supportive Mary Dyer, whose family joined her in exile in Rhode Island in 1638.

WITCHES

After Mary Dyer's willing departure from Massachusetts, Puritan leaders did not assume that the source of her and Anne Hutchinson's heresy had left with them. Although some men in the colony also held unorthodox beliefs, the women's gender made them more susceptible to suspicions of witchcraft. And so the General Court exhumed and examined a stillborn child Dyer and her husband had buried earlier that year. The fetus's malformed body purportedly signaled the consequences of holding unorthodox beliefs, an allegation repeated after Hutchinson gave birth to a stillborn child the following year. The Puritans viewed heretical beliefs as originating from malevolent forces that would warp a godly community as surely as they deformed a fetus's body.

Dyer's and Hutchinson's Boston neighbors suspected that the devil was causing the delusions that led the women to utter their heresies. The conclusion fit the logic of the Puritans' black-and-white world. If the Bible was the word of God, then who else's voice could it be that compelled these women to defy the Bible's injunctions? Necessarily, that voice belonged to Satan. The Prince of Darkness did not work entirely among women, however, and two of Hutchinson's male followers were accused too. But women suffered special suspicion, in part because of their potential role as mothers. As other courts had before, during the gathering of evidence for her trial, Boston's General Court ordered

Hutchinson searched for "witches' teats," supposedly found on those who suckled satanic imps.[6] Both Hutchinson's and Dyer's miscarriages of malformed fetuses were further evidence to their disapproving contemporaries. The later slaughter of Hutchinson and most of her children by Indians appeared as God's vengeance for the preacher's unorthodoxy. Meanwhile, Dyer, like other Puritans who were unwilling to abide by certain laws but willing to accept corporal and even fatal punishment, prompted some Puritans to suspect demonic possession. Since so many of them gave witness despite the dire consequences they faced, Quakers often faced charges of "witchcraft, treason, and being secret agents of the Pope."[7]

If the *Mayflower* and Thanksgiving narratives represent the shiny side of Puritan life in the American imagination, the subsequent witch hunts are among its darker chapters. Although Salem, Massachusetts, would become notorious for killing those believed to be witches, charges against women (and men) throughout New England fed a terrible logic about witchcraft: the discovery of one witch signaled the probable presence of others. By the end of the seventeenth century, 234 cases of witchcraft allegation had been filed in Massachusetts and Connecticut, of which 36 ended in guilty verdicts and executions.[8] Fears of witchcraft were derived partly from baggage carried from the Old World and partly from developments in the New.

Perhaps it says something about Americans that both the Puritans as religious zealots and witches as fearsome menaces cohabitate so closely in the national imagination. If the nation annually remembers the Pilgrims at Thanksgiving, witches return just as regularly a month earlier at Halloween, as well as in movies such as *The Scarlet Letter, The Wizard of Oz, The Crucible, Wicked,* and *ParaNorman.* Yet, long before Puritans settled Massachusetts' shores and New Englanders made witchcraft a capital crime, witch hunts in Old England were some of the most brutal in all of Europe. In part, fears of witches may have originated in the Christian urge to orthodoxy that continued, if not increased, from the Catholic-dominated Middle Ages to the theologically contested post-Reformation period. After all, Europeans were not uniformly Christian. Various beliefs and practices of non-Christian origin thrived among the populace, especially in rural areas. These might counter or coincide with Christian lifestyles. For instance, in England, various individuals commonly known as "cunning folk" offered magic to help in everyday matters, especially in the curing of disease. Since their ideas and actions did not fit into an orthodox framework—and orthodoxy recognized no source for good beyond God—they became suspected of tapping into evil powers when non-orthodox thought became less tolerated.[9] Nonetheless, the popularity of non-Christian perspectives lasted so long that Protestant missionaries labored to uproot them from the English countryside until at least the nineteenth century.

If Puritan intolerance proved sharp against people of their own country, it would prove more pointed still toward those of other religions. As chapter three will show more fully, Puritan conviction regarding the ongoing war between God and Satan led them to believe that the indigenous inhabitants of New England were devil worshippers, Satan's allies, and demonic instruments. Such sentiments meant that, despite the initially peaceful interactions between the surviving Indians and the newly arrived emigrants, European expansion led to friction and conflict. Even after decades of aggressive growth, Puritans blamed the antagonism on the devil. When members of the Wabanaki Confederacy destroyed the Falmouth settlement (today's Portland, Maine) in 1690, Puritans alleged that Satan was their instigator.[10]

Despite mutual relations with Native Americans and a shared European heritage, the colonists of England's southern and middle North American colonies tended to worry far less about witches than did those in New England. This was in part due to the Puritan belief that the world's history was a series of moments in a cosmic conflict between God and Satan. The pointedness of the battle heightened with an expectation that Judgment Day loomed in the near future, so individuals and communities anxiously considered the consequences of harboring wickedness. Their close-knit communities—intended to help individuals resist temptation—likely exacerbated interpersonal tensions: many of those indicted were marginal figures in their villages long before allegations of witchcraft were made against them.

Many Puritan towns were vulnerable to fatal illness, extreme winters, and/or Indian attack. Indeed, their cross-Atlantic voyage—the survival of which was not guaranteed—primed them for this insecure existence. In these difficult conditions, it might be expected that some Puritans turned to visitors or neighbors who offered special knowledge of remedies for physical or other problems, like those provided by the cunning folk back in England. But for those who believed that the gates of heaven and hell yawned so near, and that God and Satan's legions hovered everywhere, accidents and sudden loss were often believed to have superhuman causes, and those who seemed to have unfamiliar knowledge were thought to have received it from demonic lips. This helps explain how even those who successfully cured Puritans with what we would now call folk medicine could become suspected of familiarity with Satan.[11]

This shift in Puritan concerns for Satan's influence from indigenous inhabitants to their own number requires its own explanation. One year, 1692, represented the height of Salem's witch-hunting fervor, when more alleged witches suffered execution in New England than in the entire century. The prominent Puritan preacher Cotton Mather attempted to reconcile the presence of witchery not just among the "savages" of the wilderness but among God's chosen ones when he declared, "Where will the Devil show the most malice but where he is hated, and hateth, most?"[12] Not long afterward, once the fear-driven fever broke and calmer minds prevailed, Boston's leaders made yet another shift in their interpretative stance, explaining that Satan's strategy for destroying their communities did not rely on witches but on the fear of witches. With that, New England settled into a less prosecutorial attitude regarding witchcraft. But these changes belonged to a distant future that Mary Dyer would not live to see, having succumbed to Puritan persecution for her new faith in the tenets of the Society of Friends.

FRIENDLY QUAKERS

Fifteen years after Dyer had left Massachusetts for Rhode Island, she and her husband returned to England. Traveling once again to New England in 1657, she now referred to herself as a "Friend" as a result of her encounters with George Fox, the founder of the Religious Society of Friends. Whatever dissatisfactions Dyer had with Puritan perspectives that had led her to Hutchinson found a more enduring answer in Fox, who hoped that his movement would do for Puritanism what the Puritan movement sought to do for the Church of England. Fox and many of his followers set out as itinerant preachers to challenge the status quo and redeem Christianity—and society—from its errors. Infused with and enthused by this missionary spirit, Dyer made passage once again across a restless Atlantic. Not surprisingly, in Fox's and Dyer's lifetimes, the Friends would find worse persecution at the hands of Puritans than Anglicans in England meted out to Puritans.

Although emerging from Puritanism, Quakerism brought important differences to Dyer's religious life. For instance, when she joined with other New England Friends for religious meetings, they followed a singularly different routine than that of any other Puritan congregation. Gathering in a common room, she and the others present took chairs and sat in silence, their only guide being God's spirit. No clergy directed the service, no biblical passage modeled its practice, and no routinized collection of rituals steered its participants. Ideally, it was impossible to know if someone would speak and what they would say, because their words came at God's direction through what they termed "the Inner Light" or "the Inward Light." This interior force worked in individuals without regard to gender, age, social position, or biblical knowledge. While their more orthodox Puritan neighbors understood the Bible as the central template for structuring their daily lives and religious services, Dyer and her coreligionists took the book as a guide only, giving preference to the present day's revelations wrought by God's spirit within their hearts and minds over yesteryear's writings. At times their

Philadelphia: Quäkerkirche (unknown date). Courtesy of Library of Congress,
LC-USZ62–2511.

direct experience of the Inner Light brought some Friends to tremble outwardly, spurring critics to label them "Quakers."

Although God's interior direction was valued over biblical prescriptions, Friends did not discount the Bible entirely. Indeed, informed by their own biblical interpretation, many Friends committed themselves to complete pacifism, refused to take oaths, and wore only unadorned clothing. Taking the Protestant abandonment of various Catholic sacraments one step further, they also eschewed the rituals of baptism and communion. In another important theological departure from fellow Protestants, Quakers also believed in the possibility of obtaining perfection in life, overcoming the original sin of Adam and Eve that most other Christians considered to have been transcended only by Christ. Perhaps most surprisingly for the time, women were treated as spiritual equals to men. In fact, after Fox, most of the important original Friends were women. Moreover, no obeisance was shown to people of supposedly superior position either in speech or in behavior. Friends refused to doff their hats in deference to officials or judges.[13] As Dyer's life—and death—would starkly demonstrate, their radicalness did not entirely separate the ethos of Quakers from that of other Puritans, with whom they shared strident notions of witnessing their faith no matter what challenges obstructed their efforts at redeeming Christianity and the nation.

As the Friends worked to establish a godly society—to which they shared an equal commitment with Puritans—they shifted the emphasis from community and conformity to individual freedom. This did not mean that Friends gave no importance to group life—indeed, their weekly meeting for worship demonstrated otherwise—but they did not share Winthrop's sentiments about the necessity of strict communal discipline. Whereas many Puritans viewed liberality in thought as dangerous to society at large because it threatened to challenge both the community's strict adherence to God's moral order and the ordained social and political order, Friends often viewed freedom of conscience as an individual's imperative. Hence, even though the Quaker William Penn disapproved of particular religious traditions such as Catholicism, he nevertheless established Pennsylvania as a colony based on religious toleration for all. This presaged a concept that would become critical for society when the thirteen colonies morphed into the United States a century later.

FROM HERALD TO HERETIC

Dyer's return to Massachusetts in 1657 to publicly witness her faith as a Friend almost immediately led to a jail term since the colony had outlawed preaching Quaker doctrine. Although soon released, Dyer returned to her missionary efforts determined, like so many Friends, to use her persecution as an amplifier for her message. Like knowing moths lured to the punishing flames of Massachusetts law, Quakers left their safe havens in Rhode Island and elsewhere to openly and widely testify to society about the truths they found in their particular practice as Friends, despite the very real threat of martyrdom.[14] In doing so, they followed the example of Christians as long ago as the original disciples of Christ, described in the New Testament as not only proclaiming the news about him in the face of persecution, but becoming more convincing because they did so willingly and knowingly.

In the decade before Dyer's public execution in 1660, the Puritan-led government of Massachusetts faced a challenge to their ideal of the cosmic and social order. Beginning in the 1650s, fewer New Englanders began to attend, or even belong to, a church. The northeastern colonies appeared to be slipping into the religious decentralization and moral turpitude that had seemed to characterize the Virginia colony from its start in 1607 and, later, the Maryland colony.[15] Meanwhile, Quakers directly challenged not only many of the doctrines but also the rules of behavior that were common sense to most Puritans. Male Friends took to witnessing in churches and in courts, refusing to use respectful titles, doff their hats, or otherwise show deference to presumed superiors as they protested loudly against injustices. A few female Friends went so far as to shed their clothes in public, "naked for a sign" in repetition of the biblical Isaiah who walked naked for three years as a warning to Israel (Isaiah 20).[16]

Puritan leaders gave these dissenters epithets that reflected what they saw as the danger to the social order. Those who seemed to do the opposite of what the normal social order expected such as Anne Hutchinson and Friends such as Mary Dyer became known not only as heretics and blasphemers, but also as anarchists, seditionists, and traitors. The Puritans' deep fear was also evident in the extreme punishments passed by the Massachusetts government for Quakers making public pronouncements. At times, this involved cropping an ear for the first offense, cropping the other for the second, and driving a fire-heated bore through the offender's tongue for the third. Quakers in England sometimes suffered similar punishments, and at least one Friend had a "B" for blasphemy branded on his forehead, just as New Haven authorities branded an "H" on at least one other for heresy. Meanwhile, Connecticut—first settled as a colony with the Puritan settlement at

New Haven—expelled all Friends. However, Massachusetts law went a step further when it permitted Friends to be "apprehended without warrant, where no magistrate is at hand, by any constable, commissioner, or select man." Because Quakerism represented a threat to the whole of Puritan society, the General Court bequeathed broad powers to Puritans to halt its spread. One Puritan minister promoted government violence to counter such a threat—almost Catholic in its conspiratorial nature—when he wrote, "I cannot see but that the terror of the Sword of Magistracy is to be used against such a plotted, Jesuitical, mischievous Design, as this of Quakerism is."[17] Quakers and other nonconformists who challenged Puritanism thus had to choose between suffering for their beliefs, quiescence in their disagreements, or escape to safer lands.

Rhode Island became the haven of first resort for Mary Dyer, Anne Hutchinson, and other Massachusetts misfits. Indeed, such an outcast misfit had founded the colony in 1636. As was true of Hutchinson, Roger Williams's initially warm welcome from the Puritans turned icy as his nonconformist theological and social views piqued a Puritan alarm. Purchasing land from Narragansett Indians with whom he first took refuge, Williams established a new colony that tolerated heterodoxy. "Toleration" was certainly the proper term for Williams's commitment. Although he welcomed Friends, Jews, Catholics, and Baptists to his colony and allowed them to propagate their faith, he publicly disagreed with Quakerism and Catholicism. In fact, when a Quaker of no less prominence than George Fox passed through Rhode Island during his voyage from Barbados to New England, Williams challenged him to a debate. Settling for three other Friends when Fox did not avail himself of the contest (if he even knew of it), Williams engaged in the public event and then wrote a scathing critique not so playfully entitled "George Fox digged out of his burrowes." Despite this, Friends found the colony fertile ground for proselytizing, and by the 1670s Quakers were dominant religiously and politically.[18]

Despite Rhode Island's protections, the Friends' commitment to witness their faith would lead them to perilous territory. In 1656,

Massachusetts authorities imprisoned English Friends Ann Austin and Mary Fisher almost as soon as they stepped off their ship in Boston harbor. More than a month later, officials put them on a ship to the Caribbean after burning their Quaker books and checking them for signs of witchcraft. Eight more Friends arrived the next week and endured double their predecessors' prison term before expulsion. The next year, Dyer met imprisonment when her and her husband's ship from England to Rhode Island stopped in Boston. The governor allowed her release and she left the colony. Drawn by the opportunity to witness and suffer martyrdom, at least another dozen Friends followed in the next four years; authorities expelled each in turn, sometimes after severe corporal punishment. Such sanctions notwithstanding, Quaker proselytizing yielded results, with some colony residents accepting the faith. This in turn triggered more penalties, such as fines for transporting Friends into the colony and for entertaining them. Still the missionaries came, even after 1658, when a new law leveled the death penalty on Quakers who were exiled twice yet returned once again to Massachusetts.[19]

The next year, in response to this lethal rule, Dyer and three men entered Massachusetts and were imprisoned in a furniture-less cell while awaiting judgment. A letter from her husband, William, to the General Court equated its actions with the Catholic Inquisition and "the barbarous Chinese," while arguing that Anglican bishops in England afforded imprisoned Puritans better conditions. Meanwhile, Mary, in her own letter to the court, challenged the Puritans on the very biblical landscape they used to celebrate their colonies. She admonished the magistrates to suffer like the "people of God" wandering in Sinai rather than enjoy "the pleasures of Egypt" and to endure God's judgment of plagues, suggesting that Puritan Boston now played the role of England as a place of comfortable bondage that drew Puritans away from walking with God in the wilderness and establishing a true city on the hill. In addressing the court, Mary also gave voice to the exact threat the magistrates feared: that Quakers claimed spiritual insight that preempted biblical knowledge, official position, and male authority. She wrote, "Search with the light of Christ in you, and it will show you of whom, as it hath done me, and many more, who have been disobedient and deceived, as now you are." Eventually the court released but banished her and her colleagues, under threat of death should they return.[20]

Accepting the possibility of martyrdom, Dyer's two companions returned to proselytize in Massachusetts, and the General Court rearrested them. Seeking to visit the two imprisoned Quakers, Dyer arrived a few weeks later. The court ordered her arrested and all three executed. Documents circulated by the court throughout the colony proclaimed that this would protect society from a denomination that was "destructive to fundamental trueths of religion." Fear of the condemned using the spectacle of their execution to spread their dangerous ideas compelled the court to order a beating of drums as the prisoners were escorted through Boston's streets, onto the gallows, and hanged. At the last moment, the magistrates reprieved Dyer at her husband's request. However, her two friends found no mercy and ended up buried where they were hanged in Boston Common. Afterwards, Puritans and Quakers wrangled over how Providence had judged the event. When a bridge collapsed under the weight of spectators returning from the executions, one among those present considered it punishment against Quakers and their supporters in the crowd, while some Friends determined that at least one of the accident's victims died because of some malice she hurled at the condemned.[21]

The next year Dyer returned to challenge her oppressors again, brazenly entering Boston in the middle of the day. Reflecting his view of the dark forces impelling her, one merchant who viewed the scene declared, "He must needs go whom the devil drives." Quite the opposite, Dyer understood herself obedient to the god who not only sent but accompanied her to Boston. William Dyer once again wrote the General Court after their arrest of his wife. The bewildered tone of his letter suggests his own puzzlement at Mary's adamant return to a lethally unwelcome Massachusetts. He beseeched them as fellow husbands, "So am I, yea to one dearly beloved. Oh, do not deprive me of her. . . . Pity me. I beg it with tears." Officials offered Mary a reprieve should she agree to a permanent exile, but she refused. In her last letter to the court, she expressed her steadfast commitment to give no quarter to the cruelty by which they had executed her two former companions one year earlier, but to remain devoted to God, "For he is my life, and the length of my days, and, as I said before, I came at his command, and go at his command."[22] On June 1, 1660, Mary Dyer calmly accepted the noose around her neck and her subsequent execution.

LATER

The hanging of Mary Dyer and another Friend the year following represented the culmination of the Puritan government's efforts to squash religious difference. In 1661, persuaded in part by a Quaker's written recollection of Dyer's execution, Charles II prohibited the Bay Colony from executing any more Friends. Although violence against Quakers continued there (including whipping, branding, and tongue boring), with the decline in persecution, Massachusetts lost some of the attraction it had held for Dyer and other Quaker missionaries. Yet even with the dire consequences of proselytizing, Massachusetts Friends continued to gather in their meetinghouses. The Toleration Act of 1689 aided further acceptance, though no royal decree could simply erase the malevolence felt by many in the British colonies against the Quakers.[23]

When Charles II granted Quaker William Penn permission to found Pennsylvania in 1681, a colony emerged that offered religious tolerance to Friends and other groups. Although Penn's liberal attitudes toward indigenous peoples helped maintain peace for a while, the inexorable westward expansion of the newcomers inevitably sparked friction. When war came, Friends found that their commitment to nonviolence made holding public office difficult to sustain, and so their political influence waned. Meanwhile, emerging Quaker abolitionist sentiment made the southern colonies less comfortable for Friends. With their movement now losing the zeal for proselytizing and martyrdom that the first Quakers such as George Fox and Mary Dyer had exhibited, Friends

Mary Dyer sculpture by Sylvia Shaw Judson (1959), Boston Common. Under the protection of the Boston Art Commission 2013.

did not throw themselves into the jaws of persecution but followed the western frontier's expansion over the Appalachians into new territories for settlers. An era of quietism unfolded with the turn of the eighteenth century as Friends moved more firmly into silence and introspection.

Today, Friends struggle more against steadily declining membership and the stereotyped image of Quakers found on oatmeal packaging than against physical persecution. The fact that many Americans mistake Friends for Shakers or the Amish reflects how their challenge to social norms remains in the public imagination, even though what distinguishes them from those norms remains largely unknown. With an admonishment of proselytizing, its largely unstructured meeting, and commitment to the peace testimony, Quakerism remains an unusual and historically significant, though demographically small, feature on the American religious landscape. Nevertheless, the Commonwealth of Massachusetts adopted Mary Dyer's act of individual defiance as an enduring testimony by dedicating a bronze statue of her outside the state house in Boston—not far from one of Anne Hutchinson—the inscription of which identifies her as a "witness for religious freedom." Despite modern Massachusetts' embrace of its Puritan past, Mary Dyer has come to stay.

Two

Un-American and Un-Christian

Irish Catholics

Perhaps no American city appears as thoroughly Irish as Boston. Annually, the boisterous St. Patrick's Day parade provides an opportunity for Bostonians, no matter their ethnicity, to don whatever green garments they can find in their closets in order to enjoy Irish pride. Sure, New York has its parade and Chicagoans turn their river green for the day, but for Boston the parade is an annual exclamation point for an enduring embrace of Hibernian character. Irish Americans, including the Kennedy family, the Irish famine memorial off Boston Common, James Michael Curley, and the Irish Mob represent a critical cultural cornerstone for the city.

Despite today's positive association of Boston with the Irish, both before and after the Great Famine propelled desperate men, women, and children away from the famished Emerald Isle beginning in 1845, Irish immigrants found a certain hostility in Boston. For decades, suspicion, derision, and occasional violence not uncommonly came their way. And their Catholicism spurred much, though not all, of the enmity unleashed. Indeed, Catholics found little neighborliness from Puritan colonists in the years before the War of Independence. The friction they encountered with native-born Anglo Americans demonstrates how religious intolerance often involves more than just religion, and how destructive flames can feed equally well on ethnic, class, or racial fuel. Just as New England's seventeenth-century Quaker persecutions caught fire over fear of social disruption, so the Catholic persecutions two centuries later involved religious, economic, and ethnic fears, as riots in 1834 and 1844 demonstrated so terribly well.

COLONIAL ANTI-CATHOLICISM

That many Protestants throughout the original thirteen colonies were deeply infused with anti-Catholic sentiment should come as no surprise. Some Protestants knew the bitter history of the sixteenth- and seventeenth-century European religious wars that erupted across the Continent and had heard of the extremism alleged of Catholics. Especially familiar to English Protestants was the violence that blazed during the competition for England's throne in this period, which instilled a memory of terrible oppression and excesses by both sides, Protestant and Catholic. As seemingly inoffensive a publication as *The New-England Primer* expressed the deliberate remembrance of this all too well.

Along with rudimentary teachings in the ABCs, syllables, psalms, and prayers, the many different editions of one of North America's first textbooks often included a woodcut depicting a man burning at the stake. While different artists offered their various portrayals of the 1555 execution of John Rogers, the accompanying text appears boilerplate. It describes verbally what the picture portrays visually: a Protestant minister tied to a stake heaped with wood, either about to be or already engulfed in flames as his wife and children watch. The crime justifying this grotesque punishment? Rogers's refusal to disavow his Protestant beliefs. Even after the American Revolution, generations of Protestant children (and because it was so widely used, many Catholic children too) grew up on this story of religious intolerance during the short-lived restoration of a Roman Catholic English monarchy under "Bloody Mary." Indeed, at least one edition of the *Primer* included the not-so-childlike poem:

> *Abhor that arrant whore of Rome,*
> *   And all her blasphemies;*
> *And drink not of her cursed cup–*
> *   Obey not her decrees.*[1]

As "first martyr in Queen Mary's reign," Rogers's immortalized act demonstrated to students to what lengths devotees might go to defend "the gospel of Jesus Christ" and to what depths Catholic sovereigns would sink to enforce papal obedience.

Mary Tudor's intolerance was but one of other events—some real, some imagined—that stoked popular English fears of Catholicism. In 1605, guards narrowly averted the efforts of Guy Fawkes and his co-conspirators to destroy the Houses of Parliament in response to the oppression of Catholics. The next year, Parliament established an annual commemoration, later best known for the burning of Fawkes in effigy. Seventy years later, rumors of a "Popish Plot" circulated, alleging that Jesuits sought to assassinate the (Protestant) king. An order of priests and brothers, the Jesuits long featured in European fantasies of papal machinations to undermine Protestant monarchies and churches. Many stories arose describing Jesuits craftily hatching plots, often disguising themselves to avoid detection. As the previous chapter demonstrated, at least one Puritan author described Quakerism as a Jesuit-like conspiracy against the Puritan order. The following decades witnessed many similar swirls of suspicion, often promoted by the Protestant monarchy to safeguard themselves against Catholic competitors.[2] English publications and emigrants such as Benjamin Harris, the *Primer*'s original publisher, carried these sentiments with them to the New World.

The fact that more than 6 million copies of *The New-England Primer* would be published in 450 editions over 150 years—for the first half century of which it served as the only colonially published text-book—meant that the small book was able to circulate its publisher's anti-Catholic perspectives without much competition.[3] Harris had fled London for Boston in 1686, during the reign of James II, a Catholic king who objected to his stridently critical publications. Besides the Rogers image, many editions of the *Primer* featured a crude picture of the pope accompanied by the children's rhyme:

Child, behold that Man of Sin, the Pope, worthy thy utmost Hatred.
Thou shalt find in his Head, (A) Heresy.
In his Shoulders, (B) The Supporters of Disorder.
In his Heart, (C) Malice, Murder, & Treachery.
In his Arms, (D) Cruelty.
In his Knees, (E) False Worship and Idolatry.
In his Feet, (F) Swiftness to Shed Blood.
In his Stomach, (G) Insatiable Covetousness.
In his Loyns, (H) The worst of Lusts.

Although anti-Catholicism pervaded many colonies—rendering the Catholic-founded Maryland and the religiously more tolerant Pennsylvania and Rhode Island havens for Catholics—the zealotry of its Puritan heritage helped make Massachusetts particularly unfriendly. Seminal Puritan preacher and author Cotton Mather, who helped exacerbate the excesses of the Salem witch trials, wrote that "persuading of the European powers to shake off the chains of popery" was one of the goals of his church. "Popish nations" that did free themselves, he maintained, would enjoy immediate liberties and increase in wealth. Only two generations later, the Puritan and great revivalist Jonathan Edwards described Rome as "that spiritual whore, or false church" that embodied the Antichrist. These references to the whore of Babylon and the Antichrist drew mostly on the Book of Revelation, the last chapter of the New Testament, which many Christians considered (and continue to consider) a prophetic vision of God's final judgment of humanity.

Reading Revelation in a way that uses the supposed future as a tool for understanding the present, Edwards argued that the "mighty kingdoms of Antichrist and Mahomet"—Catholicism and Islam—were Satan's desperate creations to defend his grasp on humanity against Christ's salvation.

Even Americans of a decidedly more liberal stripe than Puritans and evangelicals harbored antagonisms toward Catholicism. As mentioned in the previous chapter, Roger Williams may have made a place for Catholics in Rhode Island, but this did not stop him from disagreeing publicly with Catholicism's purported tenets. Quaker William Penn did likewise in his religiously tolerant Pennsylvania, welcoming Catholics while authoring "Seasonable Caveat against Popery," a pamphlet that began, "We hope that it may not be too late to militate for truth against the dark suggestions of papal superstition." Later, patriot Samuel Adams referred in the *Boston Gazette* to Rome as "the Beast" while describing the papacy as "the idolatry of Christians" and a threat to American rights. Every November 5, dwellers of some colonial cities celebrated an annual Pope Day, during which they pulled through the streets a float bearing a repellently dressed pope and devil. This custom, echoing England's Guy Fawkes Day, went to such lengths in Boston that the city's two ends each prepared a float with a "pope" who, when he met his counterpart, set to pummel him. At the start of the American Revolution, men dressed as Lord North, the British prime minister, and General Gage, the British military governor of Massachusetts, joined the nefarious figures atop the parade floats.[4] This reflected the patriots' anti-Catholicism, as they called king and loyalists cryptopapists against colonial liberty. Undoubtedly, Catholics of the period must have felt caught in a bind of stereotypes: eschewed by patriots as inherently pro-monarchy (because of their presumed preference for absolutism) and by loyalists as pro-French and thus anti-English (because of the Catholicism of England's longtime nemesis). However, the American enmity diminished as France and colonial Catholics threw their support behind the Revolution. Generally, conditions for

American Catholics improved after the War of Independence, as signaled by the abolition of Pope Days and the end of legal restrictions against Catholics in some states.[5]

John Carroll, the new nation's first Catholic bishop, considered the change palpable. He commented on his experience visiting Boston after his appointment in 1790:

> It is wonderful to tell what great civilities have been done to me in this town, where a few years ago a popish priest was thought to be the greatest monster in creation. Many here, even of their principal people, have acknowledged to me that they would have crossed to the opposite side of the street rather than meet a Roman Catholic some time ago. The horror which was associated with the idea of a papist is incredible; and the scandalous misrepresentations by their ministers increased the horror every Sunday.[6]

Despite the changes, certain antagonisms remained, at least among some.

Although amnesty had been won in some corners of public opinion, post-Revolutionary Catholics continued to face discrimination, some of which reflected fears of their potential political power. Only Protestants could be elected to public office in North Carolina until 1835, in New Jersey until 1844, and in New Hampshire until 1876. In New York, applicants for citizenship had to take an oath denying foreign ecclesiastical authority until the repeal of this law in 1806. In New England and the South, enduring resistance sought to deny full civic rights to those who were foreign born, Catholic, and/or without property.[7] In large part, this discrimination derived from a fear of the pope's gaining control over the future of the newly independent and still-vulnerable republic. At this time, the Presbyterian evangelist Lyman Beecher declared that the papacy holds "in darkness and bondage nearly half the civilized world." (His daughter, Harriet Beecher Stowe, later contributed her own critique when she portrayed the central slaveholding characters in *Uncle*

Tom's Cabin as Catholic.) This fear of foreign usurpation helps explain why Jesuits continued to be seen as the pope's crafty disseminators of untruth and stealthy manipulators of leaders. Propelled by a regard for the apparently superhuman intellectual and political abilities of the Jesuits, conspiracy theories abounded. The extremes of these fears prompted one Protestant minister, Calvin Colton, to write *Protestant Jesuitism* in 1836, in which he argued that anti-Catholic Protestants themselves were guilty of acting Jesuitically, as were Protestant temperance and abolitionist movements.[8]

Undoubtedly, the political and intellectual antagonisms of many Protestants grew from a visceral rejection of what they saw (or, more likely, read or heard) Catholics were doing. Besides the historical corruption of the Catholic hierarchy, its purportedly oppressive control of laypeople's minds, and the supposed sophistry associated with Jesuits that contorted the truth, many Protestants also believed Catholicism turned believers away from spiritual certainties and toward material distractions. So the Protestant Americans who might wander into a Catholic church or observe a public procession would have been primed to find objectionable, perhaps even repulsive, scenes of a devotee kneeling before a statue of Mary, the smell of incense occasionally used in services, the regalia a priest might don, and the Latin-language Mass viewed as dumbly followed by uncomprehending parishioners. Not only were such scenes alien to most Protestants, but their own beliefs and practices were in fact often explained and justified in careful contrast with Catholic ones. For instance, because the Reformation upended European Christianity by focusing Sunday services more on the reading of the Bible than on the ritual of the Eucharist—thus emphasizing the word of God over the body of God—Protestant polemics often depicted Catholics as anti-Bible. In other words, many Protestants might have found it difficult to tolerate the Catholic faith because they had been raised to define themselves as the antithesis of Catholics. Nevertheless, during the colonial period explicit expressions and acts of anti-Catholicism were generally uncommon, and Catholics built hundreds

of schools and churches without opposition during the nineteenth century.[9] Yet, as the mass arrival of Irish immigrants soon demonstrated,
negative sentiments toward Catholics, especially when combined with
other prejudices, could trigger violence.

THE ETHNIC INVASION OF THE IRISH
BEFORE THE FAMINE (1800–1840)

As anti-Catholicism grew in the early nineteenth century, Irish Americans
bore the brunt of the violence. For over one hundred years on the other
side of the Atlantic, English narratives of Irish Catholic rebellions and
massacres were used by wealthy elites as warnings against populist rioters in England. Stories of rape and the mutilation of women—especially
pregnant ones—by Irishmen helped make synonymous the words "Irish"
and "barbarism." This practiced malevolence prompted Anglo Irish satirist
Jonathan Swift to publish *A Modest Proposal* in 1729, fictitiously promoting the consumption of Irish children as a solution to the island's poverty.
The pamphlet's intentional grotesqueness expressed his assessment of the
inhumanity of English attitudes and practices there.[10]

While prospects for some Irish improved after arrival in America,
many low-skilled laborers struggled for work and were plagued by poverty, hunger, and disease. Echoing the slurs of the English press, newspapers and popular opinion in many American cities portrayed the Irish
as dirty, lazy, superstitious, and driven to drink. Some newspapers made
mention of them only in the context of some perceived threat or as
the butt of ethnic jokes. English cartoonists as early as the first years of
the nineteenth century portrayed the Irish as ape-like, with a protrud-
ing mouth, a slouched back, disheveled hair, and, if male, an unshaven
face. While these satiric images undoubtedly meant to use caricature in
order to portray the alleged moral and mental deficiencies of the Irish,
they foreshadowed a future darker racism. By the middle of the century,
English and American cartoonists would regularly portray the Irish and
Irish Americans as more physically similar to Africans than to Northern

Europeans and so, in the understanding of the time, more like apes than humans.

Sensing their isolation, Irish American Catholics began to organize to protect their interests. In New York, they founded two newspapers by 1825. Following the fashion of the day, when armed civilian groups helped maintain public order in lieu of police departments, Irish Americans established militias in many cities that complemented other Irish civic associations such as hospitals, clubs, and trade unions. Their increasing political organization triggered even more anti-Irish suspicion and rhetoric,[11] thus trapping them in yet another Catch-22: recognizing their marginalization, Irish Americans organized to promote their interests, which led to more antagonism, because it suggested they were trying to be different from other Americans. Meanwhile, as the Irish became an increasingly large percentage of Catholics in America, other Americans increasingly took "Irish" and "Catholic" as synonymous. The fact that there were plenty of Irish Protestants and non-Irish Catholics as well demonstrates how stereotypes can simplistically obscure differences within groups, such as when Americans assume all Arabs are Muslim (despite the many Christian Arabs) and that all Muslims are Arab (although only 20 percent are). In efforts to avoid these attitudes, the Protestant Irish who emigrated increasingly referred to themselves as "Scotch Irish" and chose Canada as their destination.[12]

Certain Catholic responses, some due to the quickening suspicion, marginalization, and violence Catholics encountered from the 1800s onward, helped deepen the antagonisms. The persecution peaked between 1845 and 1852 when the starvation caused by the Great Famine impelled more than a million Irish to emigrate to the United States, most of them unskilled laborers and unprepared for the urban lives they now led (which contrasted with the more skilled and educated Irish who had arrived in earlier decades). Given Protestant anxieties about the power of the Catholic clergy to control the sentiments of their parishioners, public comments like those of a Louisville, Kentucky, bishop in 1860 that likened the Reformation to a "Babel-like sound and confusion of tongues" surely curried no favor among Protestants. Certainly the more mistrustful among that audience had their suspicions confirmed when a New York archbishop in 1850 more boldly declared, "Everybody should know that we have for our mission to convert the world—including the inhabitants of the United States—the people of the cities, and the people of the country, the officers of the navy and the marines, commanders of the army, the legislatures, the Senate, the Cabinet, the President, and all!"[13] Whether or not the church leaders who made these pronouncements were Irish, their boldness, coupled with the burgeoning Irish Catholic population, alarmed Protestants who felt that their country's exceptional quality derived in no small part from its Protestant—if not its Anglo—quality.

AN EXCEPTIONAL NATION

It would be overly simplistic to explain the sharp rise in anti-Catholicism of the early nineteenth century as an accidental resurgence of old prejudices. As often happens, people draw on stereotypes of the near past in their effort to understand and respond to contemporary issues. For the rebellious colonists, the hard-fought War of Independence represented only one step in the establishment of a new nation.

Patriotism served as a term to rally militiamen, the women who supported them, the politicians who organized them, and the financiers who bankrolled them. While the cries of liberty may hearten patriots through the hellfire of battle and the challenges of wartime deprivation, some more substantial vision was required by the new country's citizens to peacefully unite them despite their divergent backgrounds, ideals, and expectations. In other words, what could convince an impoverished Georgian farmer, a New York housewife, and a wealthy Connecticut shipowner that their states should not just all go their own ways socially and politically? Although they may not have used the term, nationalism would be the answer.

In a world where practically every country on the planet has a national flag, anthem, and emblem meant to help stoke sentiments of pride and unity among all individual citizens, it is difficult to remember that nationalism is still a fairly new concept. In most of medieval Europe, a monarch served to symbolize the state. Society was structured around her or him, with a series of concentric circles of status and power radiating from the royal presence. Individuals lived as subjects to the monarchy. Beginning in the eighteenth century, the notion of nationalism began turning subjects into citizens. Responsible more to one another than to a head of state, citizens together comprised the nation, serving together in its promotion and in its defense. Anyone who has watched spectators at American sports events tear up as they sing the national anthem—and the practice of singing the anthem before sporting events is itself proof of the point—can sense the impressive capability of nationalism to stir feelings of attachment, pride, and, at times, anger.

In practice, nationalism relies on people being made uniform by a certain set of characteristics, but that does not mean that universal agreement occurs regarding which characteristics these are. In the early republic, some believed that anyone of European heritage could truly be American (as opposed to just living in the United States, which millions of African and African-heritage slaves did without the benefit of citizenship). However, not all would agree, and certain Anglo Americans saw their nation as essentially defined by an English and Protestant heritage among those natively born in the United States. This helped make the narrative of the (English Protestant) "Pilgrim fathers" crossing the Atlantic and settling so important, even though Spaniards established settlements long before the founding of Plymouth, and Native Americans millennia before then. Just as their populating of the promised land made the biblical chosen people (but not the Canaanites who already dwelled there) special, Protestants of English extraction viewed their presence as providential, and that of others as potentially threatening.

The combination of anti-Catholic and anti-Irish sentiment culminated in a perfect storm of antipathy in the 1830s. The opening of the
West meant the exit of many native-born Easterners just as European
immigration surged, bringing significant numbers of new ethnic groups
to eastern cities already swelling from regional rural migrants drawn by
urban industrial opportunities. Meanwhile, in New England the Congregationalist establishment cracked and fractured as evangelicals and
Unitarians went their own ways. As the old Puritan order that had created religious, social, moral, and legal uniformity came unraveled, opportunities opened for divergent perspectives, unnerving many New
Englanders. Many continued to believe in the United States as a promised land, but they became increasingly uncertain of its direction and
increasingly distrustful of sharing it with arrivals from abroad.[14]

Many of these self-described "natives" thus became suspicious of
the non-English immigrants helping to fuel America's nascent industrial
revolution and westward expansion. As a sense of a unique America
coalesced, distinctions from Europe deepened. For many nativists, the
United States represented newness, progress, and purity in contrast with
the agedness, tradition, and corruption of the "Old World." This proved
particularly important because the popular nationalism at the time fix-
ated on the perceived vulnerability of the American republic even as it
celebrated the republic's successful founding. The assumed tenuousness
made the arrival of Old World Catholics—associated with hierarchy,
monarchy, and state religion—a matter of potentially grave threat.[15]
This would particularly hold true in "native" perceptions of Boston and
Philadelphia's Irish Catholics of the 1830s and 1840s.

BURNING CHARLESTOWN CONVENT

After days of anticipation that "it had got to be brought down," the
mob arrived on a summer's evening in 1834. Storming the convent's
front gate, they broke windows, smashed furniture, and threw clothes,
furnishings, and books outside. Pre-warned of the assault, the nuns had

TRIAL

OF

JOHN R. BUZZELL,

THE LEADER
OF THE
CONVENT RIOTERS,
FOR
ARSON AND BURGLARY.

Destruction of the Ursuline Convent by Fire.

Committed on the *Night* of the 11th *of August,* 1834. *By the*
DESTRUCTION OF THE CONVENT
on *Mount Benedict, in Charlestown, Massachusetts.*

Containing the *Arguments of Counsel, Judges Charge, &c.*

BOSTON:
PUBLISHED BY LEMUEL GULLIVER, 82, STATE STREET.

1834.

Title page of a transcription of John R. Buzzell trial depicting the burning of the Ursuline convent (1834). Courtesy of Library of Congress.

already taken their young student charges into hiding off the grounds. Some of the assailants pranced about wearing pilfered habits on their heads, while others set the expansive, three-story brick building ablaze. Apparently dissatisfied with the extent of the destruction, men returned later to topple the trees on the grounds.

By the time the Ursuline convent was built in Charlestown—across the harbor from Boston—in 1820, the growth of Catholic schools and convents was already alarming many Bostonians. However, most Catholics could not afford the Ursuline convent school, and, even if they could, they had little interest in the elite women's education it offered. Most Irish American neighborhoods consisted of slum housing for their supremely poor population. Native Yankees often viewed these impoverished slums (which presaged Charles Dickens's baleful descriptions of industrialized England) disdainfully as the source of disease and polluted water. The bishop of Boston decided to construct the Ursuline convent school to cater mostly to Protestant students as part of an effort by leading Catholics to acculturate or "naturalize" the Catholic Church in the United States by cultivating relations with local Protestant elites.[16]

Several factors played into the crowd's decision to torch the convent. For one, when the erstwhile Puritan church split in the previous century, many of the more orthodox Congregationalists considered their rival Unitarians heretics. Some even alleged a "Unitarian conspiracy," with dissenters using concealment to infiltrate and undermine Congregationalist communities. Another factor was the recent growth of a workingmen's movement in Charlestown during the 1820s that saw America as now riven by class conflict, especially as a result of Irish immigration and Catholics' alliances with aristocrats.[17] At a time when rural and foreign immigration and Western emigration brought noticeable changes to Boston, the convent symbolized exactly what these men feared.

Meanwhile, Charlestown had become a flashpoint for tensions. Known as a particularly Irish part of the Boston region, many of its taverns catered exclusively to either an Irish or native Yankee clientele.

Advertisement for the American Patriot *nativist newspaper, Boston (1852). Courtesy of Library of Congress, LC-USZ62–96392.*

The Irish patrons had a reputation for being both boisterous and of mixed gender, which bothered many Yankees. In fall 1833, a crowd of Yankee men tore down one drinking establishment after a confrontation between two local mobs led to the death of one native man. Yankee-leaning newspapers like the *Boston Post* and *Boston Atlas* started to report spurious Irish atrocities and increasingly discussed the possibility of retributive mob violence, setting expectations that this was indeed inevitable. In 1834, reports circulated of riots in Portsmouth, New York, Rochester, Philadelphia, Baltimore, and elsewhere.[18] But more serious events would soon transpire in Boston, fueled by allegations of the mistreatment of girls.

Just before the assault on the convent, word spread throughout Boston that a recent "escapee" from the Ursulines, Sister Mary John, had been forced back to her unwilling stay there. This proved the final catalyst in a city primed for a confrontation, since the narrative of yet another supposed Boston Catholic convent captive was also making the rounds, adding to an already sensationalistic set of books about this titil-lating topic. Although Rebecca Reed would not publish her narrative, *Six Months in a Convent,* until the next year, the hearsay version was already causing a stir. Sensationalist allegations that nunneries served as "priests' prisons" where clergy kept nuns for their carnal enjoyment had long circulated in Protestant countries. Scipio de Ricci's *Female Convents: Secrets of Nunneries Disclosed* (1829) made its way from England to the United States and joined a long shelf of popular anti-Catholic litera-ture. Indeed, Anthony Gavin's *Great Red Dragon; or, The Master Key to Popery*—although first published in London in 1725—proved so popu-lar that American publishers reissued it three times between 1816 and 1855, a century after its writing. One contemporary magazine noted, "The abuse of Catholics . . . is a regular trade, and the compilation of anti-Catholic books . . . has become a part of the regular industry of the country, as much as the making of nutmegs, or the construction of clocks." Another author wrote in 1838, "Indeed the class of Anti-Popery literature, including volumes, pamphlets, tracts, and newspapers, have become so numerous, that it is impossible to read them all, unless in-deed all other reading be postponed to the all-absorbing inquiry into the abominations of Romanism."[19] Reed seemed to understand the market for her alleged story. When the convent's superior wrote a counterar-gument in response to her book, Reed and her editor fired back with another before year's end.

While many themes abounded in the anti-Catholic literature, the focus on captive women proved particularly scintillating. The titles of these contemporary potboilers amply reflect their sensationalism. One particularly popular volume demonstrated the specious quality of the allegations behind many of them. Maria Monk's *Awful Disclosures of the Hotel Dieu Nunnery of Montreal,* written two years after the Ursuline convent incident, proved a best seller, with 300,000 copies sold over twenty-five years—a notable publication run. Monk detailed how she became pregnant by a priest in a Canadian convent that the clergy estab-lished as their brothel. The mother of the supposed victim later exposed the truth about her daughter, a former prostitute who had never lived in a convent but who had lived in a Catholic women's refuge until she was evicted when she became pregnant. In fact, the influential book had been fabricated with the help of a former priest and nativist men.[20]

Fascination with and allegations about convent life fit a pattern of outsiders' fixation on Catholic secrecy. Even the church confessional excited scandal. Before the mid-twentieth century, the Catholic confessional tended to be an enclosed space where laypeople penitently shared their sins with priests who, in turn, absolved them. Besides their outrage that any crime against God and humanity could be forgiven through this seemingly moral quick fix, many Protestants worried that confession also empowered priests to manipulate women and men into revealing the intricacies of their lives and influencing their choices at home, work, and the voting booth.[21] But perhaps most enticing proved to be tales of cloistered nuns. The life of seclusion chosen by many Catholic clergy had long proved titillating material for many other non-Catholics, who imagined illicit encounters between priests and nuns. Nineteenth-century America proved no exception, especially as the rising Catholic population built more convents for both the religious sisters and the Catholic and Protestant students whom they taught. Of course, the private life of the nuns meant that the scurrilous charges could not readily be denied, especially since those most familiar with the situation were likely Catholics whose identity already impeached their testimony. Reed's exposé, therefore, found a welcome audience.

The gossip about Reed's supposed escape helped prime Boston Protestants for more sensationalism. On July 28, 1834, Sister Mary John (also known as Elizabeth Harrison) took shelter at a nearby farm while suffering from delirium. Some while later her superior escorted her back to the convent, triggering rumors—circulated as well in Boston newspapers—that the nun returned only under coercion. Soon thereafter, Congregational minister Lyman Beecher delivered three anti-Catholic sermons in a single evening to capacity crowds at three Boston churches. The next night, 2,000 area residents watched a mostly working-class mob of Scots-Presbyterian bricklayers burn the convent to the ground as the school's twelve nuns hid elsewhere with their fifty students. Some rioters went so far as to open the tomb of a recently deceased nun.[22]

In the ensuing trial (overseen by Herman Melville's father-in-law), various eyewitnesses described the attack and identified some of the assailants. The attorney general prosecuting the case alleged that death threats had resulted in few cooperating witnesses. Among those who gave evidence was Rebecca Reed, perhaps called by the defense in an effort to stoke anti-Catholic sentiment by alluding to the rumors of priestly abuses. While describing her entry into the convent, she noted that she was an Episcopalian. She went on to describe how the bishop had sent her gifts of books and how the nuns prostrated themselves before him.[23] In the end, all of the men tried were exonerated. If justice found no satisfaction from the event, the booksellers certainly did. Among the resulting bestsellers was Charles Frothingham's anti-Catholic *The Convent's Doom: A Tale of Charlestown.* Speedily written and published before the end of the year, it sold 40,000 copies in its first week.[24] The author capitalized on the eager market and subsequently wrote *Six Hours in a Convent: Or the Stolen Nuns: Tale of Charlestown in 1834,* claiming that one of the convent's "inmates" was a "near relative" of his. Twenty years after the inferno, the book had entered into its eighth edition.

THE THREAT TO SECULARISM AND
THE PROTESTANT NORM

Three months after the conflagration left the convent a blackened shell, the nuns homeless, and the students without classrooms, a Thanksgiving sermon at Boston's Church Street Church continued to raise the alarm. Reverend Abel Stevens sought to remind the congregation that the Catholic threat remained potent, especially in its challenge to American republicanism. Anticipating that some might consider his remarks "as too violent," he justified his sermon and its later publication as necessary. Stevens declared, "Genuine Christianity maintains an entire neutrality on political doctrines and measures, excepting only as far as their moral character is concerned" and added, "We consider Christianity to be . . . an absolutely necessary safeguard on civil liberty."[25] This curious claim that "genuine Christianity" removed itself from politics, yet a non-oppressive political order required it, demonstrated well how many Protestants viewed their tradition as deeply enmeshed in the character of American government not despite but because of its secular quality.

Celebrating the idea of secularism proves far easier than establishing a society based on it. Demonstrating his nationalist zeal, Stevens described four blessings that distinguished the United States from other nations: "1. A representative form of government; 2. The freedom of the press; 3. Liberty of conscience; 4. Popular education." Indeed, the concern for freedom of conscience proved central to the efforts of the Constitution's framers in establishing a secular government. They carefully crafted the First Amendment to declare, "Congress shall make no law respecting an establishment of religion, or prohibiting the free exercise thereof." In this manner, Thomas Jefferson and his contemporaries sought to avoid the English system in which the Church of England served as *the* church of England, wedded to the government by subsidies while influenced by and exercising influence on the sovereign and the Parliament. Indeed, even today, England's reigning monarch serves as titular head of the church, with the power to appoint bishops, archbishops, and cathedral deans as advised by the prime minister. Bishops and parish priests take an oath of allegiance to the monarch. The framers of the Constitution may have had the examples of Anne Hutchinson, Mary Dyer, and New England Puritans in mind as well.

However, even before the War of Independence, many American Protestants considered Catholics unsuited to the liberty of conscience. The twin notions of democracy and individual freedom relied on the assumption that each man (and at this time only men—and not all men— were considered so capable) would use reason to determine both who they wanted to politically represent them and what theology they believed. Some Americans concluded that the pope's supposed absolute dominion over Catholics robbed them of this facility. Indeed, Boston's Committee of Correspondence, which included the prominent patriot Samuel Adams, concluded in 1772 that the right "to worship according to the dictates of one's own conscience" did not extend to Catholics due to their "recognizing the Pope in so absolute a manner" under the assumed threat that disobedience might lead to excommunication and murder.[26]

A half century later, Reverend Stevens railed at Catholic education and worried aloud for the republic. He viewed the Catholic endeavor to win the approval of Protestant elites by enrolling their children as reason for further suspicion, not conciliation. From his pulpit, he asked the congregation, "If Popery is favorable to education, why does it not provide means for the instruction of its own destitute children, who throng our streets, clothed in tatters and heathenish with ignorance?" The minister noted that while "Europe is disgorging the filth of her Catholic population upon our shores," it also sent—besides missionary Jesuits—generous donations for the establishment and maintenance of schools and colleges. These financial gifts, suspect from the start owing to their foreign origin, clearly were intended to help target and convert Protestant youth, as well as to control education. It would then be a short step to the pope's obtaining political control, since "they all vote alike." Ultimately, the minister advised his listeners to exercise tolerance toward all but the Roman Catholic Church.

While explicitly warning against the spread of "heathenish" ideals through Catholic education, Stevens implicitly supported the promotion of Protestant values through existing schools, despite the necessity for Catholic (and Jewish, atheist, and agnostic) children to sit through those lessons. The members and perspectives that go unquestioned in a community help create a consensus about what is normal. For those who fit the norm, norms work invisibly. In a more recent, obvious example, until the end of the twentieth century, news sources in American cities commonly described people by race or ethnicity only when they were not white. For instance, newspapers would describe politicians by name, residence, and political party but not by race unless they were African American or Asian American, to name two examples. This silently communicated to European Americans that they should expect their politicians to be white, while more loudly—even if unintentionally—telling African Americans and Asian Americans that they should not expect to become politicians. To wit, the term "European American" did not itself become widespread until the twenty-first century, even as the term "ethnic" still tends to refer only to groups who are not Anglo American. Lasagna, gyros, curries, chow mein, and burritos may all be ethnic food, but not fish and chips. Religious norms, like racial and ethnic ones, always appear more visible to those who do not fit within them. If any Boston Catholics did not know this truth before, they certainly learned it in 1834, just as Philadelphia Catholics would a decade later.

THE PHILADELPHIA RIOTS

The United States was a particularly violent place in the 1830s and 1840s. At least 200 anti-abolition riots alone embroiled the country over this period, when Abraham Lincoln noted, "Accounts of outrages committed by mobs form the every-day news of the times. They have pervaded the country from New England to Louisiana." Certainly the convent burning quelled none of the antagonisms in Boston: in 1837, when neither an Irish Catholic funeral procession nor a native Protestant volunteer firefighter group would give way to one another on Broad Street, they fell upon one another in an impromptu rumble. But even in this turbulent time, the riots that rocked Philadelphia stood out for their ferocity.[27] Reflecting the various issues involved, they came to be known by many names—the Bible Riots, the Nativist Riots, and the Philadelphia Prayer Riots—but whatever their name, the riots for the better part of a week transformed an American working-class neighborhood into nothing less than a war zone.

As Reverend Stevens's sermon suggested in 1834, many Americans viewed their education system as a keystone of the civil order. So, in 1842, when the bishop of Philadelphia, Francis Patrick Kenrick, requested that Catholic students be allowed to read Catholic-authorized versions of the Bible in classes and allowed not to read school books with anti-Catholic content, the stage was set for allegations of papal interference. The issue arose initially when the Philadelphia schools' Board of Controllers ordered the use of the Protestant-preferred King James Bible as a basic reading text in public schools. They denied the bishop's request for an alternative Bible for Catholic students, although they did make allowance for Catholic students to leave the classroom during that specific lesson. Perhaps the matter would have ended there, with Catholic students waiting in the halls while their Protestant schoolmates did their reading exercises, had not an Irish Catholic politician found one teacher who agreed to suspend all use of the Bible in her classroom. Repeating the long-standing allegation against Catholics, declamations immediately arose that the politician was seeking to "kick the Bible out of the schools," which would undoubtedly lead to godlessness and present the pope with an opportunity to impose Catholic rule. Meanwhile, Catholics bridled at the anti-Catholic messages in some school textbooks, which appeared only normal and commonsensical to many Protestant parents.[28]

Already before 1844, many of Philadelphia's Protestants had become alarmed by the rising Catholic presence in their city. Some formed organizations in response, such as the American Protestant Association, the Sabbatarian movement, and the American Republican Party. The Sabbatarians sought to protect the God-mandated Sunday Sabbath. The American Republican Party allied itself with a movement associating alcoholism and most crime with immigrants. The party favored a twenty-one-year naturalization period for immigrants, a prohibition of anyone except native-born candidates in elected positions, and the curtailment of foreign "interference" in public and religious institutions. A very conscious concern for protecting a Protestant norm was apparent in the sentiments of at least one party member who declared, "When we remember that our Pilgrim fathers landed on Plymouth rock to establish the Protestant religion, free from persecution, we must contend that this was and always will be a Protestant country."[29]

A nativist rally scheduled in the Kensington neighborhood of Philadelphia for a Friday in May 1844 seemed like just another of many protests that had ensued following the textbook controversy. Clearly choosing the site because of its Irish immigrant population, the organizers and their followers were rewarded upon their arrival with thrown rocks and garbage. That Monday, another gathering led to a tussle among protestors and neighborhood residents followed by the sound of a shot. Gunfire erupted from Irish American homes and the local volunteer fire department, the Hibernia Hose House. Nativist reinforcements soon arrived. For two hours the opponents exchanged lethal fire, while some nativists set about destroying Irish houses. Only the arrival of a large sheriff's posse finally stopped the fighting. That night and the following day a nativist mob returned to burn a nuns' seminary, only to be repulsed by Irish American fire. Irish American snipers proved highly effective, and nativists responded by burning them out of the homes where they had holed up. Once again the fighting only stopped with the arrival of a legal force, in this case the local militia.[30]

The conflict resumed the next day, Wednesday, when nativists burned more homes of Irish Americans. With native-born firemen making little effort to intervene, the nativists continued on to burn to the ground St. Michael's Roman Catholic Church. This time, when both the sheriff and the militia arrived, the nativists left Kensington for downtown, where they confronted the mayor, who protectively stood in front of another Catholic church that they threatened. Once their stones chased him out of the way, they burned that church as well. Order was restored only after the Pennsylvania governor imposed martial law over the whole of Philadelphia.[31]

Despite, or possibly because of, the devastation caused by the riots, suspicion and resentment continued to burn long after the other

"Riot in Philadelphia, June [i.e., July] 7, 1844" (c. 1844). Courtesy of Library of Congress, LC-USZ62–3536.

fires had been put out. Two months later 5,000 nativists paraded in an anti-immigration July Fourth procession into the Irish American Southwark neighborhood, where the governor, responding to rumors that the nativists would burn the local church, had allowed an Irish American militia to stockpile weapons. Over the course of a few days, a confused set of negotiations occurred that led the militia to withdraw. However, a fierce battle subsequently exploded between nativists and government forces, during which the nativists liberated two naval cannons from the Philadelphia shipyard and brought them to bear. Fortunately the firing ceased not long thereafter.[32] Casualties included twenty dead and nearly one hundred wounded.

LATER

Tensions between Irish Americans and nativist groups deepened in the decades after the Philadelphia riots as Irish immigration reached its peak in the United States. Politically, rising nativist sentiment helped establish the strongly anti-Catholic American Party (popularly called the Know-Nothing Party for the preferred answer given by members

"Uncle Sam's youngest son, Citizen Know Nothing" (1854). Courtesy of Library of Congress, LC-USZ62–14088.

to those inquiring about it). When its candidates swept into the Massachusetts legislature, they established the "Smelling Committee" in 1855 to physically search Catholic institutions, beginning with the Jesuit-run College of the Holy Cross in Worcester and then a convent school in Roxbury.[33] They also fired Irish American state workers and disbanded Irish militias. Meanwhile, as the century wore on, biology-based racism led to the increasingly pervasive linking of Irish men and women with monkeys and apes, and—by horrid association—with Africans and African Americans. This demonstrated a discriminatory connection between race, ethnicity, and religion experienced also—though in their own ways—by Native Americans, Jews, and Muslims.

However, with the turn of the twentieth century, the ethnic prejudice of the lazy, boozy, and violent Irishman gave way to the happy-go-lucky, likable, upbeat character more evident today. Although the shadow of the Troubles in Ireland occasionally cast itself over the United States as some Irish Americans supported the cause of liberating Northern Ireland from British occupation, the American Irish became another supposed model of assimilation.

Catholicism, on the other hand, has had a slower time obtaining acceptance. Suspicions of subterfuge may have lessened, but the image of Catholics as superstitious and ritualistic has proved more resistant to change, despite the substantial liberalizing and acculturating changes ushered in after the Second Vatican Council (1962–1965) that made the Mass vernacular and encouraged certain folk practices. In 1960, presidential candidate John F. Kennedy gave an address to the Greater Houston Ministerial Association in which he felt compelled to assure this Protestant body—and the larger national audience—of his freedom from papal influence:

> I believe in an America where the separation of church and state is abso-lute—where no Catholic prelate would tell the President (should he be Catholic) how to act, and no Protestant minister would tell his parish-ioners for whom to vote—where no church or church school is granted any public funds or political preference—and where no man is denied public office merely because his religion differs from the President who might appoint him or the people who might elect him.

Kennedy prefaced his remarks by noting that Americans had never elected a Catholic president, and yet they would him, an Irish Catholic from Massachusetts. While Al Smith in the 1920s came close, his reli-gious identity clearly dogged him, as nativist groups like the Ku Klux Klan made sure it would. In an important comparison, Catholic and Republican presidential primary candidate Rick Santorum in 2011 told a college audience that "I almost threw up" the first time he read these words of Kennedy's. The next year he added, "The idea that the church can have no influence or no involvement in the operation of the state is absolutely antithetical to the objectives and vision of our country." Although voicing perhaps a minority opinion among Catholics, Santo-rum's statement serves as a measure of the distance Catholics have come from feeling the need to publicly declare their secularist commitments.

Santorum did not win the primary, but his words also did not cause a firestorm of outrage that would almost certainly have occurred in pre-vious centuries. Meanwhile, surely the fact that no Protestants sit on the Supreme Court—but six Catholics and three Jews do—signals that the white Anglo Saxon Protestant establishment has fallen away and the 25 percent of Americans who are Catholic increasingly make their presence known, as they did in the 2012 presidential election. It would seem that for most Americans, Catholicism is now as rooted in the national landscape as Protestantism.

Three

Heathens

The Sioux and the Ghost Dance

Of the many epithets that Europeans subjected Native Americans to, few rankled more than the label "heathen." The term was used synonymously with "uncivilized," "wild," "black," and "red" and served to help justify, in the minds of European Americans, the mass appropriation of Indian lands, the corralling of Indians onto reservations, their coercion into Christianity, and the annihilation of those who resisted. Over five centuries of Indian-white relationships, the Sioux proved one of the most capable nations in resisting the incursions of the federal government, and their practice of the Ghost Dance religion was widely seen as a threat to the new military, social, political, and religious order of the young country.

HEATHENS

European immigrants brought to the "New World" a fair amount of baggage about how the world worked, who populated it, and what the future would hold for different groups. For many Christian immigrants until at least the nineteenth century, humanity was divided into four basic groups: heathens, Jews, Christians, and heretics. Many read the Bible as instituting at least three of these categories, since it begins with Abraham's rejection of his family's idolatry and heathenism, the eventual establishment of the Jewish people from Abraham's lineage, and the development of the Christian message through the life of Jesus Christ. As the experience of the Quakers demonstrated, various churches used the final category of "heretics" as a way of distinguishing—and making outcasts of—those whose theological perspectives challenged the norm. The completeness with which this four-part classification system structured European Christian views of humanity became particularly evident when they began to regularly engage Muslims. Instead of creating a new label, European Christians squeezed them into existing categories, portraying them either as idolatrous (despite common Islamic prohibitions against divine images) or as heretics (presuming that the Prophet Muhammad had been a Christian who deliberately split the church).

In the view of many European Christians, heretics were the enemies of the true message of the church, Jews the bypassed former recipients of God's grace, and heathens (or "pagans") everyone else in the non-Christian world. Current heathens were survivors from an early stage of the world's history that stretched from their dominion over the ancient world to their current decline before the Light of Christ. Those who continued to exist in the modern world did so out of ignorance and isolation. However, isolation was decreasingly an option. As Europeans competed against one another for global markets, raw materials, and human resources, most of Asia, Africa, Australia, and the Americas came under their control. Many of them credited their success to their supposedly superior civilization, defined in no small part by Christianity. Hence, they often dispatched missionaries to accompany their imperial and colonial projects overseas (although it is worth noting that the Anglicans organized their first missionaries to work in English villages and cities, concerned about the "heathenish" folk superstitions they found among fellow Christians).[1]

Despite the pervasiveness and stridency of negative views, attitudes toward Native Americans were far from uniform. At one extreme, the Puritans viewed them as part of the wilderness, which, being the haunt of Satan, made them his children. Pocahontas's friend Captain John Smith claimed flatly in 1612 that the Powhatan nation's chief god "is the devil" and that they "serve him more of fear than love." Ninety years later, as the Puritan minister Cotton Mather opined on how Indians came to North America, he concluded that "we may guess that probably the Devil decoyed these miserable savages hither in hopes that the gospel of the Lord Jesus Christ would never come here to destroy or disturb his *absolute empire* over them." Revivalist Puritan leader Jonathan Edwards similarly understood that before European arrival the continent had been "wholly the possession of Satan."[2] While some converted, these "praying Indians" seldom found complete acceptance as Christians among Puritans. Indeed, during the New England–wide uprising of 1675 called King Philip's War, colonists attacked, looted, and forcibly relocated peaceful communities of Christian Native Americans in Massachusetts, where antipathies raged hottest.[3] As John Winthrop expressed in 1637, it would be to colonist advantage to root out all Indians, no matter their faith.[4] While the Puritans were the most vocal about their views, distrust of Native Americans could be found in many places.

Others viewed Native Americans, like all heathens, as possibly redeemable. In 1670, Massachusetts minister John Oxenbridge accused his brethren of renouncing the possibility of grace by rejecting Indian converts. Using one stereotype to attack another, he likened their sentiments to what he considered the legalistic exclusivity of Old Testament Jews. (Of note, although he clearly favored a more tolerant attitude toward Indians, Oxenbridge remained steadfast in his opposition to heresy, especially in the form of Quakerism.[5])

On the other end of the toleration spectrum, some early Americans viewed Native Americans as living closer to nature than urban dwellers or even agricultural workers. In an age when many believed nature revealed universal truths (note how the Declaration of Independence justified rebellion based on "the Laws of Nature and of Nature's God"), Native Americans were seen as noble savages whose daily existence allowed them to better observe and deduce natural laws than most Americans of European descent could. Such was the view, for example, of James Fenimore Cooper in *The Last of the Mohicans* (1826).

The rise of Romanticism in the eighteenth century lent another twist to this valorization of Indians living in a harmonious "state of nature," unfettered by the rationalism and materialism of an increasingly urban and industrialized world. This new perspective saw "primitive," "savage," and even "pagan" as of higher value than "sophisticated," "civilized," and even "Christian." It was perhaps in this spirit that Thomas Crawford, designer of the Statue of Freedom that tops the dome of the United States Capitol, endowed the figure with a helmet "the crest of which is composed of an eagle's head and a bold arrangement of feathers, suggested by the costume of our Indian tribes."[6] Despite these more positive—if still ill-informed—views of Native Americans, efforts to convert and civilize them from their heathen lifestyles played out locally and strategically.

Although in the seventeenth century Puritans saw God's providence as directing them to master their corner of New England and two centuries later many Americans again felt God's guiding hand directing settlers to expand into the interior of North America, there was an important difference. While the Puritans focused on founding religiously self-contained settlements cut into the wilderness, nineteenth-century Americans endeavored to realize the divinely sanctioned fate of their nation as it unfolded across a continent. The patriotic nationalism that had once galvanized Minutemen and farmwives to accept the privations of war became fuel for the expansionist drive of the nineteenth century. The erstwhile colonies that had been (and still were) the terminus for overseas migration now also became a place of departure for emigrants who pinned their hopes on an expanding western frontier. "Manifest destiny" (a term coined in 1845) became the signature idea behind this movement, and men who led the expansion of the US frontier, like Daniel Boone, and those who developed and defended it, like Davy Crockett, served as heroes for more than a century (the women involved were seldom recognized).

As a result, many Christians came to see their mission as "the taming of the wilderness," "the advancement of civilization," and "the conversion of the pagans." To them, these aims served not just as prerogatives, but as duties to God and nation. Many Native American nations recoiled westward in the face of their opponents' advanced weapons and larger forces. The names on today's maps offer signposts marking the terrible multiple exoduses caused by forceful settlement. The state of Delaware and Delaware County in Oklahoma represent the two ends of a lethal forced march by one nation. The cities of Seminole in Florida and in Oklahoma mark the coerced migration of the Seminole nation from their southeastern home to their terminus in the Midwest. For other Indian groups, like the Yahi of California, contact with settlers meant their eventual extinction.

Americans today likely have difficulty imagining the popular sentiments of the nineteenth century that viewed the culturally rich Native American nations as a barely human impediment to the national destiny. Since the late twentieth century, school curricula have celebrated Indian individuals and traditions, Indian life has become synonymous with the ecological sustainability now in vogue, and several nations have escaped the poverty still endured by others through casino receipts. Meanwhile, non-Indians attend powwow dances, offer sweat lodges at summer camps, and hang dream catchers from rearview mirrors. Yet these views of Native Americans were not held by the majority of nineteenth-century Americans.

Indeed, in that century Native American heathens became the foil against which the progress of civilization and Christianity could be measured. Elizabeth Fries Ellet evinced such a view, using the role of women as a litmus test of civilization, when she described a stretch of the Mississippi River in her 1840 travelogue:

> In the wake of the "boat of fires" [a steamboat], follows the light canoe
> of the savage chief. Thus are illustrated the first and last effort of sav-
> age and civilized man. The comparison ends not here. On the deck of
> the first, woman sits, esteemed as "Nature's last, best gift," sheltered,
> caressed, and protected, with tenderest care. In the canoe, the laborious,
> degraded squaw propels her lordly chief, humble, subdued, but uncom-
> plaining. Beside the barbarous relic of heathen darkness, is the beautiful
> result of enlightened Christianity![7]

These views led many to measure the nation's improvement by the
amount of land European Americans "settled" after they displaced natives, by how many Indian children they "educated" in distant, entirely
anglicized schools, and by how many heathens were "saved" by liberating them from their benighted traditions.

While settlers, the military, and the federal government made plans
to force Native Americans to conform to the American nation and its
destiny, missionaries sought to bring them into the Light of Christ. Mir-
roring their roles in European and American overseas empires, Christian missionaries traveled just behind the wave of white encroachment
across the American landscape, seeking to save supposedly unenlight-
ened Indians from their heathen ways or to help with their transition to
modern life. In many instances, missionaries helped operate government-
established reservations. For example, in 1869 a Congregationalist missionary to the Dakota Sioux described another missionary's encounter
with Lightning-Faced Woman (Ite-wakan-hdi-win), who "was a most
zealous heathen, devoted to the imaginary beings she had, from her infancy, been taught to worship. . . . But when the Holy Spirit, as we trust,
led her to Christ, she embraced him heartily, apparently renouncing
entirely all confidence in her idol gods."[8] The conflation of "heathen"
with "idol" worshipper demonstrates how centuries-old notions regarding non-Christians still informed some Christians' views, given that the
Sioux did not use images in their practices.

AMERICA'S DESTINY AND THE
FATE OF THE SIOUX

For most settlers involved in westward expansion, the question was not just whether Indians could be civilized, but if so, whether they would accept the process willingly. The Indian agent to the Sioux in 1859 wrote reprovingly of the commissioner of Indian affairs, who only a few years earlier had complained that the tribe had responded to all the resources expended on them by being "indolent, extravagant, and intemperate." With satisfaction, the agent now reported that 200 men had expressed their embrace of civilization by forgoing their wandering, "barbarous costume," and scalp lock haircuts. But he also understood why treaty violations infuriated the Sioux and threatened these gains. He went so far as to describe them as "a deeply wronged portion of the human family." Others considered far more drastic actions necessary. In the same year, an agent in the Oregon and Washington territories proposed taking students away from their parents—whose "prejudices and superstitions" as well as "depravity and social degradation" inured them to teachers' civilizing instruction—and raising all children elsewhere.[9]

In the eyes of many Americans, the Sioux stood futilely in the way of progress. And they seemed particularly well equipped to delay America's destiny. They had readily adopted horses into their culture after the Spanish arrival in North America and, in response to pressure from their Ojibwa neighbors, had moved westward. The various divisions of Sioux—the Lakota, the Dakota, and the Nakota language groups—soon emerged from the forests of the upper Midwest, aggressively competing with other nations to dominate the expansive plains of the Mississippi River's northern watershed. Their initial contact with European Americans came when trappers and traders entered their territories, often relying on Sioux relationships to prosper. However, the rising tide of immigration into their lands—particularly spurred by prospectors attempting to join the 1849 California Gold Rush—prompted Plains

Indians to resist. A few years later, some Sioux and other leaders signed the Treaty of Fort Laramie, which assured them reserved territories, including the religiously crucial Black Hills, if they forfeited claims to land elsewhere. The 1860s discovery of gold in Montana brought renewed government intervention as it illegally safeguarded passage for miners and settlers through the treaty-secured reservations. In response to these incursions, native bands used war and civilian attacks to protect the dwindling land allowed them.

Yet armed resistance to military and civilian occupation only reaffirmed images of Native Americans as unbridled savages, as an image from about 1875 attests. The artist portrays the angry, dark-skinned Indian at the center of a tempest of white suffering. Spiraling outward from the native man's fury is a captive baby, another baby used as a flail against his own (pregnant) mother, and an arrow-pierced man whose resistance ebbs, soon to fail entirely, as has that of the dead man below him. The setting simultaneously evokes the wilderness as the action explodes from dark, tangled growth capped by a steaming cloudscape. But the shadow of a house in the background and hint of trampled cornstalks in the foreground suggest the potential of settlement, spoiled by this unexplained murderous outburst. The image effectively communicates the artist's view that Indians threaten the white effort to settle the West and tame the land at a time when many Americans would assume that native religions reflected the primitive savagery of their warriors. In fact, the refashioning of prairies into farming plots slowly destroyed the Plains Indians' ability to live independently, robbing them of their hunting range, as well as many of the basic elements of their religious traditions.

The situation worsened once miners trespassed en masse on Indian lands to access the gold reported in the Black Hills, a site specifically revered by the Lakota as Paha Sapa. The Lakota response to the illegal presence reflected the religious significance of land to this Indian nation, particularly in regard to this one place. As hunter-gatherers, living in transportable teepees in order to pursue herds of roaming bison and

"Frontier Life" (c. 1875). Courtesy of Library of Congress, LC-DIG-pga–02280.

collect seasonal plants, the Sioux were used to living on the edge of subsistence in ways that did not as sharply distinguish them from nature as many European American lifestyles did. The land, the wildlife, the weather, and the people all played central roles in how the Sioux saw the world, and this included a bevy of superhuman forces collectively known as Wakan Tanka. While prospectors and the American government valued the Black Hills for their gold, the Sioux considered them *wakan*.

A Lakota origin narrative described how the people emerged from Paha Sapa to take their place on the earth. Subsequently, they viewed it as possessed of special status (*wakan*) because of the presence of certain spiritual agents that made it a center of the people's unity. For some Lakota at least, Paha Sapa represented the center of the Earth itself, and they repeatedly returned to it for various reasons. Given these levels of significance, it was not surprising when Sioux chiefs rebuffed government efforts to negotiate relinquishment of the hills that both the initial treaty and a subsequent treaty signed at Fort Laramie had affirmed as theirs.[10]

Nevertheless, after verifying the presence of the gold, Lieutenant Colonel George Armstrong Custer sought to spook Indians of the northern plains back into compliance with the treaties broken by the government and, also, out of the Black Hills. In his vainglorious and reckless assault of 1876, he miscalculated his target on the Little Bighorn River as a small village when, in fact, it was a sprawling encampment of Sioux and Cheyenne. Lakota leaders Sitting Bull (Tatanka Iyotake) and Crazy Horse (Ta-sunko-witko) led well-organized, fast-moving, rifle-equipped warriors who annihilated the commander and his troops in the battle described as Custer's Last Stand. While other chiefs led their people back to the reservations, these two refused at first, only to surrender in the end. Ultimately, the government superseded the earlier treaties and successfully pressured some Sioux leaders to sign away half of their lands, including the Black Hills, and accept the remaining territory as a series of reservations.[11]

However, in the 1880s, tensions mounted again. Required to live on reservations too small to sustain their nomadic lifestyle and unable or unwilling to adopt the life as farmers that the government wanted for them, most Sioux became reliant on federal rations of food and clothing. The government occasionally withheld part of these rations in order to force the Sioux into compliance on various matters. Meanwhile, missionaries asserted an increasing influence, especially on the reservations. For instance, in 1875 Episcopalians established the first mission on the Lakota reservation of Pine Ridge. German Jesuits arrived in 1888 to establish the Holy Rosary Mission. Less than a century later, nearly thirty churches dotted the reservation. The variety of Christians brought a variety of sentiments about the Lakota. Even among the Jesuits there were different levels of respect and disregard for indigenous religion at various times, some disparaging medicine men as frauds, others adopting Lakota religious terms to fit Catholic theology. Missionaries sought to improve the Sioux through what we would call today "quality of life" efforts—Catholics, for instance, established schools—while also endeavoring to proselytize.[12]

Government officials often, too, deprecated native religious customs in their pursuit of another type of conversion—to "civilization." In 1882 the secretary of the interior expressed his concerns to the commissioner of Indian affairs about hindrances to civilizing Indians. These included "the continuance of the old heathen dances, such as the sun dance," multiple marriages, the destruction or distribution of property at funerals, and medicine men, whom he viewed as allies of "anti-progressive" Indians. In 1883, the commissioner forbade all these practices and the role of medicine men under penalty of fines, withholding of rations, or imprisonment.[13] Others considered civilization impossible for Plains Indians to attain. In his autobiography, Custer explicitly discredited James Fenimore Cooper's portrayal of Indians and declared, "Civilization may and should do much for him, but it can never civilize him." Without remorse, Custer explained that if civilization demands their land and Indians do not yield, "it will roll mercilessly over him . . . and the world looks on and nods its approval."[14] These circumstances left many Sioux in a difficult position, where acquiescence to current conditions would extinguish their former ways, if not their very lives, but resistance might be equally suicidal. Into this desperate situation a new religious avenue promised radical hope.

GHOST DANCING

News reached both the Sioux on reservations and the reservation-defying bands of a seer, Wovoka (also known as Jack Wilson), from the

Paiute nation of today's Nevada. The Sioux recognized some individuals among them as possessing specific powers, such as *wicasa wakan,* those endowed with powerful visions and insights who interacted with the forces collectively known as Wakan Tanka. Some groups of Sioux men traveled to hear Wovoka, who claimed to have had a vision that made possible the return of not only the bison, but all the Sioux dead, through the performance of the Ghost Dance. Various nations throughout the West, Northwest, and Midwest decided to perform the dance of Wovoka's vision, but each interpreted his message in a different manner. Some took heed of his injunctions not to fight, injure anyone, or lie. Given their warrior culture and desperate situation, the Sioux's interpretation of the Ghost Dance vision took a more militant turn. As they danced, the Sioux expected that the idyllic world returning their dead and bison would extinguish the *Wasichu,* or whites. Understandably, this was unwelcome news to the US military.

Despite the prevalence of Christianity in many walks of life, many Americans still feared the power of religion to disrupt society when unbridled. As the European wars of religion had demonstrated long ago and, according to some, as Puritan excesses had proved more recently, the unchecked passions unleashed by theological dogmatism or excited delusion could wreak havoc on public life. Now the federal government faced the potential of a new Sioux uprising fueled by the fantasy of the devastation of white civilization. National newspapers fanned pensive expectations with headlines such as "Messiah Expected to Arrive at Pine Ridge Today, When the Savages Will Fight," "Old Sitting Bull Stirring Up the Excited Redskins," and "Redskins Bloody Work."[15] Meanwhile, General Nelson Miles, commander of the Missouri division, expressed a blend of optimism and anxiety about the Ghost Dance when he opined, "It will [probably not] lead to an outbreak, but when an ignorant race of people become religious fanatics it is hard to tell just what they will do." Reflecting anti-Mormon sentiments of the time, he speculated that the Mormons had set the whole matter in motion.[16]

In response to concerns about the Ghost Dance and what the commissioners of Indian affairs judged to be primitive and self-destructive
religious behavior, many rituals were discouraged or banned outright.
Commissioners and agents condemned the self-piercings of the Sun
Dance and the communal distribution of wealth in the potlatch ceremony because they supposedly denigrated the body and undermined
personal responsibility. Many of the missionaries charged with the education and care of reservation Indians had even more concerns. In 1901,
a Jesuit missionary on the Rosebud Reservation lamented dances as "the
greatest obstacle in the way of civilizing and Christianizing these people"
because they helped maintain the old traditions, including the custom
of giving away property as presents.[17] (Of note, the fact that the reservation agent incorporated this missionary's comments into his official annual report reflects the interrelationship between government and these
early faith-based charities.)

*Dance at Pine Ridge Agency (c. 1890). Courtesy of the Denver Public Library, Western
History Collection, X-31377.*

Clearly the Ghost Dance in particular sparked concerns. The commissioner in 1890 instructed the Indian agent at the Pine Ridge Reservation, D. F. Royer, to forbid the Ghost Dance. The Sioux ignored him. Royer anxiously telegraphed Washington, "The Indians are dancing in the snow and are wild and crazy. . . . We need protection and we need it now. . . . I deem the situation at this agency very critical, and believe that an outbreak may occur at any time, and it does not seem to me safe to longer withhold troops." The interior secretary informed agents of Pine Ridge and Rosebud, "The President has directed the Secretary of War to assume a military responsibility for the suppression of any threatened out-break among the Indians." He added that if they made arrests, they should do so "with firmness and power so great as would overwhelm the Indians from the beginning."[18]

Despite the secretary's aggressiveness, others in the War Department understood Sioux concerns. In a report written in 1891, the department concluded that Indian complaints regarding the illegal seizure and settlement of their lands were justified, and that Indians had seen no guarantees that the latest treaty would be honored. Congressional delays in approving funds to fulfill the federal treaty commitments exacerbated the two years of crop failures, so that many reservation Indians lived on half or two-thirds of the rations promised.[19]

Meanwhile, some officers and government agents found little about which to worry in regard to the dance, perhaps recognizing the divergent understandings Sioux held toward it or perhaps entertaining a more nuanced understanding of apocalyptic thinking. For instance, Short Bull (Tatanka Ptecela), the Sioux who brought the Ghost Dance from Wovoka to his people on the Rosebud Reservation, explained, "I taught peace for all mankind. I taught my people that the Messiah would make all things right and that they should not make war on anyone."[20] Based on his grasp of the situation, Dr. Valentine McGillycuddy, a former Indian agent dispatched by the South Dakota governor as his advisor to the army, stated, "I should let the dance continue. The coming of the troops has frightened the Indians. If the Seventh-Day Adventists prepare their ascension robes for the second coming of the Savior, the United States Army is not put in motion to prevent them. Why should the Indians not have the same privilege? If the troops remain, trouble is sure to come."[21] Indeed, the Ghost Dance shared many compelling similarities with Adventist and other Christian apocalyptic expectations, which rarely incited a military response (a century later, the Branch Davidians— a Seventh-day Adventist sect—would prove an ill-fated exception, as chapter six describes). Tragically, however, the mix of Sioux expectations, federal agents' fears, and the march of many fully equipped troops into Sioux territory slowly spiraled toward violence.

One Oglala Sioux man, Black Elk (Hehaka Sapa), later recorded an account of what happened next in a series of interviews. Recognized by his fellow Oglalas as a *wicasa wakan,* Black Elk initially approached Wovoka's vision skeptically. However, over time he became more accepting and participated in the Ghost Dance, joining others as they danced all day long in a circle around a central pole, some brought to tears, some to laughter. Many danced until they collapsed, often pulled aside as they experienced visions that they shared once they awakened. Black Elk's experiences appeared to coincide with a great vision that he had had as a child and that had imbued him with appreciable power. He felt called to craft ghost shirts that assured those who wore them of total protection from bullets. Black Elk and his companions understood the possibility of war and believed that the agents of Wakan Tanka were endowing them with the power to fight courageously and successfully.[22]

In December, Indian police killed the important Hunkpapa Sioux leader Sitting Bull after meeting minor resistance when attempting to arrest him. Meanwhile, the agents ordered all bands roaming off the reservations to return at once and began to arrest all Ghost Dance leaders. Rumors stirred among the Sioux regarding the military's true goal. Some suggested that the troopers would disarm them; others that they would take their horses. In either case, not only would their ability to protect themselves and hunt be seriously curtailed (a perhaps life-threatening situation given a crop failure that year and the failure of agents to provide sufficient rations), but a vital aspect of Sioux male identity would be lost as well. More significantly, throughout the Sioux and other Plains Indians ran the fear that the military would simply annihilate all of them. As the Sioux attempted to make sense of unfolding events, one band of more than 300 Minneconjous that had performed the Ghost Dance in the past were intercepted by elements of the Seventh Cavalry, Custer's old troop. Their chief, Big Foot (Sitanka), who was seriously ill, peacefully surrendered. The cautious local military commander dispatched additional forces to join them. On the last night before their entry into the reservation, both groups encamped by Wounded Knee Creek on orders of the Seventh's commander, Colonel James Forsyth.

In the morning, the troop's commander had Big Foot brought to him on a litter while the rest of the Sioux men joined him for a council. During this council, soldiers surrounding the warriors attempted to disarm the Sioux. They met minor opposition as some Sioux hid their firearms under blankets or clothes. Meanwhile, soldiers searched teepees and frisked women, while Forsyth engaged in provocative theatrics meant to intimidate the warriors. Somewhere among the agitated Sioux, a shot went off, and then the massacre began. While some of the Sioux managed to regain their weapons or wrestle rifles from their opponents, the soldiers were well stationed to cut them down, some killing one another in their excitement and inexperience. Most of the warriors died in the initial minutes of the confrontation. Troopers meanwhile used pre-positioned Hotchkiss mountain guns to fire exploding shells into the encampment, blasting and riddling teepees with shrapnel that set many on fire while injuring or killing those inside. Women and children, who represented the majority of the encampment, ran for protection away from the two sets of combatants. Riflemen and artillerymen gave no quarter and cut them down. While the cannons were perhaps too far away to distinguish male from female, soldiers on foot and horseback pursued women with children for miles in order to kill them.[23] Since a blizzard soon fell over the region, many of the wounded died of exposure, though at least one child was rescued from his mother's frozen body.

Dr. Charles A. Eastman, a medical doctor of Santee Sioux heritage and an agency physician, approached Wounded Knee after the blizzard with a group looking for survivors.

> Fully three miles from the scene of the massacre we found the body of a woman completely covered with a blanket of snow, and from this point on we found them scattered along as they had been relentlessly hunted down and slaughtered while fleeing for their lives. Some of our people discovered relatives or friends among the dead, and there was much wailing and mourning. When we reached the spot where the Indian camp had stood, among the fragments of burned tents and other belongings we saw the frozen bodies lying close together or piled one upon another.[24]

Big Foot's Camp after the massacre at Wounded Knee (1891). Courtesy of Library of Congress, LC-USZ62–46006.

While exact numbers will never be known, the best estimates based on soldier and Sioux testimony suggest 30 soldiers and officers were killed in contrast with at least 300 Indian dead, two-thirds of them women and children.

CONSEQUENCES

Federal officials and newspaper reporters tended to blame the massacre on the Ghost Dance. One reporter who was present at the massacre exulted in his doubt that any of Big Foot's band, man or woman, had survived their "treachery," which the Seventh Cavalry had heroically snuffed. Viewing the dance as an unrestrained and—especially—heathenish religious practice (following on his view of them as fanatics), General Miles arrested twenty-seven Ghost Dancers. Soon after, Buffalo Bill Cody managed to get most of these released into his custody to participate in his European Wild West Show. The show advertised the presence of Wounded Knee prisoners as part of its usual theme of the savage giving way to civilization.[25]

In part, the Ghost Dance was a response to the powerlessness experienced by many Sioux—among other Indians—in the face of coerced land seizures and increasingly desperate living conditions. Federal troops had perpetuated massacres under similar circumstances against the Pomo of California in 1850, the Cheyenne and the Arapaho at Sand Creek in 1864, and the Blackfeet in Montana in 1870. In the case of Wounded Knee, a court of inquiry cleared all officers involved in the incident, and the military awarded eighteen soldiers and officers the Medal of Honor.

Although the military, the government, and much of the press held the Ghost Dancers responsible, some Americans joined Native American voices in condemning both the soldiers and the violated treaties that had led to the massacre. The New York Times described Indians as "robbed when at peace, starved and angered into war, and then hunted down by the Government." The limited political pressure that came to bear on President Benjamin Harrison forced him to enact some changes in Indian administration, but not many.[26] Meanwhile, General Miles continued to lay part of the responsibility on the Mormons, as he explained in a popular publication following the massacre. He and other officials viewed them as one among other insidious influences that fostered Ghost Dance messianism.[27] But none of this would substantially alter the fate of most Sioux.

With the death of Sitting Bull, the devastation at Wounded Knee, and the inability of the warriors and their families to survive a protracted war against the government in the winter of 1890–1891, the surviving Sioux abandoned their separate encampments and entered the reservations. Efforts continued to curtail some of their traditions. In 1892, the commissioner of Indian affairs rewrote the Rules for Indian Courts, reinforcing the 1883 prohibition on all "feasts and dances" under punishment, for a first offense alone, of losing their rations or suffering imprisonment for at least ten days. The codes buttressed the ban on medicine men, blaming them for obstructing other Indians from "adopting and following civilized habits and pursuit" by preventing "Indians from abandoning their barbarous rites and customs." Occasionally, a native group requested permission from their local Indian agent to perform a dance, who might or might not allow it. These restrictions remained in effect for six decades.[28]

Although most Sioux gradually departed from many of their customs and eventually adopted Christianity, resistance did not end entirely. The life of Black Elk is illustrative of both the pressure to conform to American religious norms and the ability—even in this vulnerable position—to preserve traditions. In 1930, John G. Neihardt traveled to the Pine Ridge Reservation to interview the sixty-seven-year-old Black Elk. Neihardt, as the poet laureate of Nebraska, sought to create a poetic cycle about native life on the plains. The aged Black Elk not only agreed to work with Neihardt but also declared him his nephew and titled him "Flaming Rainbow." Through a cumbersome but necessary relay, Black Elk spoke in Lakota, his son translated it into English, Neihardt somewhat rephrased it aloud, and his daughter wrote this down. Questions from Neihardt went through the reverse process.[29] Gradually, Black Elk narrated his life from his boyhood, through his youthful visions, to his participation in Custer's Last Stand, and ending with a rueful reflection on the slaughter at Wounded Knee and the Sioux's final resistance. The resulting volume, *Black Elk Speaks,* has become a classic—some would declare *the* classic—book on Native American religion, republished in multiple editions since 1932.

However, the Jesuit missionaries at Pine Ridge were not impressed. Namely, nowhere in *Black Elk Speaks* did Black Elk speak about being a Catholic catechist—one of the most successful on the reservation, as a matter of fact—who now went by the Christian name Nicholas Black Elk. Sensing the priests' disapproval, Nick Black Elk had a postscript penned in which he explained that Neihardt had failed to include a description of his current life. In the new writing, he portrayed his conversion three decades earlier, described his work as a catechist for twenty years, and pointedly confessed his belief in the Catholic creed and sacraments. Of particular interest, he ended his recantation of Neihardt's book by declaring,

> I know that the Catholic religion is good, better than the Sun dance or the Ghost dance. Long ago the Indians performed such dances only for glory. They cut themselves and caused the blood to flow. But for the sake of sin Christ was nailed on the cross to take our sins away. The Indian religion of long ago did not benefit mankind. The medicine men sought only glory and presents from their curing. Christ commanded us to be humble and He taught us to stop sin. The Indian medicine men did not stop sin.[30]

This declaration appeared a firm renunciation of his "heathen" past. But Nicholas Black Elk's protests proved as calculated as his reservation life.

Neihardt's notes suggest that Black Elk told him little about his Catholicism. Given their reliance for food, supplies, and access to education from government officials and Christian missionaries—who often maintained negative attitudes toward Indian traditions—many Sioux hid or even abandoned the practices and beliefs their parents had taught them. According to Neihardt's daughter, when the poet asked Black Elk why he had discarded the earlier tradition, the response was, "My children had to live in this world." So, as scholar Raymond J. DeMallie suggests, it would appear that the erstwhile *wicasa wakan* intended to use Neihardt's interest as a way of perpetuating Lakota religious life by having Neihardt do what he, by himself, could not: preserve his memories of the old ways in a published book. Black Elk continued to balance his close relationship with Neihardt—exchanging letters and working with him again during the poet's 1934 visit—with his need to assuage the concerns of the missionaries. He therefore penned another document again abusing Neihardt for not writing about his Catholic life and adding that the poet was not sharing the book's profits either. Despite these protestations, Black Elk took up dancing once again, even though the Jesuits considered it satanic in origin.[31]

While some Native Americans like Black Elk resisted the total abandonment of their earlier ways, the devastation at Wounded Knee was a death blow for the Ghost Dance. Although Wovoka rescinded his prescription to dance, American fears of a resurgence continued, enflamed occasionally by the few Native Americans who still performed it. For instance, in 1898 a newspaper reported that the Cheyenne of Oklahoma were "holding a ghost dance and making medicine." The Pawnee continued the Ghost Dance until about 1910, and some Plains Indian ceremonies still incorporate elements of it.[32] Meanwhile, the Kiowa of Oklahoma Ghost Danced at least as late as 1929. However, the Indian affairs commissioner there endeavored to end the "vicious" dance by blacklisting dancers who did not agree in writing to abandon the practice and cutting their government payments. Bending before the most powerful weapon—hunger—the Kiowa dance gradually disappeared.[33] How widely the dance declined remains unclear, but the historical record suggests that if it survived at all, it was because Indians performed it below the radar of federal officials.

Elements within the US government and American society in general have continued to demonstrate a patriarchal attitude toward Indians. In 1923, the head of the Bureau of Indian Affairs (BIA) wrote, "The Indian's spirituality is nourished by traditions as ancient as his racial infancy. Many of these are as beautiful and as worthy of historic preservation as the finest fancies of classic mythology. Many may be retained and cherished in the Indian's cultural progress, but many are benighted and sometimes degrading."[34] This official's pronouncement is part of a tradition that sees development as necessitating conformity or a necessary decline.

However, by the middle of the century, relations began to improve. In 1934, Indian Commissioner John Collier initiated the first major effort to reverse course on government approaches to Native American traditions. That year, he issued circular no. 2970, "Indian Religious Freedom and Indian Culture," which expressly forbade interference in ceremonies, languages, and other traditions. Native American liberty, he declared, must be the same as for all others.[35] This did not immediately alleviate pressure against Indian practices, but it offered a start. In 1973, the Ghost Dance returned again when a few hundred members of the Sioux nation, the American Indian Movement (AIM), and other native nations occupied the Wounded Knee site. As part of their efforts to protest and publicize the neglect Native Americans had suffered for centuries at the hands of the federal government and more recently due to the corrupt Indian government at the Pine Ridge Reservation, they decided to practice the old forbidden ritual.[36] Though reinterpreted to fit a new context, once again it served as an act of resistance, an endeavor of hope, and a forge of community in the face of political powerlessness, economic suffering, and religious denigration.

The occupation of Wounded Knee and other controversial AIM protests such as the occupations of Alcatraz and BIA headquarters have been widely viewed as helping to attract national attention to native issues while encouraging Indians around the country to reinvigorate their traditional identity and practices. Conflicts between Native American religion and national laws continue as Indians struggle against legislation that they consider obstructive of their First Amendment rights to religious freedom. Congressional efforts to redress previous wrongs through the American Indian Religious Freedom Act (1978), the National Museum of the American Indian Act (1989), and the Native American Grave Protection and Repatriation Act (1990) have gone some way to protect religious practices, ceremonial objects, and the remains of the dead. Nevertheless, some Sioux still maintain certain traditions in secrecy. One Lakota religious leader stated it plainly to scholar Lee Irwin in 1995 when he implicitly affirmed Black Elk's strategy:

> You know, Black Elk was part of a conspiracy, a cover up here among the Lakota. What he says there about the Indian religion being dead, over, was part of a plan to stop the oppression here at Pine Ridge. It worked too. After that book came out, things got better; we just said it was over, dead, a thing of the past. We had to still do it secretly, but things have gotten better. Now we can do it more openly and bring other people in. . . . I don't believe our religion is something that should be hidden or kept from other people who are not Lakota or Indian. But for a long time, we had to keep everything hidden, even from other Lakota.[37]

Perhaps the need for discretion has arisen partly because Indian "spirituality" has gone from public condemnation to popular entertainment and beyond. Publicly advertised powwows, often with attendant dances, attract not only members of various Indian nations but non-Indians as well. "Indian" things have become so popular, and potentially profitable, that a summit of Lakota, Dakota, and Nakota nations in 1993 passed a resolution against "Exploiters of Lakota Spirituality": non-Indians who market and sell Lakota artifacts and even ceremonies. So far has popular opinion swung from antagonism to attraction that AIM has sought to curtail non-Indians from posing as Indians in order to sell "authentic" items or as medicine men in order to market rituals. While it is tempting to imagine a now repentant and appreciative America valuing the medicine men it once outlawed and the native peoples it previously battled, this present moment of reconciliation must be understood in the context of a Manifest Destiny accomplished and a native continent largely remodeled according to white Christian standards.[38]

The double standard that recognizes injustice yet resists repatriating land is particularly evident in the federal government's firm denial of Sioux control of Paha Sapa, the Black Hills in South Dakota. In 1980, the Supreme Court recognized Sioux legal ownership of the land based on the 1851 Treaty of Fort Laramie, which the government subsequently ignored once the discovery of gold made the hills valuable to it. Despite the decision, the court refused to remand the land back to Indian management, offering only a cash settlement. Despite the tens of millions of dollars at stake, the Sioux have refused to accept financial compensation as a substitute for their claim to administer the hills. Ultimately, despite the many laws protecting Native American religious practices and the recognition of the Black Hills as Sioux land, the state government's interests in using the land (such as the creation of a public park) have overridden efforts by the local Lakota and Cheyenne to perform their ceremonies without restriction.[39] No longer denigrated as "heathen" or dismissed as "uncivilized"—indeed now valorized as the first Americans—and aware of their own agency to define their lives, the Sioux continue to struggle against the constraints of non-Indian religious and secular views.

Four

A Race Apart

*Jews in the Eyes of the Ku Klux Klan,
Henry Ford, and the Government*

The first effort by the Ku Klux Klan to establish
a presence in the large rural town of 5,000 failed to attract enough members. However, the organization expanded rapidly with the arrival of a
new minister at First Christian Church. His men's Bible class provided
a meeting place for the first klavern, the assemblage of Klansmen that
ultimately attracted many city residents. The local *Plain Dealer* newspaper—an early exponent of the group—freely repeated the minister's and
the Klan's perspectives, often on the front page. Some city policemen
performed their duties in full Klan regalia.[1] A few years later, a lecturer
from the Klan's Atlanta headquarters arrived and, before a 400-person
audience, espoused the ideals of "Americanism" and Christianity that
together, he argued, required a "Protestant flag" and a "Protestant government." Another lecturer/evangelist warned against immigrants—
commonly understood to allude to Jews, even as he decried allegations
that the Klan was anti-Jewish[2]—just as his predecessor had warned of
Communists.

Just a few years after the Klan's arrival, elections placed four Klansmen into four of the five city council positions, each winning their position by a margin of nearly two-to-one. The association of the Klan with the city appeared so cemented that, only three years after its arrival, an audience of 20,000 gathered in the main park among burning crosses to celebrate the initiation of 1,000 new members. Attendees arriving from outside knew they were welcome when they saw the letters KKK and KIGY (Klansmen, I Greet You) painted on the roads entering the city.[3]

The city upon which the Klansmen descended on July 29, 1924, was not Montgomery, Alabama, nor Little Rock, Arkansas, but Anaheim, California—the future home of Disneyland.

"Klanheim," as the city became known, was one of hundreds of hubs for KKK activity in the 1920s, when Klan leaders reinvented the group to appeal to Americans far beyond the boundaries of Dixie. While its anti-black propaganda was still a major pillar of the group, the organization now added a new message. They merged the anti-Catholic nativist sentiments that had led to the burning of Boston's Ursuline convent school and the rioting in Philadelphia neighborhoods with a new form of anti-Semitism. It was a unique and vitriolic cocktail of millennium-old European anti-Jewish sentiment mixed with modern, biology-based racism.

These anti-Semitic views were not restricted to the Klan, but they and Henry Ford arguably did more than anyone else to disseminate them at the time. In an age when public discussions of race freely floated into lamentable topics such as miscegenation and eugenics, public perceptions, prejudiced organizations, and government policies mutually fueled one another and quickened a cyclone of bias. This became evident particularly in the nation's immigration halls, where government officials determined who would and would not be accepted as future citizens, often based on haphazard judgments regarding ethnic, racial, and religious identities.

"JEW": RACE, RELIGION, ETHNICITY,
OR ALL OF THE ABOVE?

On a spring day in 1909, Hersch Skuratowski, having arrived that week on a steamer from Russia, appeared for a routine procedure before a board at Ellis Island. The ship's crew, responsible for recording passenger details in preparation for immigration procedures, established his nationality as Russian, his race as Caucasian, and his religion as Hebrew. The board, citing his lack of wealth, denied his entry into the United States and ordered him deported back to Russia. In their notes, they declared him a "Russian Hebrew."

Later that year, after Skuratowski was allowed to enter the United States for further legal proceedings, his lawyers protested the board's decision, claiming that his rejection had more to do with the identity of Hebrew than his lack of means, given that petitioners with similarly restricted finances were admitted that same day. In the early twentieth century, a common stereotype depicted eastern European Jews as impoverished and unwilling to labor (the board predetermined Skuratowski's economic position without allowing him the time to explain that, in fact, he owned a considerable farm in Russia).[4] This stereotype meshed with ideas of Jews as their own race, a matter that figured into immigration law because of racial prerequisite laws, which restricted citizenship to whites and blacks alone. At the time, the racial identity of Jews remained legally obscure while American Jews disputed whether or not they represented a race.

The same year, all of this came before a congressional committee, the Dillingham Commission, which was investigating the perceived threat that eastern and southern European immigrants posed to the United States. Intense debate arose on all sides as witnesses offered testimony on which identities should be recorded in immigration applications. Skuratowski's case became one of many that the commission considered in its endeavor to find answers that might recommend increased future restrictions on some groups. Were "Hebrew" and "Jew" religious identities alone or racial ones as well? Should this identity be recorded instead of national identity? Was Jewish identity different from those of other religions? A tart exchange among Senator Henry Cabot Lodge, California commissioner on immigration William R. Wheeler, and representative of the Union of American Hebrew Congregations Simon Wolf demonstrated the challenges at hand during the hearings.

> Mr. Wheeler: I must say that I never understood the word "Jew" or the word "Hebrew" to describe a religion. I have running through my mind now a half dozen prominent Jewish families in San Francisco who attend Christian churches. But we know them all as Jews.
>
> Mr. Wolf: You know them as a class, but we would not recognize them as Jews. Mr. Judah P. Benjamin has been recognized as a Jew born [sic], but he was an Episcopalian. That does not follow at all. There are any number of Jews who have become converted or who have married Christians.
>
> Senator Lodge: Do they cease thereby to be Jews? Does "Jew" become a wrong description?
>
> Mr. Wolf: They certainly cease to be Jews.

Many Jews and non-Jews of the period—and many more since then— might disagree with all of these interpretations of Jewish identity. However, Wheeler's racial identification of Jews, no matter their religious practices, instructively stands entirely apart from Wolf's belief in a self-determined religious identity, demonstrating the undecided nature of Jewish identity at this time. Complicating matters further, Wolf admitted that some Jews did recognize themselves as a race.[5] For others, the vacillations of immigration boards and the racism of the Ku Klux Klan provided proof enough of the disadvantages of a racialized Semitic identity. Happily for Hersch Skuratowski, the publicity of his case prompted supporters to offer enough financial support that he was allowed into the country.[6]

Although, like all historical biases, anti-Jewish sentiment changed over time and according to social context, the twin condemnation of the Jewish people as rejecters and crucifiers of Christ (and, thereby, of God) shaped European Christian attitudes for more than a millennium. The New Testament particularly played an important role, with some Christians reading the Gospels as more sympathetic to the Roman role in Jesus's execution than to the Jews who took part. Indeed, the Gospel of Matthew portrays the Jewish crowd—gathered before a cautionary Pilate—as so fixed on Jesus's execution that when the Roman governor finally, and literally, washes his hands of the matter, "then the people as a whole answered, 'His blood be on us and on our children!'" (Matthew 27:25). For many later generations of Christians, this legitimated the condemnation of all Jews forever, despite the Bible's depiction of the Jewishness of Jesus, his disciples, and most of his followers. However, the biblical representation of Jews as God's chosen people remained a bone of contention. Could God break the covenant with the Jews that had been forged with Moses at Mount Sinai? If not, could God condemn them to perennial punishment for their rejection of God's son?

Since the medieval era, European Christians had arrived at different answers to these questions and different attitudes toward Jews, resulting in acceptance, intermarriage, exclusion, ghettoization, persecution, forced conversion, expulsion, and annihilation depending on the time and circumstance. At the rawest end of the spectrum, the First Crusade began in 1095 and drew first blood with the slaughter of Jews in the cities along the Rhine River. Such explicit violence was often fueled by false accusations that sprang up again and again across Europe like an eternally regenerating weed: that Jews used the blood of Christian children in their ceremonies and that they stole the sanctified bread meant for the Catholic Mass in order to desecrate it. On the most tolerant end of the spectrum, at times Jews enjoyed a peaceful life among Christians and Muslims in medieval Iberia, now Spain and Portugal, where they interrelated socially, maritally, economically, and intellectually. While the level of acceptance varied, the final conquest of the peninsula's Muslim kingdoms in 1492 by the Catholic Queen Isabella and King Ferdinand brought toleration to an end. Jews and Muslims were presented with three choices: conversion, exile, or execution. The fact that even those descended from converts (*conversos*) remained as a breed apart demonstrates the Christian view of Jews as defined by blood that disallowed full acceptance as Christian converts.[7] The Protestant Reformation of the next century brought little respite to European Jews, especially given Martin Luther's virulent, biblically based sentiments excoriating them. Widespread relief would only arrive in the eighteenth century with the Enlightenment as well as Napoleon's European conquest and its subsequent Jewish emancipation.

As in Europe, colonial American sentiments shifted, waxed, and waned according to the social context, with various colonies officially tolerating Jews, yet socially and politically marginalizing them on religious grounds. For example, in the seventeenth century Dutch Director General Peter Stuyvesant petitioned the Dutch West Indies Company to expel the few Jews who had found their way to the erstwhile New Amsterdam (now New York), calling them "hateful enemies and blasphemers of the name of Christ." The company refused his request but restricted Jewish liberties to the same limited level allowed Jews in Holland, permitting them to practice their religion privately but not publicly. When the British took over the colony in 1664, conditions worsened. On the other hand, Roger Williams of Rhode Island actively invited Jews to settle there, and Newport became home to a significant Jewish congregation. South Carolina, with a thriving Jewish community, provided Jews as early as 1776 with both the right to vote and the right to hold office.[8] Nevertheless, although Jews might be legally permitted entry into Rhode Island and other colonies under the ideals of tolerance, their Christian neighbors often denied them full citizenship rights. While these discriminations followed from objections to Jewish religion, a different perception—of Jews as a race apart—would slowly become prominent in the next century and fuel the anti-Semitism of the Ku Klux Klan.

Although the notion that Jews represented a "race" existed for centuries in Europe and then in America, this term frequently meant something different than it would today. Up until the nineteenth century, many Europeans and Americans used "race" to mean any general mass of people as defined by a particular quality. Hence, the English, Irish, Germans, and Native Americans were popularly understood as races because of perceived social, linguistic, and/or geographic qualities. In this way, "race" was synonymous with the general understanding of "people" or "nation" (or what we would today call "ethnicity"), and humanity itself was perceived as representing a race apart from animals. In the eyes of many European Americans, the larger question was whether some groups counted as part of the human race at all. This was the case for many white Americans who justified the enslavement of blacks based on notions that they were not fully or, for some, even partly human. Jews, on the other hand, continued to be viewed as alien to America because of their religious identity.

In the eighteenth century, the first use of the word "race" in the English language to describe a group of people with similar physical features (including skin color) emerged. This usage slowly developed the idea that races were imbued with distinctive qualities that made them intractably different from one another. While before the Revolution, Americans generally recognized that blacks could be freemen or slaves, just as whites could be landowners or indentured servants, within a century racists would argue that blacks and whites differed almost as significantly as two species of animals. Part of the difference was physiological, so stereotypical skin color and facial (if not other bodily) features proved definitive. Part of the difference was internal.[9] Thomas Jefferson gives clear voice to these views in his "Notes on the State of Virginia" (1781), in which he deliberates on "the two races" and begins by saying, "The first difference which strikes us is that of colour." Jefferson then details the supposed physiological and behavioral qualities that differentiate blacks from whites, declaring the races as having a similar moral sense, though whites are superior in intellect and beauty. Although he cautioned readers about the tentativeness of his conclusions, Jefferson publicized them nevertheless.[10] Meanwhile, the description of Native Americans as "red men" used by Jefferson did not first arise until 1740, although whites had referred to them as a race (in the sense of "a people") long before this.

Nationalism particularly helped transform racialism—the perception of race—into virulent modern racism—the perception of a racial hierarchy among supposedly inferior and superior groups. As a more biological notion of race emerged in the nineteenth century and converged with ideas of social Darwinism, many nationalists began to imagine their nations as racially distinct from and superior to their neighbors. When the US government finally came to grips with the crime of black slavery, outlawing it nationally in 1865, it was in no small part because of the efforts of white Christian abolitionists who rejected notions of inequality based on the biblical story of Noah cursing his son Ham's children to subservience. However, racists now used "scientific" language to justify limiting rights for African Americans. The government also created a system for determining Indian racial purity in order to decide which Native Americans could receive land grants. As these racial identities began to define different groups, an implicit sense of "whiteness" developed, which made white skin color a national norm (despite black emancipation). Of note, Jefferson did not compare blacks *and* whites, but blacks *to* whites. As he words it, blacks (and red men) have more or less of any particular quality relative to whites, whom he therefore establishes as the standard of comparison or, in a word, the norm. Providing visual cues for this racial nationalism, all of the seminal personifications of the United States up to this time—the Spirit of Columbia, Uncle Sam, Citizen Know Nothing—were white.

But what *kind* of white were they? Some white Americans imagined an emerging American race brought about by the amalgamation of the white Europeans already here. But as more southern and eastern Europeans arrived in the late nineteenth century, some began to argue that American whiteness derived from northern Europeans—who were

"Holy horror of Mrs. McCaffraty in a Washington City street passenger car" in Harper's
Weekly *(February 24, 1866). Courtesy of Library of Congress, LC-USZ62–139433.*

racially described as Aryan, Nordic, or Anglo Saxon—and who were
superior to other races. Moreover, this racial nationalism could veer into
notions of racial purity, with its anxieties about miscegenation.[11]

But while some in the United States clearly did not fall into this new
category of "whiteness," others were more ambiguous. In the middle of
the nineteenth century, Irish Americans—previously marginalized owing to stereotypes regarding their Catholicism and manners—suffered
another type of marginalization when white Protestants portrayed them
as simian-like in physiology and behavior. Nativists now had another
reason for wanting to diminish Irish immigration. Debates in regard to
immigration law—which, until 1952, allowed only whites and blacks

to become naturalized citizens—led the Supreme Court to have to arbitrate regarding who was what color on a number of occasions. The racial prerequisite rules that Hersch Skuratowski encountered came into full force in the midst of this debate. The inherent arbitrariness of assigning a color to each ethnic and national group—and supposing each member of that group to share that color—became clear as the justices again and again weighed these different understandings of race. While the justices followed the opinions of anthropologists in many instances, in at least one case they ignored scientific claims that Asian Indians were Caucasians because of the biological origins they shared with most Europeans, deeming them "brown" based on the purported color perception of the average American. Meanwhile, the race of Italians, Greeks, Slavs, and Arabs remained a matter of debate. Italians followed the nineteenth-century Irish in being associated with blackness. Later, in 1942 and 1944, two different federal district courts issued totally opposite rulings in regard to the whiteness of Arabs.[12]

The race and whiteness of Jews remained a similarly contested matter. Beginning at least in the 1870s, some American Jews viewed themselves as racially distinct from, although not superior to, other Americans. There were multiple reasons for this. Sometimes such arguments for racial pride served as a defense against the threat of disappearing through assimilation. It was also a response to claims that Jews contributed nothing to civilization. However, as Wolf's testimony before Congress demonstrated, other Jews argued stridently against claims of racial distinction.[13]

As immigration brought increasing numbers of Jews, especially eastern European Jews, they drew more attention from other Americans. Between 1870 and 1900, the Jewish population ballooned from 200,000 to more than a million. Stereotypes about Jewish physical differences such as large noses and full lips eventually became a broadly accepted "commonsense" justification for arguments of biological distinction among immigration boards. By the beginning of the twentieth century it became difficult to fit the increasingly diverse pool of immigrants into

"The 'New Trans-Atlantic Hebrew line.'" Courtesy of Library of Congress, LC-USZC2–1252.

the black-white binary that had served for a century, and Jews were especially challenging to white Christian Americans.[14]

In light of all these issues, three questions arose regarding Jews: Were they white? Would they socially assimilate? And should they racially assimilate? For those who answered these questions in the negative, the presumed biological and religious distinctiveness of Jews disqualified them as Americans, as often communicated through the use of vicious stereotypes.

THE KU KLUX KLAN

Most Americans associate the Ku Klux Klan with efforts in the Deep South to terrorize blacks both in the aftermath of the Civil War and

during the civil rights movement. However sadly significant these ep-
ochs, the in-between period of Klan activity should not be overlooked,
nor should the fact that it involved not just one part of the country,
but towns throughout the entire nation. Estimates suggest that the
Klan's popularity encouraged perhaps 4 million Americans to join, from
Michigan to Mississippi, and from Atlanta to Anaheim. In August 1925,
around 40,000 pointy-capped and white-gowned men and women
loudly proclaimed their strength by marching along Pennsylvania Avenue from the US Capitol Building. Onlookers crowded four or five deep
along the curbs and waited more than three hours for the strictly organized, military-like parade to pass.[15] The Klan's presence was felt within
the halls of government as well; the organization claimed when it was at
its strongest to have helped elect at least seventy-five congressmen and
senators from five states, including Colorado and Indiana. As testament
to the Klan's influence long after this heyday, 43 percent of Americans
polled believed that KKK membership should not be an impediment to
serving on the Supreme Court when former member Hugo Black was
nominated in 1937. Despite strong opposition, he was confirmed by the
Senate and served as a justice for three decades.[16] This was in part a result
of the changes the Klan had made to broaden its appeal two decades earlier, building on a newly invoked nostalgia for the original organization.

The initial, Reconstruction-era Klan was short-lived. Formally established in Pulaski, Tennessee, in December 1865 when disgruntled
former Confederate soldiers organized to intimidate newly freed blacks
and their white supporters, it disbanded in 1869, though offshoots continued to practice enough violence that Congress passed, among other
laws, the Ku Klux Klan Act of 1871. Perhaps more consequential for
the Klan's demise, the institution of Jim Crow laws later in that decade
ensured both African American segregation and political marginalization, thus assuaging many white concerns and leading to the gradual
disappearance of the first KKK.

The formulation of a new Klan occurred in 1915, in part because of an influential and successful silent film released that year: D.

Ku Klux Klan parade in Washington, DC (September 13, 1926). Courtesy of Library of Congress, LC-F8- 40564.

W. Griffith's *The Birth of a Nation,* based on the book *The Clansman* (1905) by Thomas F. Dixon Jr. The movie depicted the KKK as a necessary response to freed blacks gloatingly dominating and undermining Southern society, preying on white women, and destroying civilization. The film related to more current concerns among many white men and women across the country in the 1910s and 1920s who apprehensively viewed the Bolshevik Revolution and rising immigration. For some, the film offered a parallel with the Reconstruction era, and the apparent contemporary necessity of a communal commitment to white supremacy, racial segregation, and Protestant supremacy.

These factors inspired William J. Simmons, a Southern-born Methodist preacher and member of multiple fraternal orders, to fashion a new organization. But the new Klan focused on more than just racial and religious identities. As American society gradually moved away from Victorian values to those of the Progressive era, the nation debated issues like alcohol consumption, marital infidelity, Catholic education, observing the Sunday Sabbath, and less constrained female sexuality.

Klan members took it upon themselves to preserve conservative values by policing their communities against these activities.[17]

After an initial faltering start, Simmons eventually developed a strategy to tap into the anxieties of his white neighbors. He went to the professional marketers Elizabeth Tyler and Edward Young Clarke, who, in turn, hired recruiters to systematically canvas men's fraternal orders and Protestant churches, earning four of the ten dollars from each of the new recruit's membership dues. These "kleagles" particularly sought ministers to join, recognizing their publicity and recruiting value. Showings of *The Birth of a Nation* and other films attempted to quicken patriotic, racist, and nativist sentiments, while the cliquish feeling of klavern membership promoted feelings of camaraderie and shared purpose.[18] In many ways, this new KKK redoubled the efforts of the old one to create an exclusive fraternity (and sorority) by reusing earlier ritualistic and costume trappings, while adding new practices that reinforced a sense of moral and patriotic exceptionality. In Anaheim, each male participant had to sign a membership card, affirming himself as "being a white, male Protestant Gentile person of temperate habits, sound in mind and a believer in the tenets of the Christian religion, the maintenance of White Supremacy and the principles of a PURE AMERICANISM."[19]

Despite the organization's vicious history, this new generation waxed nostalgic about the original Klan, defending it against charges of violence (officially sanctioned violence, anyway) while promoting its discriminatory views. A couple from the initial Klan's Pulaski birthplace, Mr. and Mrs. W. B. Romine, wrote a book that described the KKK's origins as innocently rooted in returning Confederate soldiers seeking pasttime fun, donning white robes to play on African American superstitious fears of ghosts in order to scare them at a time when blacks "were beginning to run amuck at social conditions." In a recasting of history worthy of *The Birth of a Nation* or the later *Gone with the Wind,* the authors claimed that freed slaves had no reason to challenge the order of things given that "the relation between slave and slave holder here in Middle Tennessee was nearly always one of mutual trust, kindness and friendly interest." Even while arguing that Klansmen never used violence "except in resisting violence," the Romines gave a nauseatingly casual wink and nod describing the disappearance of one member, who sought escape after sharing the organization's secrets with government officials, was intercepted by a group of Klansmen, and was supposed accidentally "to have fallen into Duck River" since no one heard from him again.[20]

The KKK thrived on secrecy. From 1867 on, members portrayed themselves as part of an "invisible empire," explicitly celebrating its influence on public life. Anaheim, California, members would give women who were prospective participants a membership request card that listed organization beliefs such as "The Tenets of the Christian Religion," "White Supremacy," "Protection of our pure womanhood," "The limitation of foreign immigration," and "Closer relationship of Pure Americanism." The card then added, "Upon these beliefs and the recommendation of your friends you are given an opportunity to become a member of the most powerful secret, non-political organization in existence, one that has the 'Most Sublime Lineage in History,' one that was 'Here Yesterday,' 'Here Today,' 'Here Forever.'" The card counseled "Discuss this with no one" and directed the reader to a contact should she be interested in learning more.[21]

The twentieth-century addition of Catholics and Jews to blacks as the targets of the Ku Klux Klan reflected a resurgence of American nativism. In the decades both before and after World War I, a surge of immigration prompted fears of poverty, radicalism, foreign influence, and job competition, especially as the government accepted an increasingly broad array of immigrants to fuel the nation's labor-hungry industries. These were the stereotypes that almost condemned Hersch Skuratowski to a forced return to Russia. The concentration of these migrants in the nation's rapidly growing and increasingly crowded cities at a time when the divide between rural and urban Americans was rapidly widening made white Protestants from farms and small towns particularly wary and led to country-specific restrictions on

"'How the other half lives' in a crowded Hebrew district, lower East Side, N. Y. City" (c. 1907). Courtesy of Library of Congress, LC-USZ62–63967.

immigration. Some questioned whether the quality of the newcomers met the standards of natives, and whether new arrivals would adopt the majority culture or stubbornly remain aloof. Simmons described unrestricted immigration as producing not a melting pot but "a garbage can."[22] One Indiana minister and Klan leader described certain foreign elements as "poison in the melting pot."[23]

However, this twentieth-century nativism differed from that of a century earlier in two ways. First, its broad antagonism against blacks, Catholics, and Jews helped bond a wide range of Protestants together, allowing them to overlook the denominational differences that might have divided them outside the klavern.[24] Second, the new nativism added race to the earlier issues regarding birthplace and overseas allegiances. In Anaheim, the KKK applications echoed this, with questions not only about foreign commitments and the religion of self, parents, and spouse, but also, "Do you wholly subscribe to the principles of clannishness between Anglo-Saxons?" Additionally, women members swore to bar racially inferior sperm from their wombs when they pledged the "protection of our pure womanhood."[25] Whereas nineteenth-century nativism had tended to define Americanness in terms of birth in the United States, the Klan's nativism excluded blacks and Jews from true citizenship because of their perceived biological race. Although European Jews may have passed as whites earlier, by the mid-1920s many Klan members—among other Americans—labeled them as a race apart.

The difference in attitudes between the first two of the Klan's twentieth-century imperial wizards demonstrates the divergence in how Jewish racial identity was imagined. The divergence between Simmons's views as the Klan's head and those of Hiram W. Evans, who succeeded him in 1922, reflected the rapidly changing attitudes of the period. Indeed, Evans's shifting stance showed how even those with strong convictions regarding anti-Semitism found drawing a distinction between Semitic and white identity nigh impossible to justify definitively and scientifically.

For his part, Simmons allowed that many Jews would qualify as KKK members due to their patriotism (and, presumably, their whiteness) but discouraged them because "the entire teaching of the Order is that our present civilization rests upon the teachings of Jesus Christ." It would be unjust, Simmons noted with feigned kindness, to admit Jews only for them to feel uncomfortable at klavern meetings.[26] In contrast, Evans in a 1923 publication described Jews as "semitic subjects" of European countries who brought their racial, religious, and social "distinctiveness" to the United States and resisted efforts to alter it. While he may have hinted at some appreciation for the purported Jewish self-isolation from those outside their "race" (indeed, he deems them "Klannish"), Evans declared that Americans owed nothing to Jews who

arrived in the United States merely as refugees and never contributed
to its development. In Evans's mind, "the white, Gentile Christian had
won the American continent by conflict and sacrifice," whereas for the
Jew, "he explored none of its forests; he navigated none of its streams."
This mythmaking, while establishing one anti-Semitic stereotype, required altering another. So Evans turned away from the denigration of
Jews as bankers and financiers (just the people many Protestant whites
before the Depression applauded for building the nation) and set out
to build a new stereotype of Jews for his 1923 publication. Describing
them as money-mongers, he alleged that they lacked influence in large
financial institutions because they kept their money to themselves, using
rules against marrying outside their group to protect their hoard.[27]

Local KKK proponents echoed this new characterization of Jews.
Reverend A. H. Moore, a Klan leader in Noblesville, Indiana, in a sermon before a crowd so large that hundreds were turned away from his
church's door, condemned Jews not only for their rejection of Jesus
Christ but also because each "holds the dime so close to his eye that
he cannot see the dollar beyond." Inserting an insidious implication,
he cautioned that Americans would do well not "to allow the Jewish
element to control the finances of the United States." Moore's congregation swelled in numbers until he could claim it as the largest in the
county.[28] In part, these allegations served to promote boycotts of Jewish
businesses, alongside black and Catholic ones. Moore's exhortation that
his Noblesville congregants "trade at home" benefited storeowners belonging to and supporting the KKK.[29] In Anaheim, one Klan member
reported that his klavern clandestinely followed the shopping habits of
members, punishing those who failed to abide by the secret marker indicating stores that were not "un-American."[30]

Consistency of argument was not a strong suit of Klan leaders, so an
eventual shift in Evans's views of Jews comes as little surprise. In 1926,
he backpedaled on his previous claim that all Jews were Semites when
he wrote an essay that distinguished two races of Jews: Western and
Eastern. He blurred the distinction between "Western Jews" and white

Americans, arguing that these Jews contributed to whatever nation they inhabited. He then went on to argue that anthropologists had declared Ashkenazi or "Eastern Jews" to be "not true Jews, but only Judaized Mongols—Chazars. These, unlike the true Hebrew, show a divergence from the American type so great that there seems little hope of their assimilation." In this and other writings, Evans argued in favor of intolerance toward groups that would not assimilate while simultaneously arguing against the assimilation of unsavory "aliens" of "low standards, low living, and fast breeding" who should not be welcome to dilute or outnumber the "Nordic stock" of true Americans.[31]

Klan members succeeded in promoting widespread anti-Semitism during the 1920s, even on university campuses. Indeed, in this period, Ivy League colleges established quotas to limit the number of Jews enrolling, for fear that the high numbers earning admission would drive away upper-class Protestant students.[32] As a result, the National Interfraternity Conference determined in 1924 that 40 percent of all its members belonged to fraternities limited to "Caucasians" and "Aryans." For instance, the Chi Upsilon fraternity at the University of Wisconsin–Madison mandated in their 1923 charter that "persons to be eligible for membership shall be male and white, of the Aryan race and not a member of the Semitic race." Their wordy specificity reflects the uncertainty surrounding the terms "Aryan," "Semitic," and—perhaps most of all—"white." This did not inhibit students from circulating on the campus stereotyped depictions of Jews as freely as they did caricatures of blacks. African American and Jewish university students formed their own fraternities in response to their exclusion, but the national conference would not recognize them. Meanwhile, on both the Wisconsin–Madison and the University of Illinois campuses in 1919, with student government approval, students established societies named after the Ku Klux Klan.[33]

Resistance to the Klan varied according to region and political will. Ironically, initial efforts to address the early Klan phenomenon helped exacerbate its spread. Newspapers featured the organization in cautionary articles while Simmons had to answer a summons to a congressional hearing. Nevertheless, membership surged. When a newspaper reprinted a Klan membership form as evidence in its exposé of the group, many readers snipped it from the newspaper's pages, filled it out, and mailed it in as hopeful candidates.[34]

Nevertheless, later anti-Klan efforts gained traction, especially after the dubious ethics of particular Klansmen became known. State legislatures criminalized wearing a mask or hood that disguised one in public, forcing Klan members to face the social scorn that accompanied membership in many places. In Chicago the chief of police barred the group from marching, and in New York City the mayor unilaterally ordered the police to run them out of town. A Cleveland ordinance leveled fines and imprisonment for belonging to an organization "tending to promote racial hatred and religious bigotry." The Irish American Mayor James Michael Curley not only banned the KKK from Boston, but had his campaign staff burn crosses during one of his speeches so that he appeared heroic in the face of a perceived threat. The antagonism went far enough that the fairly new American Civil Liberties Union cautioned officials against some of the measures. Local residents also organized. Members of the African American community and the Catholic Knights of Columbus fraternity created a citizen's committee in Atlantic City, New Jersey, that was poised to warn of Klan activity. In Columbus, Ohio, black leaders reversed a tactic used by the Klan and advocated a boycott of Klan-owned shops, while in nearby Dayton, Jews and Catholics did something similar. Meanwhile, some African American newspaper editors complained that concern arose only with the Klan's anti-Semitism and anti-Catholic sentiment, little enough concern having been raised when blacks alone were targets of organized hatred. Occasionally, community opposition turned violent, with mob assaults on Klan members and buildings in West Virginia, New Jersey, Pennsylvania, Ohio, and Illinois.[35] Despite these local acts of resistance, the Klan reached an apogee of approximately 4 million members in 1925, when Imperial Wizard Evans led his march of tens of thousands down

Washington's Pennsylvania Avenue in their show of national strength. But in the 1920s, Ku Klux Klan members were not alone among anti-Semitism advocates who broadcast their sentiments as a stern alarm of the country's peril.

HENRY FORD

In 1920, Henry Ford—perhaps America's most famous industrialist and exemplar of capitalist success—bought a local newspaper and started publishing a series of his own articles. Over the course of ninety-one issues, readers read chapters of Ford's lengthy anti-Semitic warning. That same year, he published the articles as a book entitled *The International Jew: The World's Foremost Problem.* With almost no identified sources for his evidence, Ford mounted a 250-page argument for Americans to address "the Jewish question." While the newspaper's circulation surged to a half-million readers, American consumers purchased 10 million copies of the book. Despite protests against his views by two former presidents and the Federal Council of the Churches of Christ, Ford had found his audience.[36]

What set Ford off on his tirade remains unclear. In 1915, after he led a failed endeavor aboard a "Peace Ship" to visit Europe and convince its warring governments to settle matters peacefully, he blamed one of his fellow passengers—a Jewish woman—for the disappointment. This proved to be his first public expression of anti-Semitism, and an experience to which he returned time and again as proof to him of how Jews propagated radicalism. Three years later, he faulted Jewish capitalists for his unsuccessful run for one of Michigan's Senate seats.[37]

Ford delineated the parameters of the purported problem posed by Jews in the first few pages of his book: "Financial and commercial control, usurpation of political power, monopoly of necessities, and autocratic direction of the very news that the American people read." The businesses and industries under their supported control made for a long list: periodicals, theaters, residential rentals, financing, commerce, motion pictures, grain, sugar, tobacco, liquor, cotton, clothing, and jewelry. According to Ford, Jews managed this not through evident power but by subterfuge. First, Jews invented many modern business practices, like the promissory note and the stock exchange, providing not only control over financial affairs but also the ability to move capital around a worldwide network of Jewish business. Ford also claimed Jewish racial connections made them more effective at international business. Finally, Jews manipulated governments into financial obligations that secured their control over them.[38]

This strategy, then, ensured Jewish ability to run a "super-capitalist" "super-government"—no nation controlled them, but they had a hand in them all. As a capitalist who relished his own exercise of financial control, Ford needed to distinguish Jewish commercial success from his own and that of others, just as Klan rhetoric had sought to do. Therefore, he argued that Jews, having finally managed to move beyond simply selling what others manufactured and opening industries of their own, never took advantage of scales of production to lower costs for consumers. In other words, they never contributed to the public good, as the automaker had understood his business practices to do.[39]

This urge to rewrite the past to support his allegations of Jewish historical machinations led Ford to re-describe American history. The European settlement of North America now suggested a secret story of Jewish triumph. He nixed the idea of Queen Isabella's funding Columbus's inaugural voyage, claiming that Marranos (converts to Christianity, some of whom secretly remained Jewish) had provided the cash. The same year Columbus sailed, Ford asserted, Jews founded the sugar business on the Caribbean island of St. Thomas. And a century before the Pilgrims landed on Plymouth Rock, the industrialist portrayed Jewish traders landing in South America, with Jewish businesses becoming well established on Brazil's coastline at a time when North America's shores barely supported a few settlements. Ford appeared to deliberately upset the national myth of Christian settlement and domination by portraying Jews as perennially one step ahead.[40]

This ability of Jews to act as "world-controllers," Ford argued, arose from their "unity of race continuity" that surpassed that of everyone else. Like that of others of the period, Ford's notion of "race" wavered inconsistently between a social and a biological definition. On the one hand, Jews acted as a "super-nationality" with a cohesion based on their intermarriage. Jewish success in America differentiated them from other immigrant groups like Poles and Germans who had to build their success from nothing, having arrived on the country's shores with exactly that. Immigrant Jews, however, said Ford, had wealthy Jewish backers in Europe who bankrolled their success in the United States, suggesting that their accomplishments counted for less.[41]

On the other hand, Ford implied that Jews differed biologically from others as a race. Certainly, he drew on a potent physiological metaphor when he described them as "the sickness of the German national body." More explicitly, Ford stated that "there are no stronger contrasts in the world than the pure Germanic and the pure Semitic races." Overlooking the assimilation of many Jews into German life during the previous century's Haskalah (Jewish Enlightenment), he declared that this racial discord meant that no harmony had ever existed between them. In terms of the recent world war, Ford proclaimed Jews as the sole winner, in keeping with his notion that they favored anarchy because the resulting disorder allowed poor Jews to improve their social status. In short, then, German Jews demonstrated their patriotism during the conflict not to Germany but only to themselves: "Judaism is the most closely organized power on earth, even more than the British Empire. It forms a State whose citizens are unconditionally loyal wherever they may be and whether rich or poor." This, Ford claimed, explained what he described as 2,000 years of "instinctive anti-Semitism" among other races as they recognized almost unconsciously the threat posed. Hence, he concluded, "it is probably true that the commonest real cause of anti-Semitism is the action of the international Jew," the wealthy clique of world controllers, while the victims of this response were usually poor Jews, who also tended to be the most religious.[42]

Ford insisted that similar backlash in the United States had nothing to do with Judaism as a religion. He referred to the popular anti-Semitism not only propagated by the KKK but also found throughout much of the nation's Christian majority, among whom resistance ran strong against the assimilation of a group associated with Bolshevism and the Semitic race.[43] In fact, according to Ford, Jews proved themselves far more likely to slander Christianity than Christians were to malign Judaism, especially when they falsely alleged religious prejudice in the country. As the efforts of Hersch Skuratowski's lawyers and supporters on his behalf demonstrated, Jews organized to aid immigrants and challenge discrimination. No, despite their complaints to the contrary, Ford argued, Jews were not disliked because of their religion. Indeed, Judaism's moral structure appeared similar to that of other nations in part because it had influenced so many, while, he stressed, the differences between Catholicism and Protestantism were greater than those between any branch of Judaism and Christianity.[44]

Despite these protests, Ford in his writings appeared to ultimately conclude that the religious failures of Jews had condemned them to their powerful yet wretched position. Referring to the Hebrew Bible narrative, he declared that God had directed the Jews, newly arrived in the Promised Land, to drive out the Canaanites so these natives would not infect God's people with their values. However, according to Ford's reading, the Jews decided to ignore this directive and enslaved the Canaanites instead, trading a "preference of material mastery over spiritual leadership." This decision has haunted Jews ever since and, once exiled from the land of Israel, compelled them to seek their material benefit by exploiting those around him. Ford left ambiguous a claim he made about the perennially unsatisfactory life imposed on Jews since then: "Some explain it Biblically as the curse of Jehovah upon His Chosen People for their disobedience to the discipline by which He would have made them the Prophet Nation of the world." Whether this curse follows the mistake with the Canaanites or the rejection of Jesus Christ as Messiah remains unclear. In any case—and with evident unawareness of

Peter Stuyvesant's restrictions—Ford noted darkly that Jewish prosperity in New Amsterdam and then New York had made some Jews consider it "the Promised Land foretold by the Prophets."[45]

Ford's articles culminated in his sustained reiteration of the classic twentieth-century anti-Semitic tract "The Protocols of the Elders of Zion." The industrialist coyly described how an American academic obtained a manuscript in Russia that appeared to have been a document read by the father of Jewish nationalism, Theodor Herzl, at the first Zionist congress in Basel, Switzerland. In keeping with the meritless assertions he makes throughout the articles and book, Ford's argument for the validity of "The Protocols" relied on a circular logic: "It is too terribly real for fiction, too well-sustained for speculation, too deep in its knowledge of the secret springs of life for forgery." Ford went on to explain how the text outlined a program for Jewish world domination in which Jews control legislatures, legal systems, and economics, just as they supposedly did in Bolshevik-controlled Russia. The result would undermine the foundation of all nationalisms, leaving only "Judaization."[46]

However, the erosion of societies' bedrock did not stop there, according to Ford. Through the promotion of freedom of conscience and the deliberate discrediting of "Gentile clergy," Christianity would be wrecked. Rabbis and ministers would forge a religious union that "would of necessity dispose of Christ as a well-meaning but wholly mistaken Jewish prophet." Meanwhile, Jewish movie studios created films, Jewish music producers promoted jazz, and Jewish clothiers introduced "sport clothes," all meant to undermine the morality of young Americans. With words dripping with malice, Ford suggested that such products should bear a tag, as a piece of apparel would, that read, "Made, introduced, and exploited by a Jew." All of this led Ford to declare the "International Jew" and his allies "as the conscious enemies of all that Anglo-Saxons mean by civilization."[47] For this reason, in his estimation, Jews had never assimilated elsewhere and would never do so in America. In fact, they preferred to live apart and create their own ghettoes.[48]

In the decades following the publication of his anti-Semitic thoughts, Henry Ford was perhaps less famous for them than for the remark "History is more or less bunk." Clearly his interpretation of the past and the promiscuity with facts evident in *The International Jew* proved that he meant what he said. Although he later renounced his anti-Semitic remarks, evidence suggests that he never abandoned his opinions. The extent of his influence may be difficult to calculate, but it would not appear that his anti-Semitic remarks cost him readers. Much to the contrary, the circulation of the *Dearborn Independent* rose from 72,000 copies per week when he began his essays to 7 million in 1924.[49] And the "Protocols" would gain a committed readership in the United States. Meanwhile, in 1938, on a trip arranged by one admirer, Ford traveled to Germany to receive a medal from the Third Reich. Adolf Hitler praised Ford, as demonstrated by his favorable mention of him—the "one great man" holding out against Jews' control over American labor—in the first edition of his two-volume manifesto *Mein Kampf* (1925 and 1927).[50]

CONSEQUENCES

Anti-Semitism in this period was grounded in new, biological notions of race. Despite problems in fashioning a coherent scientific argument to support this view, many white Protestants portrayed Jews as essentially different owing to physiological differences. The ascent and popularity of the Ku Klux Klan and Henry Ford's anti-Semitism testify to this, while the similarly virulent anti-Jewish tirades of the "radio priest" Father Charles Coughlin in the 1930s demonstrate how such sentiments could animate Catholics too. When Jewish liberalism and financial success appeared to threaten the white Protestant-shaped majority culture of the United States, detractors would dismiss them as the product of a racially degenerate people.

However, the increase in intolerance sparked other responses as well. In light of Henry Ford's prominent remarks, goodwill committees supporting interfaith cooperation arose among Jewish and Christian communities. In various cities, Catholics used the Vatican's official eschewal of anti-Semitism to reject Father Coughlin's invective. More regionally, Indiana Jewish leaders forged alliances with the press, politicians, and Christian clergy to discredit and, over time, undermine the Klan.[51]

As a result of efforts like these, the Klan's efforts in Anaheim soon dissipated, like a match that flares intensely into flame but quickly burns out. After less than a year in office, the four new councilmen faced a re-call election after the public realized that the Klan had secretly supported their campaigns. The newly organized anti-Klan group U.S.A. Club assembled its own slate of candidates, which the *Plain Dealer*'s rival, the *Anaheim Gazette,* supported. While plaintively noting that some had alleged the paper to be under Jewish or Catholic control, the *Gazette* portrayed three of the four of its candidates as Presbyterian, Episcopalian, and Methodist. This suggested that the newspaper sought to uphold the Protestant norm by promoting the candidates' mainline Protestant credentials and avoiding the association with Jews and Catholics even as its editors castigated the Klan for its denigration of religious minorities. Voter turnout reflected the level of concern among the town's citizens about Klan involvement: out of about 4,600 registered voters, 4,178 voted.[52] The four Klan candidates lost.

Meanwhile, the Orange County *Plain Dealer*'s efforts to smear anti-Klan advocates cost it dearly. One victim—the pastor of a local church—sued the newspaper for its allegations that he was a drinker and disloyal to the country. Facing a humiliating loss in court, the editors accepted a settlement that included a front-page repudiation of its former allegations against the minister and an admission of the newspaper's alliance with Klansmen to degrade him and back the embattled councilmen.[53] The same front page also announced that the *Plain Dealer* had been sold to its other rival, the *Anaheim Bulletin,* which noted that publication of the *Plain Dealer* would end that evening.[54] Meanwhile, Anaheim civic leaders designed a strategy to further weaken the Klan. Starving it of public attention, both the *Bulletin* and the *Gazette* stopped reporting on Klan activities, while the city council prohibited the distribution of handbills and required registration by groups attempting to recruit within city limits.

The four years between the rise of the invisible empire in Anaheim and its debacle with the recall election demonstrate how many of the city's citizens agreed with the positions it advocated but found that the name Ku Klux Klan proved too much of a stigma for most to bear. By the 1930s, the Klan had all but disappeared from Anaheim and from the rest of the country,[55] yet the National Origins Act, which sharply curtailed the numbers of southern and eastern European immigrants and prohibited Asian immigration entirely, had passed in 1924. This legislation, with its implicit restriction on Jewish and Catholic influx, remained in effect for twenty-eight years. The Klan's outrageous customs, ceremonies, and declarations may have left them on the fringe of mainstream opinion, but, nevertheless, their claims about America as a fundamentally—and imperiled—white Protestant nation were shared by many.

As evidence of the distance the country has—and has not—traveled since the 1920s, note that in 2013 the comedian Seth Mac-Farlane, while hosting the annual Academy Awards ceremony, built a comedy routine around the claim that Jews restrict Hollywood success to themselves. In one short sketch, an animated teddy bear told the self-identified Catholic actor Mark Wahlberg to fake a Jewish identity, declaring himself Jewish in name (Theodore Shapiro) and by deed (financially supporting Israel). The bear anticipated that his ruse would pay off "when they give me my private plane at the next secret synagogue meeting." Clearly, the comedian relied upon his audience's familiarity with the very old allegation to make the joke work. While many audience members undoubtedly shrugged off any claim made by a digitally animated stuffed animal as an obvious farce on the allegation of Jewish control, the actors' performance of the joke failed to communicate clearly whether the humor pivoted on mocking the prevalence of this stereotype or on its repetition by a child's toy. Either way, the incident demonstrated that such allegations remain very much alive and incendiary.

Five

Fanatics

Secular Fears and Mormon Political Candidates from Joseph Smith Jr. to Mitt Romney

"American exceptionalism" is a fixture of election campaigns in the twenty-first century. A 2010 poll demonstrated that 80 percent of Americans believe that their nation's history and Constitution give it "a unique character that makes it the greatest country in the world." A majority considered that this quality imparted a special duty to be the foremost global leader.[1] For many, this uniqueness stems from a special covenant with God that showers the United States with particular blessings but requires it to rise above the imperfect morality of its neighbors. Long after the Puritans borrowed the theme, immigrants were viewed as attaining a promised land after escaping their homeland's oppressions (economic, political, or religious). This self-understanding, inspired by the Hebrews' journey from Egypt to Canaan in the Book of Exodus, helped to create the idea of American exceptionalism that portrays the United States as "a light unto the nations" and "a city upon a hill."[2] How ironic, yet how quintessentially American, that the Church of Jesus Christ of Latter-day Saints—perhaps the nation's most rapidly expanding home-grown religious movement—has suffered persistent prejudice over the course of its nearly 200-year history for holding precisely this belief regarding its own community.

During that history, three Mormons have campaigned for the presidency of the United States. In each instance their church affiliation has become an issue in a manner not usually suffered by Episcopalian, Methodist, Lutheran, or other mainline Protestant candidates. While the fate and success of Mormon candidates has improved over time, the "Mormon question" that inevitably arises reflects how their traditions continue to be suspect even as Mormons increasingly fit popular American norms.

JOSEPH SMITH, LDS ORIGINS, AND THE PRESIDENTIAL CAMPAIGN OF 1844

Joseph Smith Jr.'s family moved from his birthplace in Vermont to Palmyra, far upstate in New York, just as one of America's series of evangelical wildfires scorched the social and religious landscape. Various Protestant ministers sought to evangelize ("proclaim") through popular meetings or revivals that would prompt attendees to accept God in a public moment of conversion. Evangelism blazed so intensely in Smith's region that it became known as the Burned-over District, and the nearby meetinghouses of the mainline Protestant congregations would have reflected revivalism's impact. Presbyterians, Methodists, and Baptists in the region saw their memberships swell.

As a teenager, Smith wrestled with the truths presented by these various churches. Then he claimed to have a vision of God and Jesus Christ that settled the matter. The revelation condemned every Christian denomination as corrupt and counseled Smith to remain pure by staying away from them. Yet, as the Quakers had discovered two centuries earlier, claims of divine inspiration often pose an unpalatable challenge to established religious authorities.[3] When the adolescent Smith confided his experience to a preacher, he found his vision stridently rejected. After all, if a layperson could discern God's will in a minute's revelation, what was the worth of a minister's years of training or a denomination's centuries of convention? Put another way, how could socially sanctioned traditions (or hierarchies) stand up against divinely inspired insight?

A few years after this initial revelation, Smith had another vision in which an angel named Moroni revealed that a set of golden tablets were buried near his home. In 1827, he unearthed them under Moroni's direction. After three years translating them with the use of special stones, Smith published the content of these tablets as the Book of Mormon, a book he declared would supplement, not replace, the Christian Bible. The Book of Mormon narrated the history of the Israelite prophet Lehi who, under God's guidance, had fled Jerusalem just before its conquest by the Babylonians in 586 BCE. According to early Saint interpretation, he settled in a new promised land: North America. There, his sons established two competing lineages, the virtuous Nephites and the sinful Lamanites, the latter of whom became associated with the Native American peoples. Although Christ's appearance among these two groups after his resurrection helped reconcile them for centuries, their enmity later returned, and the Lamanites annihilated all the Nephites but one. This survivor, Moroni, preserved the history and religion of his people so that God might reveal it. Moroni came to Smith in an angelic form, having transcended his human condition. Through his claims that God communicated various spiritual insights and community directives to him directly, the prophet had both embraced the concept of direct revelation and verified his assertion that his was the true church.

In addition to a growing following, the publication of the Book of Mormon in 1830 spurred public derision toward Smith in his small community. After an alarmed local newspaper published—without permission—parts of what critics called the "Gold Bible" even before the book left the press, some locals organized a boycott against its sale. The local Presbyterian church partially suspended Smith's mother's and brothers' membership when they refused to denounce it. Nevertheless, the newly published book drew the attention of an increasingly wide circle of newspapers starting in Palmyra and expanding to Rochester, New York City, Vermont, Ohio, and beyond. Journalists and editors used terms like "blasphemy," "fanaticism," "priestcraft," "fraud," and "superstition" to describe the volume. Many early detractors denied that Mormonism had any relationship to Christianity at all, refusing to call it "heresy" and instead denouncing it as a fake religion invented to dupe the innocent. Mark Twain later weighed in with a critique of the work's readability, dubbing it "chloroform in print."[4] Despite such critiques, Mormon missionaries found ready audiences for the incipient church and its book—especially on America's western frontier.

In the same year as the initial publication of the Book of Mormon, the Church of Jesus Christ of Latter-day Saints (LDS)* found itself sharply at odds with existing Christian denominations. Although Smith initially described it as only a complement to the Bible, he later called the Book of Mormon a purer book than the Bible, which centuries of scribal corruptions and church politics had malformed.[5] Conflict also emerged around the story of Moroni, which represented a serious divergence from mainstream Protestant theology. Toward the end of his life, Smith explained that Moroni's transition from human to celestial being reflected every individual's potential spiritual evolution. In fact, he argued, God once existed as a man like any other. This declaration, which made the existence of multiple deities plausible, and other revelations stirred more opposition to the LDS, some of it within the church itself.

In 1831, in an effort both to escape the hectoring of his New York neighbors and to establish an American Zion, Smith joined a Mormon community founded by missionaries in Kirtland, Ohio (today a Cleveland suburb). Relative to other contemporary challenges to the

---

*The church initially went by the name Church of Christ, taking the LDS title in 1838. As a title, "Mormon"—deriving from the name of a prophet—originated as a derogatory term used by critics but was gradually embraced by church members who otherwise have referred to themselves as "Saints."

status quo, the Mormons were generally optimistic and constructive, establishing new communities among converts and settlers.[6] Simultaneously, with Smith's encouragement, other Saints migrated to Missouri, where Independence was declared the new Jerusalem. In both places, antagonism soon mounted between resident non-Mormons and the new arrivals.

In 1838, following business and other failures there, the prophet left Kirtland, along with most other local Mormons, for Missouri. Despite the presence of a preexisting Mormon community in Missouri, antipathy toward the movement thickened quickly after the newcomers' arrival. Christians had long used the charge of "fanaticism" to signal that a religion was out of bounds, using the term for movements that appeared to go too far in religiously reshaping the world. Fearing that such groups would tear society apart in their energetic zeal, Missourians directed their antagonism toward Mormon settlement. Soon, both Mormons and non-Mormons had raised militias, with each side sporadically attacking settlements of the other. Finally, the state governor leveled an ultimatum that the LDS community "must be exterminated or driven from the state if necessary for the public peace" (an order that remained legally in effect until rescinded in 1976).[7]

The next year, most of the Missouri Mormons moved on to Commerce, Illinois, which they renamed Nauvoo. There they enjoyed years of success until—one decade after the church's formal establishment—overall membership topped 20,000.[8] The Illinois state legislature practically granted self-government to the local Mormons, even allowing them the ability to raise the Nauvoo Legion, their own militia. Such militias were not unusual in the United States at this time, but this legion began to worry the region's non-Mormons.[9]

Despite belief within the church that the imminent, millennial return of Christ would end human governance, by the 1840s Smith had outlined a new form of government, which he termed "theodemocracy."[10] Not a pure theocracy, this style of democratically elected government recognized the importance of individual voting but also the supremacy of God's laws. Under the shadow of mob assaults against Mormons and others across the country, Smith sought protection for the autonomy of minority communities. In keeping with Thomas Jefferson's republican ideals, the prophet viewed religious communities as nurturing the moral ability of their various members, which would guide them to elect proper representatives to government. The LDS understood the need for democracy on the state and national levels of government even as it supported authoritarian rule within the church itself, where Smith was the recognized, uncontested leader of the religious community.[11]

In January 1844, Smith declared his candidacy for president of the United States. He explained that the move, in part, was meant to improve the political visibility and pull of the church among Americans.[12] But before Smith's national campaign got very far, he ran into trouble in Nauvoo. Upset about his recent revelations allowing men multiple wives, the potential elevation of humans to godhood, and the possibility of multiple deities, some Mormons rebelled and established a dissenting press in town. When the newspaper criticized the presidential campaign, Smith and other Mormons declared the publication a public menace, prompting a mob to storm the press, destroy it, and burn the newspapers they found.[13]

The burning of the press ultimately ignited a firestorm of unrest, fueled by other issues—both local and national—that quickened the volatile atmosphere in and around Nauvoo. The various surges of revival in the United States both before and after the War of Independence, as well as that conflict itself, had all helped galvanize the nation into a mindset that challenged hierarchical, authoritarian structures with ideals of individualism and equality. This individualism motivated dissenters in existing denominations to fracture them into smaller churches, as Puritanism initiated in the late sixteenth century and to which it was later subject. At the same time, nationalism cultivated a group identity, prompting some tolerance of one another among some of these splintered Christian groups, even if they did not always show the same forbearance toward non-Protestant communities like Catholics, Jews, and Native Americans.[14]

Joseph Smith's visions and the Book of Mormon represented a challenge to many of these popular features of American life. His teenage vision of God and Christ that warned him to reject all churches as corruptions did not bode well for a future of pluralism and toleration. In many ways, the Church of Jesus Christ of Latter-day Saints represented a return to a Puritan ideal: a single, exclusive church—enjoying a covenant with God and considering themselves God's chosen people— rejects mainstream denominations and migrates to find safe haven.[15] Indeed, just as English Puritans viewed New England as their future utopian city on a hill, so some Saints understood Independence, and then Salt Lake City, as their new Jerusalem. However, the LDS differed in one major way from its predecessor: the Puritans were suspicious of those, like Anne Hutchinson and the Society of Friends, with personal visions, while the Saints accepted one as their prophet, president, and lieutenant general.

Smith's multiple roles reflected how the early LDS community extended the theocratic structure of the church into everyday life. Smith headed the church's religious, political, and military organizations as a revered figure, contradicting the populism of Andrew Jackson's presidency that celebrated the individual autonomy of common folk to fashion their destinies and elect their own leaders. The frontier life of Illinois in the first half of the nineteenth century redoubled these sentiments as individuals and families sought to carve an independent existence for themselves from their rough environment. For the LDS, good society arose "through a covenant with God that created a people," while many Americans understood government as akin to a contract among individuals. What particularly concerned many non-Mormons was the Saints' merger of all leadership—secular and religious—into one man. Within a few years of their Nauvoo settlement, Mormons used bloc-voting tactics to elect Smith as both mayor and municipal court chief magistrate, even as they recognized him as prophet, president, and lieutenant general of the local militia. While members of the LDS community used democratic means to attain civil positions, many non-Mormons saw their control of municipal institutions as inherently authoritarian, thus threatening ideals of individualism and egalitarianism.[16] Similar concerns fed contemporary fears of papal control, which helped fuel anti-Catholicism on the East Coast, especially in Boston and Philadelphia. But whereas nativists fretted about Catholics grabbing the gears of power for the pope's external manipulation, many non-Mormons—and increasing numbers of disaffected Mormons—worried about Smith's endeavors to establish a theocracy in the heart of America.

Even as he prepared his national presidential campaign, Smith's most immediate problem appeared to be a dissenting group in Nauvoo who disagreed with the prophet's recent changes and sought to found a reformed church that would avoid the threat to secularism that they, like many LDS critics, saw in Smith. In a recently established newspaper meant to provide an alternative public view to that of the local Mormon paper, they objected to the newly introduced polygyny, viewed their erstwhile leader as a "fallen Prophet," and "repudiated Smith's plan of uniting Church and State." It is important to note that this endeavor to decouple religious authority from political authority did not mean they wanted to completely separate religion from politics. Indeed, one dissenter wrote in a neighboring town's newspaper, "We verily believe in the sentiment that 'Resistance to tyranny is obedience to God,' and with the arms and heart that God has given us, we will fearlessly and faithfully maintain our rights."[17] He clearly viewed ethics, law, and politics as inherently *connected with belief*, though not as entirely *directed by belief*.

This distinction is important, because without it this dissatisfied Mormon's views might initially appear contradictory as he expresses one method of balancing religion and politics in public life. He, and many others during this period, considered it a religious duty to defy those who would entirely conflate religious and political power. Although religious people cannot be expected to leave behind their consciences, beliefs, and sentiments before entering balloting places, it should come as no surprise that some draw a line between their religious and secular commitments, resisting any "inappropriate" religious encroachment into public life, and vice versa. In order to maintain such distinctions—so crucial for balancing the country's religious pluralism and commitment to secularism—the nation has needed properly behaved, rational religious communities that create both devout congregants and cooperative citizens. Nineteenth-century Protestants struggled with suspicions toward revelation and miracles, which appeared irrational and thus dangerous to a nation dependent on its citizens' individual powers of reason, yet fundamental to the origin of Christianity. Many resolved this seeming paradox by arguing that revelation and miracles belonged to the biblical period and that a Protestant Christianity guided by reason existed today.[18] Ultimately, Smith answered these dissenters' challenge in a manner that triggered the very collective violence he had sought to protect against.

The prophet had long warned against "mobocracy" for good reason. In the 1830s and 1840s, Illinois suffered from the same gang riots that embroiled the eastern states, with Mormons participating in them as well. In the case of the newspaper riot, Smith had planned for and prompted the assault on the dissenting paper's offices using a kind of government mob: rallying the Mormon-dominated city council to legitimate his calls for the press's destruction as a public nuisance and prodding them to assign the local police to the task. He had attempted to flee once he realized the opposition the newspaper attack had fomented, which was the culmination of the growing mistrust of him, his recent revelations, and his non-secular government practices. However, Smith reconsidered and submitted to local authorities, who imprisoned him and other leaders in a nearby Carthage jail. Before his trial, however, a mob stormed the prison and shot him and his brother. He fell from his cell's window, his escape prevented by a mortal wound. The prophet and his presidential ambitions died on the Illinois soil that night.[19]

The Mormon community spent the next five years regrouping from their loss before embarking on a new westward flight from persecution,

"Martyrdom of Joseph and Hiram Smith in Carthage jail, June 27th, 1844" (c. 1851). Courtesy of Library of Congress, LC-USZ62–765.

this time to build a kingdom near the Great Salt Lake in Utah. However, their troubled relationship with the United States followed them.

REED SMOOT AND THE QUESTION OF MORMONS IN THE SENATE

While Mormon dissenters did break away and found their own churches after the 1844 death of the prophet, the LDS remained a visible, and troublesome for many, force in the United States in the ensuing decades. Brigham Young, who was working in Boston for Smith's presidential campaign at the time of the murder, returned to Nauvoo and ultimately became the next church president. Later, he led a large group to Utah, where he served as both LDS leader and federally appointed governor. There, he oversaw the church's public prescription of polygyny and its efforts to establish an autonomous kingdom, further antagonizing the church's detractors and culminating in the arrival of federal troops sent to keep an eye on the Mormons and counter their population growth by encouraging non-Mormon immigration. Tragically, the Mountain Meadows Massacre of 1857 helped inaugurate this period of tension, as Mormons and Paiute Indians slaughtered more than one hundred emigrants passing though Utah to California. This provided both more fodder for national outrage against the LDS and further legitimation of federal watchfulness over the territory.

The election to the Senate in 1903 of Reed Smoot, who simultaneously held one of the highest offices in the Church of Jesus Christ of Latter-day Saints, seemed an important milestone in the gradual acceptance of the church by the rest of America. Just a decade earlier, Congress had finally ratified Utah's petition for statehood, after denying several previous efforts. Yet far from being an unqualified success, Smoot's election brought more unwanted attention to the church, as accusations of polygyny and theocracy resurfaced. The victorious Smoot endured four years of hearings as his congressional colleagues debated whether or not to deny him his Senate seat. Though the LDS had formally recanted polygyny and fully recognized federal authority, American cultural memories kept anti-Mormon prejudices alive, and the Smoot hearings helped refresh and reinvigorate the biases that had once led to the murder of Joseph Smith.

A confederacy of Protestant churches organized much of the opposition to Smoot. Declaring their intention to protect "Christian America," their members filled the hearings as spectators and flooded their representatives with letters (some Congressmen received a thousand letters on the topic daily). Meanwhile, the press maintained close coverage of the events and opined on "the Mormon problem," as they termed the collective allegations of multiple marriages, theocracy, and anti-Americanism.[20]

Protestants were willing to lead the charge against the LDS Church because most had not yet felt the pinch of conflict when duty to church conflicted with allegiance to the state. Enjoying the Protestant cultural and legal norms that had existed since independence, Episcopalians,

Methodists, Baptists, and others in mainline churches encountered little interference in their efforts to fashion a Christian America. This would change by the end of the twentieth century, when a growing secular movement and changing cultural values resulted in challenges to municipal governments displaying Christmas manger scenes and legal restrictions on the teaching of creationism in public classrooms, spurring on cries of government oppression of religion. However, at the time of the Smoot hearings, many Protestants felt little conflict in criticizing the religious lives of Mormons and urging the government to levy restrictions on them. In telling contrast, few identifiably Catholic or Jewish groups joined the condemnation, perhaps in part because of their own experiences with a government imbued with Protestants and Protestant norms.[21]

Although the fourteen senators assigned to run the hearings sought to understand contemporary LDS beliefs and practices, they investigated a wide range of old suspicions leveled at the movement. Originally seeking to establish a literal kingdom of Saints, the Utah settlement under Brigham Young had experimented with social features deliberately at odds with the mainstream norms. These included economic communalism, unusual rituals, and secret oaths. Similarly utopian communities of Puritans, Mennonites, Shakers, and the Amish had sought comparable goals in previous centuries, as the Branch Davidians would later in the twentieth century. Although Congress, the press, and the public focused somewhat on the continued nonconformism of a few Mormons, it attended far more to old suspicions regarding polygyny and the influence of the LDS leadership in political matters.

While Smith and the church leadership practiced multiple marriages during the first decade of the church, a public proclamation of the LDS's official stance waited until Young had led the remaining community to Salt Lake. Young took the prophet's lead in declaring "celestial marriage" (as the church termed the plurality of wives) the highest sacrament, and one with eternal consequences, since it was essential for achieving godhood. The practice often figured centrally in non-Mormon derision of the LDS as being backward and retarding civilization. Delegates at the Republican convention of 1856 declared Mormon polygyny, along with slavery, as the "twin relics of barbarism."[22] As the Saints struggled with the animosity directed toward them, celestial marriage became a defiant marker of LDS identity. However, over time the church recognized that the issue served to frustrate their efforts at obtaining statehood, and, in 1890, LDS president Wilford Woodruff declared that a new revelation abrogated the earlier one that had legitimated the practice. The federal government in turn reversed its opposition to statehood and pardoned all participating in preexisting Mormon polygynous marriages. While the instances of polygyny declined, some church authorities continued to surreptitiously sanction it until 1910.[23]

At the same time that polygyny was waning in the LDS community, fascination with it in the rest of America continued. This derived in part from a surge in Protestant nationalism and a contemporary movement to improve the rights of women, which could cut against Mormon women in various ways. Despite more than a half century of effort, the women's suffrage effort had managed to win the vote in only one state by 1890. Yet, in the name of undermining polygyny, evangelical women supported successful federal efforts in 1887 to remove the voting rights Utah women had exercised for nearly two decades after the LDS territorial government had enfranchised them.[24] Later, many non-Mormon women saw the Smoot hearings as an opportunity to protest the alleged mistreatment of women in plural marriages. Mormon B. H. Roberts had already stirred polygynist controversy when elected to Congress in 1898. While the important church post he held brought some measure of suspicion on Roberts, the dealbreaker was his two marriages. Congress refused to allow him to take his seat in the House of Representatives, and a year later he served five months in prison because of them. Unrepentant, he married another woman when released. The Roberts case proved a prelude to the Smoot controversy, priming many to rally against seating a Mormon in the Senate.

"How will this destructive monster be allowed to live?" by Frederick Burr Opper. Detail from "A desperate attempt to solve the Mormon question" in Puck (February 13, 1884). Courtesy of Library of Congress, LC-DIG-ppmsca–28293.

In 1903 the Woman's Home Missionary Society of the Presbyterian Church organized against Smoot's election and hosted a speech by a converted Mormon who damned the senator-elect. She suggested that, given his status as an apostle in the church, Smoot was "the seat of the disease."[25] At the same time, the National Congress of Mothers dispatched to each Senate member a letter declaring that Smoot had taken "treasonable" vows to the LDS Church "to which he owes first allegiance" and "whose president and members are teaching and practicing polygamy."[26] Like the anti-Catholic agitators of the previous century and the detractors of Jews, Branch Davidians, and Muslims to come, these critics used one stereotyped behavior to portray the LDS Church as lacking allegiance to the United States. Even a fairly favorable interview with Smoot in the *Hartford Courant* the same year defended him against charges of multiple wives yet found his claim that religion and politics proved no more mixed for him than for any other senator "not quite ingenuous." "The country has not had time yet to forget the days and ways of Brigham Young," the journalist wrote, even as he declared this should not obstruct Smoot from taking his Senate seat.[27]

"I imagine it must be a perfect Paradise," by Joseph Ferdinand Keppler. Detail from "A desperate attempt to solve the Mormon question" in Puck *(February 13, 1884). Courtesy of Library of Congress, LC-DIG-ppmsca–28293.*

Smoot was a confirmed monogynist, but because he was a member of the Quorum of the Twelve Apostles—the church's second-most authoritative body—many across the country remained suspicious of his capacity to act independently from the church. In part, this concern arose from a worry about monopolies, coming as it did on the heels of the antitrust efforts of the 1890s. Corporate monopolies threatened freedom of choice and individuality, so religious monopolies appeared similarly dangerous.[28] As the hearings came to an end, Senator Shelby Cullom of Illinois declared that he was satisfied that Smoot—like most Mormons—had not engaged in polygyny, but that the church's hierarchy continued to threaten the nation.[29] To some, these suspicions were confirmed when it was revealed that Smoot had declined an earlier run for Senate after his fellow apostles in the Quorum of the Twelve withheld their approval. They saw his willingness to run in 1903 after approval was finally granted and the church hierarchy's subtle dissuasion of Mormon Democrats from opposing the Republican Smoot as further evidence of the church's control.[30]

Smoot's defenders relied on the guarantees of the Constitution to argue their case. An article in the *Washington Post* sought to preempt arguments against Smoot by declaring him a monogynist, quite at odds with Roberts's polygyny, which had prevented him from taking his seat in the House. Referring to the First Amendment, the article's author continued on to declare stridently, "There is no established church in the United States, nor is there likely to be any soon. Every sort of belief and unbelief stands on a precise equality in voting and office holding in this country. Several of them—Episcopalianism, Presbyterianism, Unitarianism, atheism, and others—have been represented among the Presidents."[31] The journalist countered prejudice with pluralism.

In the end, the Smoot hearings involved one hundred witnesses who generated 3,500 pages of testimony. After four years of investigation, the committee recommended expulsion by a count of seven to five. However, with President Theodore Roosevelt's support, a majority in the Senate voted in support of Smoot.[32] He retained his congressional seat for thirty years. Today, an LDS website uses a quote ascribed to Reed Smoot as exemplary of devotion to Mormon priesthood.

> Many people encouraged him to run for president of the United States. But they told him he would have to give up his religion because people at that time would not elect a Mormon for president. He said, "If I had to take my choice of being a deacon in The Church of Jesus Christ of Latter-day Saints, or being President of the United States, I would be a deacon."[33]

The question of Mormon membership and presidential ambitions would not end with him.

After the Smoot trial, the LDS Church continued to work to fit mainstream expectations, receiving public support only after it deferred to federal law by renouncing polygyny, proved its civic commitments by recruiting soldiers for the US military, and denied any political agenda. For instance, the negative attention of the Smoot hearings prompted the

church leadership to prohibit new plural marriages in 1904, but continued scrutiny led to more rigorous enforcement in 1910.[34] The success of this strategy would prove itself sixty years later when George Romney ran for president.

THE PRESIDENTIAL CAMPAIGNS OF GEORGE ROMNEY AND MITT ROMNEY

By 1968, George Romney had taken one successful political step after another, largely unencumbered by anti-Mormon sentiment. From 1954 to 1962 he had served as chairman of the American Motors Corporation before becoming Michigan's governor in 1963. In 1966, George entered the contest for the Republican presidential nomination and initially dominated the polls. Yet when surveys just before the race's first primary projected a thumping defeat, he withdrew before the voting even commenced.

While the candidate's declaration that he had been "brainwashed" by US generals into supporting US involvement in the Vietnam War was seen as the biggest impediment to victory, his Mormon identity played a much smaller role. The press certainly mentioned it during his gubernatorial and presidential campaigns (in part because he sometimes spoke of it). However, the journalists speculated more frequently about how AMC's stockholders and board of directors might influence his decision to run for office than about how the church hierarchy might do so. While some of the nation's newspapers may have had concerns about his religion, newspapers such as the *Chicago Daily Tribune,* the *Hartford Courant,* and the *Washington Post* tended to characterize George's affiliation positively, if at all. Many matter-of-factly explained his role as stake president of Detroit (which they equated with the role of a bishop). Others described his religion as responsible for favorable personal qualities. One article described George's quest for "guidance beyond that of man" through fasting and prayer on the eve of a press conference announcing his decision regarding a run for governor.[35] "He has the Mormon's honest passion for work and getting things done," one journalist glowed.[36] Yet another journalist noted how the candidate tithed his income to the church and "in an industry noted for hard drinking and tough talking, Romney neither drinks nor cusses."[37] Although the news media mentioned George's birth in Mexico, it gave little attention to the fact that his grandparents moved there to practice polygyny (his son, Mitt, would later describe them as escaping "religious persecution" in his political autobiography).[38] Indeed, the country had travelled a long distance from Reed Smoot's first election. Before 1951, with only one exception, the only Mormon members of Congress represented Utah. In every term since then, at least one Mormon has been elected by voters of another state to the House of Representatives, if not also to the Senate.[39]

While the theological and polygynist heritage of the candidate's Mormonism might not have mattered, a more troubling question arose regarding the church's attitudes toward race, especially as George's run for governor swung into gear. Newspapers increasingly noted how the LDS Church's constraint on black leadership was proving contentious to Michigan's African American voters.[40] Until it was renounced through a revelation in 1978, a longstanding LDS doctrine declared that Africans (and, thus, African Americans) were stained by the curse of Cain and thus prohibited from serving as priests. Nevertheless, George Romney's strong record of support for civil rights undoubtedly helped allay some of these concerns, and the issue did not stop him from winning the governor's seat, nor did it appear as an important factor in his future, failed presidential campaign. All of these issues demonstrated how the public identification of George Romney as a Mormon did not burden his campaign with unanswerable allegations stemming from stereotypes. The diminishing power of these stereotypes meant that the candidate could rise above them through the force of his character.

Four decades later, Mitt Romney followed his father's lead in becoming governor of his state after a successful career in business and then in pursuing the presidency. Although Mitt succeeded where his father failed—clinching the Republican nomination in his second presidential bid—his Mormon identity proved far more consequential, demonstrating the changes in America's religious and political landscape since 1968.

Mitt Romney's Mormonism was an issue starting with his first foray into politics. In the 1994 Massachusetts senatorial race, incumbent Ted Kennedy's campaign sought to sow mistrust about Mitt's racial and gender attitudes by focusing on his church's former—but by then long ended—restriction on blacks, as well as current exclusions of women from the priesthood (something the Catholic Kennedy had to admit continued in his own church). Ted's nephew, Massachusetts representative Joseph Kennedy argued, "I believe very strongly in the separation between church and state. But I think that if a particular church has a belief that blacks are second-class citizens, and that's the stated belief of the church, or that women are second-class citizens, I mean you ought to take a look at those issues." In response, the Catholic archdiocese of Boston condemned this strategy, the *Boston Globe* retreated from its earlier interrogation of Romney's religion, and Kennedy's allegations began to result in a decline in popular support. The Kennedy campaign eventually found it necessary to back off of its religion-baiting effort in order to win the race, further showing the limited popularity of anti-Mormonism, at least in Massachusetts.[41] Although Mitt's senatorial campaign ultimately failed, he later succeeded in becoming Massachusetts' governor (2003–2007) before preparing for his first national campaign.

The role of Mitt Romney's religion in his two presidential races differed somewhat. In 2008, Republican opponent Mike Huckabee catered to religious conservatives when he asked a string of questions regarding LDS beliefs, including "Don't Mormons believe that Jesus and the devil are brothers?" In 2012, candidates proved less willing to make religion a central issue, although some had their surrogates hint at it. Mitt himself showed little willingness to showcase his faith. His 2010 political autobiography *No Apology: The Case for American Greatness* mentions it only three very brief times: his Mormon great-grandparents' flight to Mexico, Mitt's missionary work in France, and his counseling work as a bishop. This reflected Mitt's strategy of publicly embracing his Mormon identity but refusing to discuss any particulars about the church or his practice. Some were unwilling to let it go at that.

Influential Texas megachurch preacher Robert Jeffress—a supporter of presidential contender Rick Perry—declared Mitt Romney "not a Christian" at a 2011 Christian conference and denounced the LDS as a cult.[42] Jeffress had already demonstrated his anti-Mormonism when, during the 2008 primaries, he declared that Mormons, "Muslims and Hindus worship a false god."[43] Concurrent with Jeffress's remarks, Bryan Fischer, a director at the American Family Association, argued that Mormons, like Muslims, did not deserve First Amendment rights because they supposedly understood Christ differently than had the nation's founding fathers.[44]

Among Democrats, Montana Governor Brian Schweitzer in April 2012 wondered publicly about the possible impact that "his family coming from a polygamy commune in Mexico" would have on Romney's campaign. Romney responded by defending his grandfather as a monogynist, while a spokesperson for Democratic contender Barack Obama—who, like Romney, had a polygynist great-grandfather and faced critics' questions about his religion—quickly eschewed raising issues about any candidate's religion.[45] Meanwhile, an assembly of pro-Obama black ministers in the Greater Hampton Roads Christian Leadership Conference of Virginia crafted and distributed a voting guide offering side-by-side comparisons of the two candidates' supposed views. The last page, detailing religious differences, declared Mormons' purported belief in progression to godhood, in Jesus as a married man, and in the refutation of the notion of the divine trinity.[46] Among media commentators, Bill Maher on HBO and Lawrence O'Donnell on MSNBC each took opportunities to ridicule elements of polygyny, the MSNBC anchor declaring it Joseph Smith's invention to excuse his adultery.[47]

In light of these types of attacks, various political pundits—and undoubtedly Mitt's consultants—pondered the potential of a John F. Kennedy–like speech in which Romney would declare that his Mormonism would not interfere with his presidential responsibilities. The fact that he never offered such a declaration perhaps demonstrates that his campaign recognized Mitt's larger problem for conservative voters was not appearing too Mormon but not Mormon enough. This possibility reflected how successfully the LDS had repositioned itself on the shifting American religious landscape as no longer a self-ruled utopian community but now a standard-bearer for conservative moral values. The church's prominent role in the 2008 passing of California's anti-gay marriage Proposition 8 offered ample evidence of this. Although many observers debated whether or not evangelical Christians considered the candidate's religion a boon or a bane, the greater obstacle to their support appeared to be his inconstant commitment to conservative values relative to abortion and gay rights.[48] As Southern Baptist leader Richard Land explained, "If his stance on life and his stance on marriage had been consistently what the stance of the Mormon church has been, he would have far less doubts among social conservatives."[49] Again, even though many conservative Christians may not have considered the LDS Church truly Christian, they valued the conservative family and social values it appeared to promote.

The fact that the 2012 primary race for the Republican presidential nomination included two Mormons and two Catholics out of eight remaining frontrunners—and that the eventual ticket would pair the Mormon Romney with the Catholic Paul Ryan—reflects the altered prospects both religious groups have undergone in the past century. (Indeed, the Democrats' vice presidential candidate was Catholic, too.) Less than a half century ago, both anti-Mormonism and anti-Catholicism shared suspicions of authoritarianism, since rigid hierarchies structure both churches. None of these issues played a significant role in the 2012 campaign.

Nevertheless, both the 2008 and 2012 campaigns proved how popular suspicions about Mormonism remain. Jon Krakauer's best-selling book *Under the Banner of Heaven: A Story of Violent Faith* is only one of the more successful recent books critical of the LDS Church whose titles blare for attention. These include *Deception by Design: The Mormon Story*; *The Mormon Cult: A Former Missionary Reveals the Secrets of Mormon Mind Control*; and *The American Muhammad: Joseph Smith, Founder of Mormonism.* In anticipation of the 2012 election, one author penned *Mitt Romney and the Mormon Church: Questions.* The author describes the book as "a brief review of the Mormon corporate empire and the power it holds over high priest and presidential candidate Mitt Romney, whose family has been a part of the Mormon Royalty since the Church's creation."[50] The old themes of hierarchy, authoritarianism, and priestcraft remain, as the campaigns demonstrated as well.

Whether or not these themes significantly influenced the electorate, many Americans remain dubious about Mormonism, even when they admit their ignorance about the LDS Church. A 2011 poll by the Brookings Institution showed that more than three-quarters of Americans believed they knew little or nothing about the religious practices and beliefs of the LDS Church. Nevertheless, 41 percent felt sufficiently well informed to declare that they did not consider Mormonism a Christian religion. While 67 percent said they held wholly or mostly favorable views of Mormons, these numbers remain low compared to two other groups historically discriminated against. Jews and Catholics regularly hold acceptance rates of about 84 percent.[51]

In 2012, a Pew poll found that only a bit more than half of Republican voters viewed Romney as a Christian. Among white evangelical Protestants it was about a third. Although Republicans' view of Mormonism as a religion correlated with their support for Romney in the primaries—those less likely to view the LDS as a Christian church were less likely to vote for him—it had no impact on their preference for him above the Democratic candidate, Barack Obama.[52] The poll's statistics provide additional evidence of the shift of Mormons from religious eccentrics to religious conservatives in popular perceptions, helping explain the Romneys' electoral successes, even if they did not obtain their ultimate goals. As the authors of the Brookings report concluded, "It appears that Mormons' family life, work ethic, traditional values, and pronounced conservative leanings do more to shape evangelical attitudes toward them than does their theology."[53] This is an important observation: factors other than belief shape the lives of religious people and the perceptions of them by those outside their tradition.

The shift in American voters' attitudes since the Smoot hearings at the beginning of the last century may reflect the decline in the white Anglo Saxon Protestant ideal that once dominated American politics.[54] While the poll above proves that some Republicans choose Christian candidates over non-Christian ones, other polls show that American voters appear most interested in personal ethical attributes and less in particular religious membership. However, they also value an important convergence of the two qualities. A 2012 Gallup poll found that Americans were less likely to vote for an atheist presidential candidate than any other type of well-qualified candidate, including a gay or lesbian one (68 percent). Although 80 percent of respondents said they would vote for a Mormon, 94 percent for a Catholic, 91 percent for a Jew, and 58 percent for a Muslim, only 54 percent would select an atheist. While polls clearly demonstrate that a preponderance of citizens view *some* religious commitment as essential for the personal qualities required for the nation's highest office, this too is in flux, having risen from a mere 18 percent when the question was asked in 1958.[55]

AFTER THE ELECTION

Mitt Romney's tie for second in the 2008 Republican nomination race and his win of the nomination in 2012 demonstrated conclusively what George Romney's political fortunes already had hinted: Mormons have won increasing cultural recognition and acceptance through the occasional success of members in gaining notoriety. Beginning in the 1960s and '70s, the popular singers Donny and Marie Osmond brought their toothy winsomeness from their Provo, Utah, home to a national (and international) audience as singers, actors, and television stars. When Ronald Reagan dubbed the Mormon Tabernacle Choir, which sang for his 1981 inauguration, "America's choir," he reflected the views of those who consider the 360-member group an American musical icon. The short-running (1978–1979) yet long-remembered *Battlestar Galactica* projected Mormon history into a science fiction future with a planetary exodus searching for a lost tribe in a promised land. Even if its more successful successor (2004–2009) reprised some Mormon themes more accidentally than Glen A. Larson's original did, it nevertheless helped increase attention on the impact of the Saints on popular culture.[56] Meanwhile, Stephenie Meyer's *Twilight* series of books (2005–2008), then films (2009–2012), reaffirmed that message with a nationally bestselling story, perhaps only slightly more improbable in its portrayal of a girl falling in love with a vampire than that its unwed high school protagonists eschew sex and alcohol. This cultural prominence only reflects the Mormons' demographic size: today, the Church of Jesus Christ of Latter-day Saints represents the fifth-largest denomination in the United States, with about 6 million members. Nevertheless, anti-Mormon representations remain evident in popular entertainment (at least). Perhaps the surest, if most unlikely, sign of the church's contested acceptance in the American mainstream is offered by the skeptical creators of *South Park,* who have managed to fashion a hit Broadway musical entitled *The Book of Mormon,* which critics have alternatively decried as a cynical lampoon and embraced as an endearing endorsement of its eponymous subject.

Six

It's Not a Religion,
It's a Cult

The Branch Davidians

Few who were alive at the time could forget the scene. It ranks with iconic images of unfolding living horror like those of the napalm-burned girl in Vietnam, the fleeing students of Columbine High School, and the downwardly telescoping towers of Lower Manhattan. On April 19, 1993, incredulous Americans watched as their televisions showed billowing orange flames consuming the Branch Davidian compound outside Waco, Texas. The inferno cast upward churning black smoke that expanded above the buildings like a funeral shroud. As if stunned by the horrid scene, military helicopters circled in mute helplessness as seventy-four people, including twenty-one children, perished in the fire and smoke inside. One woman, her clothes on fire, ran out of the inferno only to try to run back inside when approached by law enforcement agents.

The history of Christianity is replete with the stories of communities like the Branch Davidians who remove themselves to some extent from the society that surrounds them in order to pursue what they consider a more Christ-centered existence. Many have taken the fact that Jesus "withdrew himself into the wilderness, and prayed" (Luke 5:16) and Jesus's injunction in the Gospels that his followers "are not of the world, even as I am not of the world" (John 17:16) as model statements for their seemingly eccentric lifestyles. Perhaps motivated by the Gospel narratives of Jesus's forty-day retreat into the desert wilderness, Saint Antony lived the solitary life of a hermit for twenty years in Egypt until he emerged to organize the first community of monks among other hermits in the year 305. These monks accepted a rule of behavior to guide their practices of prayer and austerities. Eventually, orders of monks developed in the Roman Catholic Church, each with its own rule for living in a secluded community. Eastern Orthodox Christians also built monasteries, and today an entire Greek peninsula is governed by twenty of them, the oldest of which is more than a millennium old.

The United States has its own host of secluded, communal traditions. Some represent continuations of ancient models, such as the silent life of work and meditation practiced in the Trappist abbeys situated in Spencer, Massachusetts; in Moncks Corner, South Carolina; and outside Dubuque, Iowa. Others exemplify newer utopian traditions emphasizing communal lifestyles that radically challenged mainstream America, even if the communities did not wholly seclude themselves from that society. Shakers arrived in the thirteen colonies just before the Revolution and established communities of men and women who lived in strict celibacy, pooled their possessions, and perfected skills of handicraft. The fame of "Shaker style" furniture and interior design has outlived the movement itself. Later, a community of "Bible Communists" built a home for themselves in Oneida, New York, where they practiced a socialist lifestyle that included the notion that all men were married to each woman, and vice versa. More enduring than most utopian communities, the Amish also arrived in North America in the eighteenth century. They built communities guided by the *Ordnung*'s strict rules, the transgression of which could lead to an individual's shunning by the entire group, including her or his family. Their rebellious lifestyle of eschewing most electrical and, for some groups, mechanical devices strives to avoid the evils they see in the society surrounding them. Despite the extreme nonconformity practiced by such groups—perhaps even because of it—local and state tourism officials often tout sites associated with them, such as the Shaker villages of New England, the Oneida communities of New York, and the Amish groups of Pennsylvania. Although their visible challenge to the status quo has prompted some neighbors to respond pensively (and even confrontationally) to these groups, a wider public has embraced them as wholly American, as part of the national landscape of religious pluralism.

So how did the peaceful group that called themselves Branch Davidians and built a compound in the flat plains of north Texas come to be the target of an armed assault by scores of Bureau of Alcohol, Tobacco, and Firearms agents that left four agents and six Davidians dead? And how did the fifty-one-day siege that followed culminate in the firestorm that immolated most of this community? For many news commentators, law enforcement officials, and other Americans, the answer could be summarized in one word: cult.

CULTS: TO BE OR NOT TO BE?

The Peoples Temple, Heaven's Gate, the Unification Church, the Family, and the International Society for Krishna Consciousness (aka the Hare Krishna) have all been alleged to be cults, just as the Branch Davidians were. But despite its popularity, the term proves harder to define than to use. In one sense of the word, "cult" refers to the intense veneration of an object—such as the "cult of youth" or "cult of secrecy"—or of an individual—such as the "cult of personality" that purportedly arose around figures like Lenin, Mao, and Castro. (The second usage hints at the negativity often associated with the term, since when Americans use the term in reference to the popular veneration of national leaders, they tend to restrict it to foreign ones who are politically antagonistic to the United States. One seldom hears, for instance, of the cult of Kennedy or

Reagan.) In another sense, the word describes a minor ancient or "primitive" religious group such as the "Dionysian cults" of ancient Greece or the "cargo cults" of Melanesia. Finally, in its most common use today, "cult" is the label applied to small religious groups organized around a charismatic leader that isolate their members from the larger society and demand belief in unconventional (sometimes destructive) ideas. Overall then, discounting its reference to ancient groups, the term has an overwhelmingly negative association.

Americans maintain a laundry list of iconic cult leaders, publicly reread by journalists each time another small group galvanized by someone's magnetic personality fractures the social compact. "Cults" became a front-page issue starting in the 1970s as a result of a number of high-profile incidents involving charismatic leaders and their followers. In 1969, Charles Manson and his Family committed the gruesome murders of five people, including the actress Sharon Tate and her unborn child. A decade later, Jim Jones directed his Jonestown community of more than 900 in Guyana to commit suicide by drinking poisoned Kool-Aid after murdering a visiting US congressman. Dissenting members were shot. Other incidents like the suicide of Marshall H. Applewhite and Bonnie Nettles with most of the rest of the Heaven's Gate group in 1997 (supposedly allowing them to reach an alien spaceship following a passing comet) reaffirmed for many Americans that any group labeled "cult" by the media, authorities, or anti-cult "experts" was suspect and potentially dangerous.

Given the prominence of at least one small breakaway religious group in our popular national-origin myth, it may surprise some that they provoke such suspicion. Although in their day the Pilgrims did not call themselves "Separatists," "Puritans," or even "Pilgrims," as we saw in chapter one, they rejected what they viewed as the failure of the Church of England to properly realize the Protestant Reformation's ideals. Successive English kings persecuted the faction, forcing members to flee abroad, ultimately leading them to establish colonies along the cold waters of New England's shoreline at Plymouth, Boston, and New

Haven beginning in 1620. In their new towns, the settlers required church attendance, outlawed blasphemy, and demanded dedication to communal life. Massachusetts colony residents mostly accepted John Winthrop's social and political ideals, and his legendary leadership—although not unchallenged—extended for almost all of the twenty years before his death. The well-known expulsions of Roger Williams and Anne Hutchinson—if not the lesser-known trials of Mary Dyer—indicate their hostility to divergent religious perspectives (indeed, as already discussed, Winthrop and many of her former neighbors proclaimed the later murder of Hutchinson and her children a retributive act of God). Nevertheless, every November, American families suffer traffic-jammed highways and passenger-crowded airports to return to family homes for the reenactment of a Pilgrim meal and the reaccreditation of Pilgrims as exemplary Americans, even though the group's separatism and intolerance would likely make them suspect as a cult today.

The exemption of the Pilgrims, Shakers, and Amish from the label "cults" suggests that the application of the word says more about those who apply it than about those it purportedly describes. This is to say that the label "cult" serves more as a mirror of the expectations and self-understandings of those who use it than it acts as a lens by which to understand the unpopular groups it pretends to describe. Understood this way, we can then recognize the popular American perception that religions—in contrast with cults, their upside-down mirror image—are large, long-established groups whose practices and beliefs are appropriate, whose leaders are conventional, and that do not require their members to sacrifice their individuality. Since the difference between a "cult" and "proper religion" relies on such ambiguous distinctions as how long a community has existed and how appropriate its practices appear, efforts to label a religious group as one or the other become an entirely subjective judgment. Ultimately, then, "cult" simply marks particular religious groups as unconventional and disliked. This is not to suggest that there are not destructive religious groups, oppressive communities, or malevolent leaders. However, scholars of religion generally have recognized that the subjective nature of the term does not justify its use, preferring instead the term "new religious movement" (NRM) to neutrally indicate recently formed groups that often share some similar qualities, such as small size, charismatic leadership, challenges to the status quo, and the suspicion and scrutiny of larger society. The history of the Branch Davidians displays most of these characteristics.

ORIGINS OF THE BRANCH DAVIDIANS

As already demonstrated in regard to the Pilgrims, a key feature of American Protestantism—perhaps of Protestantism throughout its history—is the fracturing of denominations into separate churches, if not wholly new denominations. Many Americans consider religions to be hidebound phenomena, entrenched in tradition and conservative by nature. While many religious communities value books, leaders, and traditions of their past, it would be a mistake to confuse this with stasis. In fact, when new religious movements form in order to better realize the conditions they considered to exist among their predecessors, they may pursue radical changes in their status quo. In doing so, these new communities commonly face the double bind of ostracism from the denomination from which they secede and suspicion from society at large. The Branch Davidians encountered just such conditions in their short history.

The Branch Davidians originally stemmed from Seventh-day Adventism (SDA), a Protestant denomination that arose in the nineteenth century. The Adventists' name reflects two key dimensions of their belief system. "Seventh-day" refers to their affirmation of Saturday as the Sabbath sanctioned in the Hebrew Bible and thus demonstrates their strict biblical literalism. "Adventist" signals their expectation that Christ's imminent return will serve as the prelude to the end times. The Seventh-day Adventists were born in the ruined anticipation of Christ's arrival that the preacher William Miller had declared would occur around

1844. Later, Ellen Gould White and her husband helped couple Millerite doctrines with health proscriptions and created a new organization that became so popular that its churches could be found throughout the United States by the end of the century. One White follower, John Harvey Kellogg, made Battle Creek, Michigan, the movement's headquarters and the center of his thriving cereal business.

Seeking reform of the Seventh-day Adventist Church, Victor T. Houteff and roughly seventy others created the Davidian Seventh-day Adventists and, in 1935, settled outside Waco, Texas. Houteff's expectation of an imminent apocalypse following his interpretation of the Bible—the Book of Revelation in particular—continued the Adventist millennialist heritage with its history of great disappointments. Meanwhile, Houteff and his community had to struggle with the hostility of the Seventh-day Adventists who rejected his provocative message, which included both allegations that the mother church had allowed corruption by conforming too much to worldly expectations and warnings of the imminent return of Christ.

Houteff and his followers started from scratch in building the infrastructure for living at Mount Carmel, as they called their community. This included using their land to meet their needs for food and lumber. While they never attempted complete isolation, self-sufficiency was an ideal. Thus, although some members earned wages in the surrounding areas, those residing at Mount Carmel mostly made do with a currency produced there, symbolizing their disconnection from mainstream America. In other ways too they marked their secession: marriage forbidden with outsiders, restrictions on types of clothing, and the prohibition of ball sports. While these separatist ways could be considered markers of difference with mainstream American Christianity, they can also be seen as indicating the pursuit of a less-traveled—yet wholly familiar—Christian road. The Davidians built their spiritual and material lives around the example of Jesus and his apostles, taking Jesus as the Son of God and savior of humanity. They read the same Bible as many Protestants, although they differed in regard to some of the conclusions they drew in their interpretations of it. These conclusions led them away from existing communities so that they could create the best conditions to welcome the end of days.

The "Davidian" component of their name referenced the kingdom of David. This simultaneously gestured to the ancient God-sanctioned kingdom described in the Old Testament and the expectant rule of Christ anticipated by various passages from both the Old and New Testaments, according to Houteff's interpretation. This period to come, foreseen by the prophet John of Patmos and recorded in the Book of Revelation, is called by Christians the Apocalypse: a time when what has been hidden is revealed (indeed, "apocalypse" derives from the Greek word for "revelation") and the future brings a new reality. An initial era of extreme difficulty or tribulation begins the Apocalypse and culminates in the return and rule of Christ. This rule gives "millennialism" its name, referencing the thousand years of peaceful existence before the final judgment of all humans—living and dead—following the ultimate defeat of evil by a returned Jesus Christ. Millennialism has served as a critical component in various American Protestant movements, threading through the histories of the Puritans, Mormons, Jehovah's Witnesses, and Seventh-day Adventists, even as they disagreed about whether Christ's return occurred before or after the millennium.

Davidian expectations that the Apocalypse was imminent relied upon Houteff's understanding of the Bible, which he combed for passages that would shed light on the expected advent of Christ. A minor crisis erupted in 1955 when Victor Houteff died without establishing the precise time of this event. However, his wife, Florence, stepped in and pronounced a date in 1959. Nearly a thousand Davidians from around the world arrived at Mount Carmel in anticipation of the event, many severing all their social ties and unburdening themselves of their possessions. Needless to say, they faced another "great disappointment" on the magnitude of the Millerite setback a century earlier. The resulting storm of despair drove away all but about fifty believers. None of this garnered much national news coverage.

In the subsequent turmoil, the Davidian's eight factions competed against one another, with the Branch Davidians—which had formed in 1955 under Ben Roden's leadership—eventually gaining the upper hand. Roden bestowed the name "Branch" in reference to the passage in Isaiah 11:1, "There shall come forth a rod out of the stem of Jesse, and a Branch shall grow out of his roots."[1] Although Roden changed the organization of the Davidians in certain ways, his own authority as leader continued to rely on his ability to interpret the scriptures in insightful ways, as had Houteff's authority. But authority does not exist in a vacuum: it relies upon the recognition of legitimacy by those who follow. Ultimately, the most charismatic or patriarchal leaders are powerless without the consent of those who are willing to accept their leadership. This held true for Lois Roden, Ben's wife, who claimed and was rewarded the mantle of leadership after the death of her husband in 1978. However, while she proclaimed the power of a divine vision granted to her, her son George asserted his own prophetic authority. Into this volatile mix entered a new personality, Vernon Howell, with his own declaration of authority.

DAVID KORESH: *A* MESSIAH, NOT *THE* MESSIAH

Vernon Howell, a member of the local SDA church, first arrived at Mount Carmel to work as a carpenter. While his provocative prophecies eventually drove the SDAs to withdraw his membership, the same pronouncements prompted most Branch Davidians to embrace his spiritual guidance, demonstrating again the contextual nature of authority. Indeed, Howell ultimately obtained the sanction of Lois Roden to succeed her as community leader. Characteristically, George Roden rejected this, and a terse exchange of allegations culminated in a terser exchange of gunfire. The rivalry was finally decided by two unlikely arbiters: tax collectors and court judges. While George's intractability and threatening outbursts against judges landed him in jail, Howell paid Mount

Carmel's back taxes, and the Branch Davidians under his leadership reoccupied the site in 1988. Howell quickly moved to reestablish an orderly life there, maintaining the tradition of preparing for the Apocalypse. The earlier Davidian choice of the name "Mount Carmel" reflects their end-time expectations: this was the biblical battleground where the prophet Elijah confronted the false prophets of the idol god Baal (1 Kings 18). Since the community's founding by Houteff decades earlier, the Davidians—and now the Branch Davidians—viewed their home under the expansive skies of central Texas as a place of preparation for the impending battle between truth and falsehood, right and wrong, Christ and Antichrist.

While they rebuilt many of the more decrepit parts of the compound that had been inadequately maintained under Roden's control, the community's devotion to living at Mount Carmel still meant a dedication to a difficult life, without central heating, air conditioning, or even, in many areas, plumbing. Nevertheless, the community got back to at least partially homeschooling their children, cultivating their own farm, and working for wages. Despite their separatist preference, the community remained integrated into society in Waco and beyond. For instance, among other enterprises upon which the Davidians' finances relied was the purchase of components that allowed Howell to retool semiautomatic rifles into automatic rifles (which was legal, so long as the guns were registered). He then openly sold these at the gun shows commonplace in Texas. Although their isolation was not complete, it did allow most members to focus on the purpose for which they joined the community: to learn from and participate in the world Howell foresaw through his biblical interpretation. Convinced that he could guide them through the text to reveal God's plan and will and also drawn to the shared values of Mount Carmel's moral community, members accepted the rudimentary living conditions of the compound in the barren landscape surrounded by the long horizons of central Texas.

If Mount Carmel's name was meant to be meaningful, so was the new one Vernon Howell chose for himself. By renaming himself "David

Koresh," he signified that through his interpretation of the Bible he understood himself as a God-guided leader, directed to sire a select generation of children. "Koresh" referred to Cyrus, the king of ancient Persia whose vanquishing of Babylonia set free the Jews exiled there after the Babylonians had subjugated them. The song "By the Waters of Babylon," based on Psalm 137 and performed by modern singers like Jimmy Cliff and Don McLean, relates the sorrow of captives pining for a return to their home. David Koresh saw himself as a savior, sent by God to prepare a chosen few at the time of the Apocalypse, which, as most SDA members believed, would soon be at hand. With this worldview, Koresh considered himself a messiah spoken to and directed by God, although with a decidedly small "m" that did not contest Jesus Christ's large "M" messiahship. The Hebrew term *messiah* (*christos* in Greek) literally means "anointed one" and initially referred to the anointment of a king with oil as an indicator of his sanctity. Hence, Isaiah 45:1 describes Cyrus as a messiah. However, the term also could be applied to God-chosen people of stature without political power, such as when Psalm 105:9–15 refers to the familiar biblical figures of Abraham, Isaac, and Jacob as "messiahs."[2] In sum, Koresh thought that God had anointed him to lead a group out of the captivity of modern American Babylonia, just as God had anointed Cyrus to free the Jewish captives in ancient Babylon and return them to their homeland.

Who would comprise this group? Koresh sought to create and prepare a community that *together* would not only welcome Christ back to the world but would help trigger his return. Known as premillennialism, this belief in Christ's reappearance as the harbinger of the millennium may appear odd even to many Christians, yet it has long been prevalent among conservative Christians. Indeed, Columbus sailed with the hope of prompting this event, since by fulfilling certain biblical prophecies he would help spur the Antichrist's arrival. He indicated as much in 1500 when he wrote, "God made me the messenger of the new heaven and the new earth of which he spoke in the Apocalypse of St. John after having spoken of it through the mouth of Isaiah; and he showed me the spot where to find it."[3] Since him, Mormons, Jehovah's Witnesses, and the SDAs also have made the notion central to their theology. Meanwhile, the book and film *The Late Great Planet Earth* (1970, 1979) and *The Omen* series of films (1976–2006) are among various productions that have helped popularize these ideas. With this millennialist urgency, Koresh and some of his followers vigorously proselytized around the globe, especially among SDA members. The Mount Carmel community grew as new initiates from the United States, Britain, Australia, New Zealand, and other nations joined in preparation for the end of contemporary world order.

Meanwhile, Koresh's name change also alluded to another preparation within the community: what he called "the House of David." Part of this looked backward, to the exemplary reign of the biblical King David, the presumed ancestor of the next messiah. Part of it looked forward, to the creation of a new generation of the lineage.[4] While Koresh's exact intentions remain unclear, there is evidence that he sought to rear twenty-four children to serve as the "four and twenty elders" who venerate God on the heavenly throne, as described in Revelation 4:4 and elsewhere. Although Koresh required celibacy of even his married members (whose marriages he had dissolved and who bunked in gender-specific quarters), he fathered children by several women: some of them were the legal wives of followers, and some of them were the teenage daughters of followers. The details of these liaisons remain unclear given that some allegations about them originate both from disgruntled members who had left the community and from distraught relatives of members. Nevertheless, Koresh's adultery and sexual relations with minors would become a provocation to the surrounding society, were investigated by authorities, and helped fire popular indignation when reported by news media.[5]

As in Houteff's time, Branch Davidians followed the unorthodox views of their leader as necessary for their apocalyptic preparations. Koresh primed the community to eventually relocate from their separatist compound in Texas to Israel, where they would prepare for and greet

Christ's return while bracing themselves against the accompanying oppressions of Satan. Instead of declaring a specific date for the advent of the Messiah as William Miller and Florence Houteff had done earlier, Koresh explained that the "Tribulation" preceding the Savior's arrival was already in effect, using world events as examples of the confusion and conflict that Revelation purportedly describes. Much like Columbus and some Christian groups, the Branch Davidians did not consider themselves mere observers of the end-time but participants who were shaping events. Hence they expected that their migration to Israel would trigger a great war in the Middle East that would, in turn, prompt Christ's return. Agreeing with Koresh's interpretation of the Book of Revelation, they expected that these events would bring martyrdom to some of their community even as they rallied 144,000 righteous ones to survive the Tribulation. In the millennial aftermath, the twenty-four children of the House of David would live in a world from which Christ had temporarily expunged evil.[6]

How was Koresh able to convince people to abandon their lives and move as far as half a world away to central Texas? What could he say that would persuade husbands to let him sleep with their wives and persuade parents to let him impregnate their teenage daughters? Ultimately, most Branch Davidians followed Koresh because they agreed with his view of scripture and of the world. Acquaintances do not describe a man with a magnetic personality. He dressed in an unassuming way, often went unshaven, and "seemed a regular guy," according to at least one former member.[7] However, Koresh's masterly exegesis or interpretation of the Bible imbued him—in the eyes of the Branch Davidians—with authority because he could illuminate matters in the text that had initially been invisible to them. In a long Bible study following dinner each night (which sometimes went on until morning) and in others held occasionally at other parts of the day, Koresh would expound at length on particular Bible passages, stringing together verses from various books and explaining their combined meaning, all the while appealing to a particular logic of interpretation. Community members often found these spellbinding, and the truths they supposedly revealed only deepened their regard for and trust in Koresh.

Their leader convinced the Branch Davidians that only he had the insight to bring out the hidden facts of the text, in part because, as a prophet, he received continuous revelations from God. These revelations helped guide not only Koresh's biblical interpretation but also the larger direction of the community because his understanding of the Bible influenced his understanding of events. And the opposite was true, too, since happenings unfolding around Mount Carmel suggested that certain expected parts of the Book of Revelation were coming to pass. A basic key to Koresh's success in attracting new members to the community depended on their recognition of his exegetical authority. The many Seventh-day Adventist churches that turned him away often did so because they could not square his interpretations with their own worldview and thus could not accept his authority. But those who embraced his authority accepted that no other interpreter of both the Bible and world events could make better sense of both.

But the focus on the unusual quality of Koresh's leadership only offers half an answer as to why his dedicated followers gave up so much to live at Mount Carmel. The other half of the answer lies in the very Christian message and lifestyle that this community offered. As with the original Davidians (and most Christians), the Branch Davidians understood the Bible to offer divine guidance to a humanity struggling with the usual challenges of survival, family, neighbors, economics, morality, sexuality, and politics. The focus of news sources and law enforcement on the unconventional aspects of their community life meant that the many more conventional qualities of these Christians were ignored (even though these more common Christian beliefs and practices might appear as absurd to many non-Christians as Davidian traditions often did to mainstream Christians). Belief in Jesus as the savior Christ, whose historical life on Earth was foretold by the Hebrew Bible and described in the New Testament, and who heard and responded to the prayers of the devoted made the Branch Davidians the same as most Christians.

The choice to join them, then, arose more from the recognition of their similarity to other Christians than from their difference.

Of course, most Americans had a far harder time appreciating Branch Davidian beliefs, given that they did not believe that the world as they knew it was gradually disappearing in the convulsions of the age. Having dismissed the factuality of Koresh and the group's claims, the newspaper journalists, federal law enforcement officials, and American audiences who gradually focused on the group in the early 1990s needed a different interpretative frame in which to picture the Branch Davidians and Koresh. "Cult" would serve mainstream society not only as a label for the Davidians, but as a signal of peril and a call to action.

CREATING A CULT AND THE INITIAL ASSAULT

In 1991, the Australian television show *A Current Affair* launched an investigation of the Branch Davidians after former member Marc Breault piqued their interest. Breault had joined the Davidians after listening to some of Koresh's Bible study sessions. However, Koresh's later justifications for bedding the community's women laid the first seed of doubt in his mind, and upon his exit from the group Breault made various unsuccessful efforts to pitch his story to media in the United States before his eventual success in Australia. The television show portrayed him as a heroic "cultbuster" who faced extraordinary dangers in leaving the group—"You don't just leave a cult, you have to escape. . . . One wrong move could mean a bullet through the brain"—and then dedicated his life to save others from Koresh's "poison." Despite the fact that several others had departed from the community before him without threat to their well-being, *A Current Affair* made Breault's exit a perilous endeavor fraught with mortal danger. Later, members of the Branch Davidians explained that Breault, who was seeking a ministry among the Seventh-day Adventists when he met Koresh, had vied for the leader's position. Nevertheless, Breault's narrative gained an increasingly wide audience as he pursued media contacts, organized former Branch Davidians, and tried to persuade government and law enforcement authorities in both Australia (where he settled) and the United States to act. He finally got the attention of both the media—the producers of *A Current Affair*—and law enforcement—members of the Bureau of Alcohol, Tobacco, and Firearms (ATF)—who consulted him as part of their investigation that would legitimate the attack.[8]

Meanwhile the newspaper most local to Mount Carmel, the *Waco Tribune-Herald,* had begun its own investigation, also relying heavily on Breault's testimony while cooperating with the ATF. The paper's editor, in explaining his initiative to publish the seven-part "Sinful Messiah" series, said, "It was time to let the public know of this menace in our community,"[9] despite the fact that the county sheriff later described the Branch Davidians quite differently.

> We had a bunch of women, children, elderly people—they were all good, good people. They had different beliefs from others, different beliefs than I have, maybe. . . . I was around them quite a lot, they were always nice, married, they minded their own business, they were never overbearing, they were always clean and courteous. I liked 'em.[10]

These local experiences paled, however, before the colorful descriptions of the Branch Davidians as a cult, implicitly equivalent with danger.

These two media projects on the Davidians incidentally coincided with an ATF investigation and assault preparations. The bureau took the Australian report as a background source in support of its incursion, interviewed Breault, and discussed their interests with the *Tribune-Herald.* At the ATF's request, the newspaper's editor withheld publication of the series—titled "The Sinful Messiah" in reference to Koresh's admission of sin and claim to be a messiah—until just before the bureau's assault, when he became impatient and began publishing it anyway.[11]

These collusions between the media and law enforcement had three immediate effects. First, local media figures were already attuned to ATF preparations for their assault on the Branch Davidians' Mount Tabor compound and were thus primed to respond with intensive coverage. Second, the agency enjoyed media verification of its charges regarding weapons violations and child abuse. The heavy reliance upon disgruntled former Branch Davidians, one of whom had turned to the media possibly to excoriate Koresh after a failed bid to replace him as leader, helpfully skewed the reporting to support the bureau's allegations. And third, when the ATF assault resulted in casualties among their agents (and among the Davidians), the agency had media immediately available to broadcast its version of the fatal events, while it curtailed the ability of the Davidians to publicly provide their own account.[12]

On February 28, 1993, before the Branch Davidians felt directed to affect their relocation plan, three military helicopters passed above Mount Carmel, taking fire according to the government and firing into the building according to Davidian survivors. Then two pickup trucks pulling cattle trailers stopped outside the compound's entrance, and fifty or more heavily armed ATF agents poured out, some running toward the front door and others using scaling ladders to enter the second floor. The ATF launched this assault—codenamed "Operation Showtime"—on the community in an attempt to serve an arrest warrant on David Koresh and a search warrant for alleged weapons violations regarding the potentially legal upgrades that turned semi-automatic rifles into automatic weapons. The stakes were high for the ATF, since the bureau faced budget hearings in a few months, not long after a bungled, fatal standoff with a small white supremacist group and allegations by female agents of sexual harassment. So they may have preferred the showy assault covered by journalists (whom they alerted to the raid) rather than the discussion Koresh offered to clarify matters regarding his gun upgrades.[13]

Tipped off by both an undercover agent among them whom they had already suspected and the movement of law enforcement agents, the Branch Davidians were prepared to defend themselves against what they viewed as an attack. The resulting firefight ended only after six Davidians and four ATF agents lay dead, and others were wounded, including Koresh. With many of its agents pinned down near or on the compound, the ATF agreed to a ceasefire offered by Koresh that allowed both sides to recover their dead and injured. The process by which the ATF decided to assault Mount Carmel using overwhelming force and equipment borrowed from the military in order to serve warrants demonstrates how a public and governmental marginalization of the Branch Davidians occurred through the efforts of news media, disaffected former members, and government agencies that intertwined around the fear of cults.

ENTER THE "CULT SPECIALISTS" AND THE ANTI-CULT MOVEMENT

The *Tribune-Herald*'s "Sinful Messiah" series often used the language of "brainwashing" when interpreting its interviews with nearly a score of former community members. This reflected the preexisting interest in cults and the role of self-proclaimed cult experts of the anti-cult movement in framing the public narrative about various new religious movements. As the failed attack transformed into a long-term siege, many of these supposed specialists sought to capitalize on this opportunity to promote their services and successfully influence media, if not law enforcement, representations of the Branch Davidians.

When news and entertainment media began focusing on so-called cults in the 1970s, some individuals sought personal advantage from commenting on and removing members from new religious movements. Besides the tragic Manson Family murders and Jonestown suicides, the rise of the Unification Church of Reverend Sun Myung Moon and the International Society of Krishna Consciousness (the Hare Krishna) of Swami Prabhupada convinced Americans that leaders of these groups were seeking to ensnare their sons and daughters, if not their husbands and wives, in an inescapable community turned so inward as to deny anyone outside. Before long, the cult phenomena spawned the anti-cult movement.

The emergence of a market for supposed specialists and disaffected former members to comment in print, on air, and during police investigations—as well as to proffer services to concerned parents and other family members—nurtured the self-promotion of various "expert" individuals and groups. Anti-cult groups like the Cult Awareness Network (CAN) sowed suspicion about small religious communities that seemed to veer away from popular norms. As a collection of professional "deprogrammers," CAN became one of the most prominent representatives of this movement. They alleged that charismatic leaders brainwashed their followers, robbing them of their individualism, and condemned them to mental servitude and social isolation. Over time, self-styled deprogrammers advertised their supposed skills of breaking a cult's mental hold and liberating individuals to "think for themselves" again, often relying on coercive methods to abduct and reeducate the "cult victim." The sensation generated by these anti-cult activists—amplified by news and entertainment media—created a popular game of guesswork on whether or not various new religious groups such as the Hare Krishna, the Peoples Temple, and the Japanese Buddhist Soka Gakkai were cults. Eventually, in response to this disturbing trend, professional associations of psychologists and sociologists denied the possibility of brainwashing, and scholars of religion refuted the notion of cults. Certainly leaders can be manipulative and groups can apply social pressure, but individuals cannot be made into automatons bereft of any independent thought. Nevertheless, the tantalizing mixture of secrecy, megalomania, and manipulation so perfectly caught the popular imagination that the cult phenomenon remained fixed there, even informing the ways in which the Federal Bureau of Investigation (FBI) would manage the standoff with the Branch Davidians.

Hours after the ATF's abortive attack, the FBI took tactical control of the situation, establishing a ring of law enforcement officers and armored vehicles around Mount Carmel and beginning negotiations with David Koresh. The FBI attuned its strategies to a "blockade/hostage" scenario. This model cast Koresh as a charismatic, maniacal cult leader who had brainwashed his followers to act contrary to their will.[14] Such a conclusion paved the way for members of the anti-cult movement to enter the situation as "authorities" to whom the FBI turned in order to better comprehend the dynamics at play. In its effort to understand the circumstances, the FBI sought out a variety of sources, including behavioral scientists, medical experts, and the now-published *Tribune-Herald* articles.[15] In the meantime, ex-Davidian Marc Breault and two self-described "cult experts" offered their unsolicited help. The federal agency listened to what these three had to say, but—according to their after-action report—did not engage in extended discussion with any of them. However, these and others like them became authorities to whom news outlets turned for insights. By doing so, broadcast and print news outlets cast the standoff as one of law enforcement against a cult of programmed followers led by a manipulative, possibly psychotic, demagogue, while describing their sources as authorities working with law enforcement. Although the FBI may not have entirely bowed to this portrayal, many of their tactics conformed to what the "cult experts" recommended.

As opposed to most of the other specialists to whom the FBI turned for advice and consultation, the "cult experts" promoted themselves— sometimes enthusiastically. Throughout the siege, Breault attempted to insert himself into the unfolding events. Living in Australia, he first made contact with the FBI through the State Department. Although the bureau decided not to contact him because he had no up-to-date information and was speaking with the media, they compiled everything Breault had written about the Branch Davidians. Not to be rebuffed, Breault repeatedly sent e-mails to the FBI offering advice, including the idea that a radio debate between him and Koresh be broadcast to demonstrate his superior understanding of the Bible. By the end of the year, he co-published a book entitled *Preacher of Death: The Shocking Inside Story of David Koresh and the Waco Siege.*[16]

Rick Ross, a professional "deprogrammer," also vied for FBI and media attention. Within a week of the initial confrontation, he contacted the FBI to offer his insights about cults and the Branch Davidians. The ATF had already consulted him the month before their assault on Mount Carmel[17] and had interviewed people whom he recommended.[18] During the siege, he moved into a hotel in Dallas, then shifted to one closer to the action in Waco, all the while doing interviews on local television and CNN. Perhaps recognizing belatedly the spurious quality of Ross's expertise, the Department of Justice's after-action report defensively states, "The FBI did not 'rely' on Ross for advice whatsoever during the standoff. The FBI interviewed Ross only at Ross' request, and politely declined his unsolicited offers of assistance throughout the standoff."[19] However, research by scholar Nancy Ammerman—who provided the Department of Justice at their request with an assessment of the FBI's strategy after Mount Carmel's incineration—suggests that the FBI's denial is somewhat disingenuous. As their own records demonstrate, the FBI discussed the situation with Ross twice over the course of the siege and engaged in tactics similar to those that he proposed would undermine Koresh's authority within the Branch Davidians—despite the fact that agents determined that Ross "has a personal hatred for all religious cults" and would like to help law enforcement "destroy a cult." Meanwhile, neither the ATF nor the FBI made concerted efforts to engage academic scholars of religion, despite the fact that some faculty at neighboring Baylor University had studied the Branch Davidians and understood how Koresh spoke through biblical paradigms.[20]

Meanwhile, the language of cults and the expertise of cult specialists, punctuated by testimony from disaffected former members, dominated news reporting from the start. Even before the conflict, CAN affiliates served as sources for the "Sinful Messiah" series, which repeatedly referred to the Branch Davidians as a cult.[21] National newspapers routinely did the same, suggesting that even normal aspects of life seemed topsy-turvy. For instance, the *New York Times* reported how children's lives at Mount Carmel fit "a routine that is by turns harrowing and almost eerily pleasant." The same article described Breault as "one of the few former cult members willing to offer warnings about Mr. Koresh," suggesting pressure not to do so.[22]

The cumulative effect of these allegations, voiced by self-accredited experts and broadcast by news agencies, was evident in media and law enforcement explanations following the horrifying end to the siege. After the conflagration, the *Washington Post* covered the Clinton administration's response to the tragedy. Attorney General Janet Reno, who took responsibility for the decisions that preceded the fire, explained that the ATF had initially acted on reports of weapons violations and assertions that "babies were being beaten." The FBI had believed the same, despite the lack of evidence regarding the latter allegation. The article went on to quote a counterterrorism negotiator who sympathized with the FBI officials making the final decision: "You're talking about a cult. You don't know how fanatical they are going to be."[23] The public consensus that the Davidians fit the cult stereotype promoted by anti-cult experts meant that news media often dismissed the counterevidence offered by many of their neighbors, their families, and even behavioral scientists. The Davidian children reportedly appeared well adjusted, Koresh demonstrated affection as well as strictness, and the group was not at risk of mass suicide. Such testimony notwithstanding, the collusion between media, law enforcement, and cult specialists laid the basis for the echo chamber that soon crystalized around public discussion of the Branch Davidians. The repeated assumptions, often lacking in or countered by evidence, forged a mutually reinforcing set of assumptions that became increasingly unquestionable with each day of the fifty-one-day standoff.

APOCALYPSE NOW

Repelling the ATF with gunfire only to be besieged by the FBI, the Mount Carmel community was thrown into turmoil as the cosmic denouement they had expected seemed to have arrived earlier than anticipated. Surrounded by a ring of federal law enforcement officers, badgered by helicopters and armored vehicles, and deprived of communication and electricity, Koresh and his fellow church members returned to the Bible's apocalyptic books to gradually reinterpret their situation. They concluded that the end-time they had anticipated for the near future—after they had relocated to Israel—had come to pass now. While some Branch Davidians elected to leave during the fifty-one-day siege, most decided to stay, steeling themselves for the final assault they knew would come.

Based on the information they obtained from behavioral specialists and supposed cult experts, the FBI responded to the standoff using strategies developed for a hostage/barricade scenario. In other words, the bureau viewed Koresh as a possible psychotic who held the other seventy-three against their will in a compound made impervious to entrance or exit. This approach targeted Koresh as the lynchpin of the situation: weakening him would strain his hold over the hostages, and they might fight their way free. Initial efforts to negotiate with Koresh had resulted in some community members and all but Koresh's children leaving Mount Carmel. Some of these adults were immediately arrested for their part in the firefight with the ATF agents. The indictment of two elderly women for attempted murder brought a chill to the negotiations when the Davidians heard about it on CNN. Koresh made a promise of surrender if a tape of his teachings was broadcast and then, after it aired, backpedaled—claiming it was God's decree—to the mounting frustration of the FBI negotiators. Ultimately, Koresh decided that he would leave the compound once he finished writing a God-directed manifesto interpreting the opening of the seven seals in the Book of Revelation.

This need to wait for Koresh to receive divine inspiration did little to bolster the diminishing patience of the law enforcement officials waiting on the siege perimeter surrounding the "Wacko from Waco," as some in the press and public called him. Opting for a more aggressive strategy meant to make the Branch Davidians both feel increasingly helpless and view Koresh as decreasingly powerful, the FBI made various, escalating provocations. Electrical power and telephone access were cut. Massive lights shone on the compound all night to

"A helicopter makes a low pass over a banner that was unfurled from a window by Branch Davidian cult members at the compound near Waco, Texas on Friday, April 9, 1993. The banner reads: '1st Seal, Rev. 6:12, PS 45, Rev. 19, PS 2, PS 18, PS 35 KJV,' which refers to several verses from Psalms and Revelation in the Bible. KJV refers to the King James Version of the Bible. Authorities refused to comment on the significance of the banner." (1993). Associated Press/David Philip.

deprive residents of darkness. Huge speakers assaulted their ears with the sounds of Tibetan chanting, Nancy Sinatra singing "These Boots Are Made for Walking," and the slaughter of rabbits, making sleep in Mount Tabor nearly impossible. Armored vehicles circling the compound gradually moved into closer and closer orbits, directed at one point to crush Davidian cars under their grinding caterpillar treads. Despite the warning of at least two FBI agents that these tactics might be counterproductive, they continued.[24]

Responding to the initial interpretative confusion of an assault against them occurring earlier and on a different continent than they had expected, the Branch Davidians shifted their expectations to conform to their current situation. They turned their anticipation that they would be the target of Babylon's forces and some made martyrs in Israel into a reinterpretation of the Bible. Babylon had caught up with them in Texas before their overseas relocation. The six killed by the ATF represented the prerequisite martyrdom preceding the opening of the final seals that culminated in Christ's return. Rather than undermining Koresh's authority, the FBI's actions did exactly the opposite, affirming his declarations that the Davidians would suffer for their righteousness and making it appear that the Apocalypse would unfold not in the near future but now. Meanwhile, the FBI suffered its own crisis of interpretation, although it did not know it.

Even as they unwittingly reinforced Koresh's authority within the compound, once the FBI decided that social power and psychosis, rather than religious vision, motivated Koresh, they forfeited the ability to understand what he and his proxies said during telephone conversations with federal negotiators. The Department of Justice's report on the catastrophe reflects the FBI's views of Koresh's use of the Bible. Instead of recognizing how his understanding of the Bible overwhelmingly shaped the lens with which he viewed this and the next world, agents viewed him as engaging in subterfuge. Perhaps most tellingly, the report notes, "Each time the negotiators would attempt to steer the conversation to substantive matters, Koresh would simply keep preaching what the negotiators called 'Bible babble.'" Clearly, for Koresh and those adults who elected to stay with him, no matter could be more substantive than the events the Bible predicted and the actions it prescribed. But the FBI willfully would not understand this. Describing one of a number of instances when Koresh subjected negotiators to an hour-long sermon, the report noted, "This 'Bible study,' as with Koresh's other preaching and sermonizing, rambled and made little sense, except perhaps to his followers."[25] Without any background in religious discourse or movements, the FBI negotiators and their commanders could not appreciate that Koresh was only speaking to those who shared his biblical commitments. Law enforcement officials kept demanding that he speak about the situation as *they* understood it, not as *he* did. In essence, although they both used English words, the two sides of the standoff at times spoke two different languages as divergent from one another as Swahili and Swedish. Comprehension by either side was often hamstrung, though not impossible, even as Koresh made slow but steady progress on his exegesis of Revelation, the completion of which he said would allow their surrender.

The last recorded conversation between Koresh and federal negotiators tragically bears out this problem in translation. Henry, the negotiator, persists in telling Koresh that he should lead everyone out of Mount Carmel. When Koresh replies that he does not control everyone in the compound, Henry disagrees.

> Henry: And you're willing to send out thirty people.
> Koresh: Look . . .
> Henry: Fifty?
> Koresh: Whoever wants to go out can go out.
> Henry: No, no, no, no. Don't tell me *that*. Tell me that you're sending somebody out.
> Koresh: I'm not going—You see, you don't understand about these people yet.
> Henry: And you don't understand about the people here yet, *either*.[26]

Until the sad end, the FBI remained committed to the view that Koresh, having commandeered everyone's will, held them against their best interests while in pursuit of his own.

But the transcript also shows the root of a far deeper misalignment of worldviews. While Koresh and Henry discuss broken promises on both sides, Henry chides Koresh for not surrendering when he agreed and Koresh responds from his perspective that God instructed him to defy his earlier agreement with the FBI. He senses Henry's disregard for this possibility.

> Koresh: Look, you denounce the fact that I have a God that communicates with me. That's the first mistake. . . .
> Henry: Nobody is saying anything about your religious beliefs, your thoughts, your ideas, or anything like that.
> Koresh: But you *are*.[27]

For Henry, Koresh made the decision to stay, just as he made all the decisions in the standoff, and his followers remained at his direction. This approach, so central to the FBI's training for a hostage/barricade situation, inherently dismissed Koresh's claim that God directed him and that the community members made their own choices. Koresh, an intelligent man standing in a position of peril, had a better grasp of the challenges of misunderstanding than did the FBI negotiators who were presumably trained in communication; he recognized the terms shaping FBI perspectives. "We've not been your everyday kind of cult. We've not been your everyday kind of terrorists, which I'm sure you're familiar with having to deal with," Koresh said.[28] While the Branch Davidians' messiah repeatedly showed insight into the framework shaping FBI perspectives, the latter had no place for even the *perception* (let alone the reality) of a person that a god could communicate with. The result tragically proved the truth of sociologist W. I. Thomas's dictum: no matter how unreal it may appear to others, if people define a situation as real, then it is real in its consequences for them.

As the next step in the strategy to ratchet up pressure and increase a sense of insecurity, two modified M60 tanks breached the walls of the compound buildings at select locations and inserted a potent CS gas. For six hours the hulking metal vehicles crashed through the compound's thin pink and white walls, forcing the inhabitants to watch the demolition of their home and community. Some members died after one collapsing wall crushed them. Then, around noon, flames appeared at various places, flames that swiftly grew to envelope the entire compound. One woman raced out, her clothes on fire. When well-meaning law enforcement agents approached to help her, she turned to run back in. Another woman exited, sent by Koresh to protect the manifesto that he had just completed. The FBI insists that Branch Davidian members purposely set fire to Mount Carmel despite constant reassurances from Koresh that suicide would not be an option. Other investigators have argued that the CS gas used becomes combustible at the high pressures at which the tanks pumped it into the enclosed structures, and that the

"Fire engulfs the Branch Davidian compound near Waco, Texas, April 19, 1993. Eighty-one Davidians, including leader David Koresh, perished as federal agents tried to drive them out of the compound. A few weeks earlier four agents from the Bureau of Alcohol, Tobacco and Firearms were slain in a shootout at the site, and six cult members were found dead inside. Hearings into the raid and its aftermath are scheduled to open in the House of Representatives" (1993). Associated Press/Ron Heflin.

ferret rounds used to introduce more gas ignited the CS gas. Because the FBI bulldozed the few remains of Mount Carmel soon after its demise, a definitive conclusion may never be reached. In any case, of the eighty-five people in the compound at the commencement of the final assault, seventy-four perished: immolated, suffocated by smoke, crushed by debris, or asphyxiated by the CS gas. Seventeen of them were children.

IN THE END

In film footage documenting the Branch Davidians' fiery demise, the Davidian blue and white flag, emblazoned with a Star of David, can be seen ripping away from the compound's flagpole. Soon after, the ATF, aggrieved by the deaths of its four agents, symbolically reclaimed Mount Carmel for Texas and the United States by running a US, a Texas, and an ATF flag up the pole.[29] One senses in this move that federal agents viewed

"The Texas flag and the ATF flag hang by one corner with the U.S. flag over the site where the Branch Davidian compound once stood in Waco, Tx, May 4, 1993. Investigators are still searching the area for bodies from the April 19th fire. The bodies of 72 people, including cult leader David Koresh, have been removed so far" (1993). Associated Press/ Ron Heflin.

the suspicious self-isolation and unconventional self-determination of the Branch Davidians as a challenge to the American social order, a challenge confirmed by allegations of adultery, polygyny, child abuse, drug manufacturing, and weapons stockpiling. Before the last flaming wall collapsed to the fire-scarred earth and despite the apparent tragedy that had just occurred, someone sought to assert victory on behalf of the United States and Texas by raising flags to flutter above the still-flaming remains.

Just as the Branch Davidians used their unique flag to mark Mount Carmel as apart from the United States, the popular use of the term "cult" to describe the Branch Davidians allowed Americans to safely distance the group and their theology from more common American concepts of Christianity. This protected mainstream Protestants and Catholics from suspicions that "normal" Christians might become similarly dangerous by exceeding the accepted limits of religion in their lives and in society. As mentioned earlier, American history is rife with offbeat Christian groups that have challenged the norms of their surrounding society. Indeed, the history of Christianity is rooted in the belief in a man who, according to numerous Gospel passages, actively flouted the conventions of his society and urged his disciples—if not all of his followers—to do the same. While many Christians would like to imagine that their lifestyles answer the question "What would Jesus do?," others—such as Anne Hutchinson, Mary Dyer, and Martin Luther King Jr.—have believed that his teachings and actions demand a life of deliberate provocation toward a complacent society until Jesus's ideals are achieved. If cult stereotypes were difficult for the Branch Davidians to defy in media portrayals of them before the conflict started at Mount Carmel, they proved impossible to escape once the media, law enforcement, and purported cult experts built a largely unchallenged portrait of them as such.

The Davidians, previously uninterested in convincing anyone other than fellow Seventh-day Adventists of their beliefs, lost all opportunity to communicate their perspectives once the FBI cut their telephone lines. Although some members of the media asked more probing questions about the group after the catastrophe, in the preceding months organizations and individuals with an interest in crafting an unsympathetic image molded most public perceptions of the group. Media outlets particularly turned to professional provocateurs as so-called experts in their efforts to capitalize on a news spectacle. The effect was palpable: One 1993 survey found that, of those polled, 72 percent approved of the final attack. Another survey showed 95 percent of those asked thought Koresh was responsible for the tragic end of the siege.[30]

Today, the Branch Davidians serve as a lesson for people of two quite different perspectives. In the first case, they represent the dangers of religion when it becomes too much a part of a person's life, when one's religious community appears too far apart from mainstream America (a curious perspective for Christians to take, given the life Jesus exhorted his disciples to lead in the Gospels, which alarmed both religious and government officials). In this view, Koresh led a destructive doomsday cult hell-bent on its own destruction, an end that was inevitable from the start given Koresh's worldview and control. From another perspective, the disaster at Waco represents an imperious government's massacre of those asserting their rights of religious expression and gun ownership. Among those with this view was a visitor to the siege perimeter during the standoff, a young man by the name of Timothy McVeigh. Sitting atop the hood of his car among bumper stickers proclaiming the need for gun rights, McVeigh calmly described to a student journalist how the government had overstepped its authority from the start of the conflict. Two years to the day after the burning of Mount Carmel, he made another statement, detonating a self-manufactured explosive that shattered the facade of Oklahoma City's Federal Building and killed 168 people, including nineteen children.

While "cults" as a media sensation have diminished significantly, the popular use of the term abides. Although the Cult Awareness Network buckled under a broadside of lawsuits by those claiming harm from its operations (including a man involuntarily "deprogrammed" by Rick Ross) and was bought in bankruptcy court by the Church of Scientology,[31] Ross, undeterred, continues to offer his services to those suffering mind control, as he advertises through a website. The Rick A. Ross Institute of New Jersey, a nonprofit organization, also provides archives, videos, and lectures on cults and abusive relationships. Demonstrating the term's use beyond professional provocateurs, the iconic evangelist Billy Graham's website listed religions he considered cults until 2012. Its removal coincided with the Mormon Mitt Romney's nomination as the Republican presidential candidate. Nevertheless, when users enter the names "Hare Krishna," "Islam," "Hinduism," "Unitarians," and "Mormon" into the website's search engine, it returns various topic threads, including "How do I recognize a religious cult?"

For most Americans, the claims and practices of a religion other than their own (if they have one) must appear fairly alien. After all, each derives from a view of this world (and others) usually based on a relationship with unseen, superhuman agents engaged by the community relative to a past and a future that bear little resemblance to mainstream understandings and expectations. This might make some of their choices in practice, lifestyle, home, and family appear inexplicable, if not irrational. The term "cult" serves as a social expression of this failure in understanding, and also in acceptance. Mainline American Protestants may understand Mennonites or Orthodox Jews as little as they understood the Branch Davidians, but these two groups have the benefit of longevity in the American religious landscape. Having found historical acceptance in the mainstream portrait of "religion in America," they do not need to publicly defend their choices. Bereft of an education in the history of religions, which public schools usually avoid due to secular concerns, most Americans do not have the tools with which to intellectually engage new religious movements as other than weird and wholly different from what they know. And so, Mormons—despite their century-and-a-half history—find their "cult" standing ambiguous on Graham's website because they are just now finding admission into the American pantheon of religions that jealously guards its doors of acceptance, if not understanding.

Although contestations continue among the movement's various splinter groups, a small Branch Davidian community continues at the Mount Carmel site. Their modest white church stands adjacent to the buried ruins of the earlier compound. The survivors of Koresh's group, like other Americans who eschew the easy, self-apparent answers offered by the "cult" label, continue to struggle with their understanding of Koresh, his vision, and his community's fatal ostracism from America.

Seven

The Sum of All Fears

Islamophobia and Anti-Muslim Sentiment Today

Sunando Sen looked down the tracks of the elevated station, anxious for the next train to arrive so he could continue his commute. The open platform made the December air cold to breathe as he waited, but he could see a Number 7 approaching. A violent shove from behind threw him down onto the tracks and the arriving train crushed him to the screams of fellow commuters. According to police, when caught just before New Years 2013 Erika Menendez admitted to the murder, claiming in so many words, "I pushed a Muslim off the train tracks."

The fact that Mr. Sen was not Muslim, but had been raised Hindu, might not have disappointed Menendez, since she also stated to investigators, "I hate Hindus and Muslims ever since 2001 when they put down the twin towers." Although her statements do not explain why she connects Hindus with the 2001 attacks, the history of American anti-Muslim sentiment suggests that it has something to do with a common stereotype portraying Hindus and Muslims as people of similar complexion.[1]

Coincidentally or not, in the weeks leading up to this murder the New York–based group American Freedom Defense Initiative (AFDI) posted a series of advertisements throughout the New York transit system. In station after station, their ads juxtaposed an image of one of the 9/11 World Trade Center explosions with a quote from the Quran. This followed a similar set of campaigns in four other cities that used large public transit ads to declare, "In any war between the civilized man and the savage, support the civilized man: Support Israel, Defeat Jihad." Although it is difficult to know whether or not the placards helped motivate Mr. Sen's murder, they validate the virulent anti-Muslim views shared by Menendez and others.

The organization behind this radical advertising campaign has long been in the Muslim blame game. In fact, that is all the organization endeavors to do: warn non-Muslim Americans about Muslims who supposedly threaten them. Although lone (non-Muslim) gunmen like James Holmes, Wade Michael Page, and Adam Lanza have killed many more people in the United States than al-Qaeda has since 2001, Islamophobic groups like the American Freedom Defense Initiative (AFDI) believe Islam itself is the key threat upon which their fellow citizens should focus.

Meanwhile, according to the FBI, in the months immediately following the 9/11 attacks, American Muslims went from the second least likely religious group to report hate crimes against them to the second most likely. The parade of hate crimes against Muslims has tragically run through the many news cycles of the past decade. And while there has been an overall decline in hate crimes since 9/11, the FBI tracked a 50 percent increase in reported anti-Muslim hate crimes in 2010, the year when congressional electioneering and Islamophobic organizations helped make the improperly termed "Ground Zero" mosque a national issue.

Just a sampling of events in the months preceding the Sen murder demonstrate the extent and viciousness of Islamophobic and anti-Muslim violence. In October 2012, near Tacoma, Washington, an intoxicated man pummeled a Sikh taxi driver so fiercely that he ripped out part of his beard and dislodged one of his teeth. The assailant had confusedly believed the Indian-born victim to be Iranian or Iraqi. In November, an attacker assaulted a man opening a Queens, New York, mosque for prayers. As he repeatedly stabbed his victim, he told him that he did not like Muslims. Also in Queens in the same month, two men beat a seventy-year-old man after asking whether he was Muslim or Hindu. In December, a man walked into the Fremont, California, Islamic Center and threatened to kill everyone with a gun.[2]

Meanwhile, it is not unlikely that Wade Michael Page, the shooter responsible for killing six Sikhs in Oak Creek, Wisconsin, during this period had thought he was attacking Muslims. Just as Hindus such as Mr. Sen have been victims of verbal and physical assault because assailants conclude they are Muslim based on their skin tone, bearded, turban-wearing Sikhs have repeatedly suffered assaults after being misidentified as Muslims since 2001. In fact, the first fatality of 9/11 backlash was a Sikh gas station owner murdered a few days after the attacks by someone who sought, in his words, to "kill the ragheads."[3]

Also in 2012, during the month-long Islamic celebration of Ramadan, Muslim institutions came under attack across the country. On August 4, 2012, teenagers assaulted a Haywood, California, mosque, throwing fruit as Muslims prayed inside. The next day, a man destroyed the sign outside a Rhode Island mosque. One day later, an arsonist burned to the ground a mosque in Joplin, Missouri, a month after another arson attempt. The next day, pigs' legs were thrown at a site where Muslims had gathered for prayers near Chino, California. On August 10, a gunman shooting a pellet rifle damaged a mosque in a Chicago suburb. The next day, an attacker threw acid at the College Preparatory School of America, an Islamic school in another Chicago suburb. The same day, vandals shot paintballs at an Oklahoma City mosque.[4]

This incomplete list of anti-Muslim acts in late 2012 demonstrates both the virulence of American Islamophobia and how it repeats many of the themes of religious intolerance outlined in our country's history. Nativism, racism, theological disagreement, secular anxieties, gender concerns, fears for civilization, and allegations of disloyalty have pervaded the remarks of media commentators, campaigning politicians, and ordinary citizens in recent years. Islam is now a singular menace in the eyes of many Americans: the sum of all fears. They justify their anger against and fears of Muslims through historical prejudice—some of which was formerly aimed against groups with whom they identify.

To my dismay, I discovered for myself how easy it is to recycle deprecations once aimed at one's own religious community and redirect them toward others. One evening, after discussing Islamophobia with an interested, well-educated audience, during informal conversation one of the audience members, a Jewish doctor, described how the news that two prominent American universities had accepted Saudi donations to establish independent Islamic studies programs unsettled him. "It's like me injecting myself with tainted blood," he said. The analogy between money from Saudi hands and a deliberate shot of diseased blood shocked me, given that the Holocaust was driven in no small part by Nazi fixation on blood purity and was typified by inhumane medical experimentation. "That doesn't surprise me at all," a colleague in Jewish studies replied after hearing the story. "The oppressed often take the terms of their oppression and turn them against others." This may also explain the reuse of slurs regarding racism and sexism in the Mormon Church by the 1994 campaign of Irish Catholic Ted Kennedy.

As a co-author and I have described elsewhere, the term "Islamophobia" refers to unjustified social anxieties toward Islam and Muslim cultures. The word motions toward a socially shared sensibility, not a psychological condition of an individual. As opposed to personal fears of spiders, snakes, and heights, Islamophobia originates from and is sustained by a group. The appropriateness of the term stems from this anxiety, so deeply engrained in a community that it can trigger a defensive anger and hatred.[5] However, this should be distinguished from "anti-Muslim sentiment." Although this form of prejudice may not at times be entirely distinct from Islamophobia, it remains important to note that in the United States, as in Europe and elsewhere, bias against Muslims does not wholly arise as a response to the precepts, practices, and sensibilities of their religion but can also manifest itself through perceived differences in race, ethnicity, clothing, facial features, skin complexion, and/or place of origin. After a brief consideration of the historical roots of Islamophobia and anti-Muslim sentiment, we will examine specific events between 2008 and 2013 that demonstrate the intensity of these forms of intolerance.

INHERITED DISTRUST

Islamophobia and anti-Muslim sentiment in the United States did not originate with the 9/11 attacks, the al-Qaeda attacks against Americans in the 1990s, or even the Iranian hostage crisis before that. Like anti-Catholic sentiment, these attitudes arrived on the American continent packed in the intellectual and emotional baggage of European settlers. Like anti-Jewish attitudes, Islamophobia stems from a history that is over a millennium old.

In an age of religiously defined empires such as Orthodox Christian Byzantium and Zoroastrian Persia, the rise of a Muslim Arab competitor in the seventh century was not surprising. However, when the new empire expanded rapidly to encompass most of the lands between Persia and Spain within a century, it seemed to prove something else. Christians until then had enjoyed centuries of successes that they believed were directed by the hand of God. Since the first century their proselytizers had founded churches in increasingly distant realms, and by the fourth century the Roman emperor converted, making Christianity the official religion of the empire. So when North Africa—an important Christian region and home of the venerable Saint Augustine—gradually converted to Islam after Muslim Arab armies conquered it 400 years later, many saw it as the work of Satan. The loss of Jerusalem, Bethlehem, Nazareth, and other biblical sites associated with Jesus's life further added to this perception.

As some European Christians began to learn more about their foes—who followed military and religious success with commercial and scientific accomplishments at a time when Europe was trapped in the Dark Ages—the more alarmed they became. Unlike the pagan enemies the Christian Roman Empire had once battled, the Muslim enemy believed in Jesus: just not as the Son of God. To the slight degree that medieval European Christians knew anything about Mediterranean Muslims, they understood that the Quran named many of the patriarchs and prophets of the Christian Bible (and the Hebrew Bible): Adam, Noah, Abraham, Moses, David, and Solomon all appear. But while acknowledging Jesus as an exemplary man and recognizing his virgin birth from Mary, Muslims considered him one prophet among others. More importantly, they viewed a succeeding prophet, Muhammad, as an even more exemplary person, one who channeled the word of God into written form as the Quran. Many Europeans saw Muhammad as a heretic, a former Christian who had warped the truth for his own gain. For this sin, Dante cast him into the second to last circle of hell in his fourteenth-century *Divine Comedy*, where a demon retributively and repeatedly cleaved him head to groin with a sword: punishment for splitting the church. Meanwhile, Christian Europeans also portrayed the Prophet as a hedonist whose sexual proclivities went beyond the pale.

Although most medieval Europeans would have had no contact with Muslims, the fervor surrounding the Crusades deepened hostility to Muslims, whom Europeans began to label collectively as "Saracens." In 1095, in an effort to drum up enthusiasm for a Christian invasion of the biblical Holy Land, Pope Urban II made a steady stream of appeals to his fellow Latin Christians to fight the Saracens and liberate Jerusalem. He urged Latin Christians to lay aside their antagonism to each other and fight the "Turks and Arabs," "pagans," "infidels," "barbarians," and "a despised and base race, which worships demons." The 60,000 to 100,000 men, women, and children who answered his initial call viewed themselves as "taking up the cross" in an armed pilgrimage to the land of Christ. The reality of the Crusades often diverged from the ideals of liberation said to have motivated them. Bigotry against Jews resulted in members of the First Crusade annihilating whole communities in some cities in the Rhineland (now contemporary Germany) and forcibly converting Jews in others. Nevertheless, the crusader ideal remained potent. During the seven centuries after the mixed success of the First Crusade, various Christian Europeans depicted their political and economic conflicts with Turks and Arabs as "crusades," as was the case with the Iberian Peninsula's Reconquista.[6]

While Muslim, Christian, and Jewish merchants, pilgrims, and scholars frequently came into peaceful contact, when their leaders conflicted with one another, they sometimes used religion in order to better mobilize support. Most of the Muslim-ruled states of the Iberian Peninsula practiced an official tolerance of the Jewish and Christian populations who intermixed and intermarried with Muslims during the medieval centuries, but Christian sovereigns, seeking to conquer the peninsula, portrayed their campaign as a crusade to liberate "Christian" Iberia, which had been under Moorish rule for centuries. This culminated with Isabella of Castile and Ferdinand of Aragon, who conquered the last Moorish kingdom in 1492 and enforced conversion or expulsion of most of Spain and Portugal's Jews and Muslims. The newly victorious monarchs immediately financed Christopher Columbus's voyage in part to open an eastern front against the Holy Land's Saracen occupants by going through Asia, which the explorer understood as part of his God-directed role in triggering the Apocalypse. Columbus's unexpected encounter with the Americas scuttled that plan, leaving the interpreter of Arabic and Hebrew he brought along with little translating to do.

So, even before they realized where they were (given Columbus's certainty that he had reached Asia), the first European explorers arrived in the "New World" ready to combat a Muslim enemy. Ironically, not long after they realized that the Americas had no Moors or Saracens, Christian colonizers started populating them with Muslims. As many as one out of five Africans enslaved for North American and Caribbean labor was Muslim, although the brutal conditions of slavery largely erased any Islamic heritage that might have been passed to future generations.[7] Nevertheless, just as anti-Catholicism remained latent among English colonists despite the relatively few Catholics in most of the thirteen colonies, so Islamophobia remained latent among European American Christians.

The evidence for this was clear at the time of the American Revolution as the new nation's leaders worked to build a new system of representative government. The country's founders made passing, usually desultory, mention of Muhammad as a historic figure. In 1787, John Adams negatively contrasted "the despotism of Mahomet" with the democratic institutions of ancient Greece. Three years later, Benjamin Franklin lampooned American pro-slavery arguments by putting them in the mouth of a fictional North African Muslim pirate, satirically justifying the enslavement of Christians according to purported Islamic injunctions. He intended to outrage his audience by comparing the broadly accepted American practice of slavery with the unacceptable thought of Christian captives in Muslim hands.[8] In 1810, John Quincy Adams wrote his father in regard to Napoleon Bonaparte, who he suggested might model himself on the example of Muhammad as a fanatical leader self-promoted as "a being of a superior species" deserving worship.[9] Clearly, educated men of the new United States peppered their rhetoric with shallow caricatures of Muhammad and of Islam, less out of an understanding of the Prophet and Muslim traditions than through the use of European-inherited stereotypes as foils for democracy, constitutionality, freedom, and reasonable religion.

As they wrote laws promising religious tolerance for the newly independent nation, these leaders often mentioned Muslims in order to demonstrate that inclusivity covered *even* Muslims. This moved Muslims from the extreme antagonist of America's ideals to the extreme example of America's pluralism, which included even "infidel" Muslims and Hindus, whom few suspected to live on the continent. Theophilus Parsons noted that the Massachusetts Constitution he helped draft in 1780 was meant as "the most ample of liberty of conscience" for "Deists,

Mahometans, Jews and Christians." In his Bill for Establishing Religious Freedom, Thomas Jefferson sought protection for "the Jew and the Gentile, the Christian and the Mahometan, the Hindoo and infidel of every denomination." During debates regarding the nation's Constitution, fellow Virginian Richard Henry Lee declared that "true freedom embraces the Mahometan and Gentoo [Hindu] as well as the Christian religion."[10] Including imaginary Muslims (and Hindus) represented a litmus test of tolerance.

The new republic soon faced its first international crisis. Franklin's choice of North African Muslims as his satiric foil for American Christian slavery had not been accidental. Along the southern Mediterranean coast, the Barbary States, formerly under Turkish control, took captives from ships of nations that did not pay them tribute. When the fledgling United States decided to defy these demands and went to war, many citizens viewed their enemy as "Turks," "Mahometans," and "infidels." Religiously stereotyping the pirates was a way to rally Americans and denigrate the enemy. Period images portraying the heroic fight of naval

"Desperate conflict of American seamen under Decatur, on boarding a Tripolitan corsair," detail (1851). Courtesy of Library of Congress, LC-USZ62–3760.

officer Stephen Decatur against Tripolitan forces made liberal use of stereotypes such as the Arab headdress and large, crooked noses.

While some Americans used antagonistic rhetoric to emphasize the
country's tolerance toward Muslims, others used it to caution against
too much tolerance. The younger Adams's comparison between Muhammad and Napoleon's fanaticism paralleled the allegations against
the early Mormons as "fanatics." Many Americans in the nineteenth
century used their understanding of Islam to make sense of Mormonism. Just as Muhammad supposedly duped Arabs with an invented
Quran, so Joseph Smith had fooled followers with the concocted Book
of Mormon. Both purportedly posed as prophets to enjoy religious
leadership, political control, military support, and lots of wives. American Christians used Muhammad in similes and metaphors in order
to describe particularly potent domestic threats,[11] as, for example, in
the title of Bruce Kinney's cautionary book, *Mormonism: The Islam of
America* (1912). A century later, another book *The American Muhammad: Joseph Smith, Founder of Mormonism* by Alvin Schmidt, advertised itself as a comparison between two prophets whose messages went
against biblical Christianity.

In early America, Islamophobia remained a latent prejudice until
activated by a specific moment of political, economic, and/or religious
conflict. The next two centuries offered ample opportunities for this,
especially in the late twentieth century: the 1973–1974 OPEC oil embargo, the 1979–1981 Iranian hostage crisis, the 1991 Gulf War, and
the various Israeli-Arab conflicts. Some of these represented non-reli-
gious confrontations between Americans and Middle Easterners over
oil, influence, and Zionism in which fears of Islam and Muslims nevertheless surfaced.[12]

The horrific terrorist attacks of September 11, 2001, and the
American-led invasions of Afghanistan and Iraq released sentiments
that not only borrowed from this unhappy anti-Muslim heritage but
also created new sources of prejudice. Arguably, previous American
Islamophobic and anti-Muslim expressions arose when people who

Display comparing American sailor and a Barbary corsair. Aksana Volfson/USS Constitution *Museum, Massachussetts (2007).*

genuinely knew no better drew from a common fund of inherited stereotypes. Such has been evident in a recent exhibit at Boston's USS *Constitution* Museum describing the Barbary War (1801–1805, 1815–1816). One of the main displays juxtaposes a slim, innocent-looking, and unarmed American sailor and a hulking, hirsute, and well-armed North African corsair festooned with the stereotypical accoutrements of a Muslim man: scimitar raised to strike, curved knife positioned in waistline, thick beard, turban, and scowling face. Another display contrasts this image of the North African corsair with a picture of an American privateer. While the curators may have thought they undermined a stereotype by describing the corsair and privateer in very much the same language—and, hence, suggesting that corsairs had their American counterparts—the calm, debonair demeanor of the European American sitting at his desk contrasts markedly with the leaping, sword-wielding North African.

While this portrayal likely drew on innocent, perhaps even well-meaning intentions, the new millennium has witnessed very willfully distorted information about Muslims and Islam.

BARACK OBAMA, ISLAM, AND RACE

The 2008 election of Barack Obama as the first African American president represented another milestone passed on the road toward American egalitarianism. When Obama took the stage in Chicago that November evening to give his victory speech, he cast his personal success as the success of all Americans, but of African Americans in particular. Addressing the entire audience, he declared, "But above all, I will never forget who this victory truly belongs to. It belongs to you." He then went on to describe one voter, Ann Nixon Cooper, whose 106-year life span meant "she was born just a generation past slavery; a time when there were no cars on the road or planes in the sky; when someone like her couldn't vote for two reasons—because she was a woman and because of the color of her skin." His speech merged popular myths of American technological and social progress, making the political inclusion of all Americans as inevitable as the invention of automobiles.

Unmentioned in Obama's speech is the fact that—despite this celebration of mounting inclusivity—nationalism implicitly relies on exclusivity: not everyone can be American, and Americans supposedly differ from citizens of other nations. The democratic nation-state separates the undocumented and unqualified from the true citizens and requires that those citizens subvert all of their interests and loyalties to the nation. The names Benedict Arnold, John Wilkes Booth, and Lee Harvey Oswald are known almost as well as those of George Washington, Abraham Lincoln, and Rosa Parks because they rejected these conditions.

A disappointing number of the conservative challenges to Obama's election played off the expectations of patriotic dedication while relying on prejudices against blacks and Muslims. Exemplified by the "birther" movement, these critics pursued two strategies. The first sought to raise doubt regarding Obama's legal qualification based on allegations that he was born outside the United States. The second was to argue that Obama acted unpatriotically, thus proving his non-citizenship no matter what the legal records say. These accusations include false claims that he was the first president not to lay a wreath in Arlington National Cemetery on Memorial Day, unfounded allegations that he removed the American flag from the tail of Air Force One, and doctored images purporting to show the president and his wife pledging allegiance to the flag with their hands on the wrong side of their chests. Perhaps the most persistent effort was the allegation that Obama is a closet Muslim.

Of course, even had Obama been a Muslim, it would have had no legal bearing on his presidency. The Constitution's framers settled the debate regarding whether or not even a Muslim could be elected, with Article Six explicitly stating "no religious Test shall ever be required as a Qualification to any Office or public Trust under the United States." Despite this history, voter expectations of religious affiliation have led to a de facto test in recent elections. The Catholic, Protestant, and Mormon backgrounds of the major 2012 presidential candidates were widely reported.

Recent surveys have shown that roughly half of Americans are less inclined to vote for candidates who identify as Muslim. In light of this, some conservatives challenged the authenticity of Obama's self-identification as Christian, implicitly or explicitly declaring him a secret Muslim. During the 2008 election, e-mails circulated widely that described Obama's supposed education in an Indonesian madrasa, pictured him in a turban, and alleged that he took his oath of office on the Quran. These suspicions, exchanged through social networks, created a vicious feedback loop: Obama's patriotism was at odds with his (supposed) Islamic commitments, but his unwillingness to admit to being a Muslim made him inauthentic as both a candidate and an American. Hillary Clinton's primary campaign had to ask two volunteers to resign after it became public knowledge that they had distributed an e-mail alleging Obama to be Muslim. The e-mail read in part, "The Muslims have said they Plan on destroying the US from the inside out, what better way to start than at The highest level."[13]

During the 2012 election, his Republican competitors avoided outright assaults on Obama's Christian identity, preferring to allege that he is "acting like a Muslim," has been "soft on Muslims," and has "given Islam a pass." Newt Gingrich, for example, claimed that "President Obama is very quick to apologize for Islam while he attacks the Catholic Church." Some practiced a strategy of retroactively soft-pedaling their own provocations in an effort to insulate themselves from criticism even as they garnered media attention. After Gingrich made the remarks above, his spokesperson assured reporters that the candidate believed that Obama was a Christian.[14] In early 2012, then-candidate Rick Santorum condemned Obama's "phony theology," purporting that it was not based on the Bible. Later, when pressed by reporters, his campaign dissembled that Santorum was not calling into question his competitor's Christianity but was identifying his commitment to a secular theology of government.

The increasing Muslim population has also led to increased Islamophobia. Overwhelmingly associated with Arabs and other people of non-European heritage, Islam and Muslims both have long represented to many Americans the intertwining of racial and religious apartness and threat. Beyond the challenges of purportedly unprogressive Muslim practices such as women wearing hijab, the perceived foreignness of certain skin complexions haunt Muslim immigrants and their descendants. Although some races attain "honorary whiteness" in America, this goes to show that only whiteness and blackness tend to represent authentic Americanness. The presence of other people of color may signal inclusivity in the United States, but they rarely become part of the American norm,[15] as demonstrated by hostility toward the Jewish "race" described in chapter four.

In the 2008 campaign, various commentators declared that Obama was not "really black" or questioned whether or not he was "black enough." For some, his white mother ameliorated his blackness, while

Rush Limbaugh claimed that Obama's Kenyan father was not black but Arab. Limbaugh told his radio audience, "He's Arab! You know, he's from Africa. He's from Arab parts of Africa. He's not—his father was—he's not African-American. The last thing that he is is African-American."[16] Since the 9/11 attacks, Arabs have lost the honorary whiteness once accorded them by immigration policy, if not by mainstream society. Until 1952, various laws barred particular non-white racial groups from becoming American citizens, so petitioners literally had to show their bodies for the court's assessment of their skin color. As was the case for Jews, courts sometimes judged Arab individuals as white, sometimes as yellow.[17] The continued sense of Arab alienness was clear at a 2008 rally for candidate John McCain. When an audience member declared, "I don't trust Obama. I have read about him and he's an Arab," McCain took the ethnic slur in stride as he sought to deflect the criticism of his competitor and said, "No ma'am, no ma'am. He's a decent family man."[18] The popular allegation that Obama was a closet Muslim helps make sense of this bizarre insistence that he is Arab African, not black African. Besides demonstrating how "American" has been equated most firmly with white and black, the charge also shows how Americans have equated Islam with Arabs despite the fact that only a fifth of all Muslims are Arabs.

Because Americans associate the United States with whites and blacks, and Islam with non-whites and non-blacks, American Islamophobic discourse has frequently overlooked the Muslim victims of 9/11 and the Muslim members of the armed forces. This perception runs so deep that during the 2008 race Obama proved unwilling to defend Muslims' constitutional right to hold elected office. It is significant that it was an African American veteran—Colin Powell—who finally did so, implicitly drawing on his credentials as the leader in an earlier war against Saddam Hussein, stridently reminding Americans about the constitutional protection against a religion test, and explicitly using the grave of a Muslim soldier in Arlington National Cemetery as a marker of authentic Muslim Americanness.

It is useful to contrast the allegations about Obama's authenticity with those about fellow presidential contender Mitt Romney. There were few challenges to Romney's American identity during either his 2008 or 2012 presidential campaigns, despite suspicions among some Americans about whether Mormonism is a religion or a cult. If anything, the LDS suffers in public perception because it is *too* American. For some, its birth less than two centuries ago in upstate New York means that the LDS does not stem from an ancient past in a distant land as do "genuine" religions such as Hinduism, Buddhism, Judaism, Christianity, and Islam. Ironically, it is its overwhelmingly non-Hispanic white racial composition[19] that has proved to be the greatest liability for Mormon candidates. Since at least his 2008 presidential campaign, Romney has had to repeatedly answer allegations of racism in Mormon communities, especially due to the late admission of black men into the priesthood. That Mormons took fourteen years following the passage of the Civil Rights Act to curtail their institutionalized racism might seem trivial given the centuries of systematic discrimination throughout the United States preceding 1964. Nevertheless, for many, this fact is one of several that proves the inauthenticity of Mormonism as a religion, though not of Mormons as Americans. If anything, while his religion's past ties to racial prejudice may have made Romney appear less Christian, in the eyes of many this made him seem all the more white and authentically American. In contrast, Obama's bogus Muslim identity and mixed racial heritage convinces some that he is authentically neither Christian, nor black, nor American.

Polls demonstrated the effect these concerted disinformation campaigns had on at least some voters. Sociologist Charles Kurzman has tracked more than two dozen polls taken since 2002 and finds that, on average, while increasing numbers of Americans view Islam unfavorably, the increase in favorable sentiment toward Muslims peaked in 2008 and—coinciding with the Islamophobic and anti-Muslim election campaigning that year—began to decline.[20] Between 2009 and 2010, the percentage of Americans believing Obama to be Muslim increased from 11 to 18 percent. The numbers were highest among conservative Republicans and white evangelical Christians. The fraction of Americans believing him to be Christian dropped in this period from nearly half to little more than a third. More alarming, a 2013 poll showed that 13 percent of Americans believed their president to be the Antichrist.[21]

PROFESSIONAL ISLAMOPHOBES, THE 2010 ELECTION, AND MANUFACTURING THE "GROUND ZERO MOSQUE" CRISIS

As a prayer leader of a mosque in Lower Manhattan since 1983, Imam Feisal Abdul Rauf wanted to create an Islamic center that would relieve overcrowded conditions and replace the lost prayer space workers once used in the World Trade Center towers. The new center, referred to as "Park51" and "Cordoba House," would stand two and a half blocks from Ground Zero, only two blocks closer than an existing mosque. The well-publicized plans—discussed in the *New York Times* and on Fox's *O'Reilly Factor*—were uncontroversial at first. Indeed, conservative talk show host Laura Ingraham concluded a 2009 interview of Daisy Khan, Imam Rauf's wife, with the remark, "I like what you're trying to do."[22] When the plan came before the requisite community board in May 2010, they voted twenty-nine to one in favor of the center (ten members abstained).

The day after the community board approved Park51, the *New York Post* ran a story provocatively entitled "Panel Approves 'WTC' Mosque."[23] Simultaneously, Pamela Geller, founder and executive director of the group Stop the Islamization of America (SIOA), posted an essay on her website entitled "Monster Mosque Pushes Ahead in Shadow of World Trade Center Islamic Death and Destruction."[24] The next day, she announced a campaign to stop the project. On May 13, Andrea Peyser began her *Daily News* column by declaring, "A mosque rises over Ground Zero. And fed-up New Yorkers are crying, 'No!'" She declared that the center would open on the tenth anniversary of the attacks, and she promoted a protest planned by SIOA, an organization (described by the Southern Poverty Law Center as a "hate group") that she characterized as a "human rights organization."[25] Soon an op-ed article by columnist Diane West in the *Washington Examiner* proclaimed, "The second attack on the World Trade Center is coming" in the form of the Cordoba House, named after "an early caliphate that, of course, subjugated non-Muslims."[26] By June, conservative politicians like Newt Gingrich, Sarah Palin, Rudy Giuliani, and Tim Pawlenty jumped onto the bandwagon as its momentum increased.[27]

The media helped to speed this parade of panic along. In a July 2010 blog, a conservative commentator declared that Cordoba House "isn't about honoring the dead [of 9/11], but celebrating their deaths." He suggested that Park51 would be a beachhead for Muslims in America. "They wish to launch new terror attacks and forcibly convert Americans to their way of thinking and believing. What will we gain by allowing this to happen?" In August, *National Review Online* blogger Jim Geraghty and *NewsBusters* managing editor Ken Shepherd compared building Cordoba House to establishing the "Dylan Klebold Memorial Nurse's Office" in Columbine High School. Later, Fox News commentator Dick Morris declared that "these Sharia mosques . . . have become the command centers for terrorists" before adding, "so this one would be, too." The next day, *Fox Business* host Eric Bolling proposed that it "may be a meeting place for some of the scariest minds—some of the biggest terrorist minds."[28] By the end of August, commentator Glenn Beck tied the Islamic center with the alleged efforts of Muslims to implement sharia in the United States,[29] and Rush Limbaugh connected the debate to the upcoming elections in November.[30]

Limbaugh's leap was a calculated one. Just as the Know-Nothing Party of the 1850s sought to galvanize nativist concerns regarding Irish and German Catholics into electoral success, so many conservative candidates in the 2010 campaign sought an edge over their opponents through Islamophobia. Both the reactionary media commentary and the political opportunism implied subtly or boldly that all Muslims promoted sharia, violence, and forced conversion as a matter of faith. For instance, Nevada's Republican Senate candidate Sharron Angle declared that "Muslims want to take over the United States" and implement sharia. New York's Republican gubernatorial candidate Carl Paladino declared that Muslims are not Americans and that Cordoba House was to be "a monument to those who attacked our country." At least some of these detractors worded their allegations in a way that championed a Christian supremacy for the United States. At the same time that North Carolina's Republican congressional candidate Renee Ellmers called Park51 a "victory mosque," she described her districts' residents as uniformly "good, hardworking, Christian people." Ilario Pantano, an Iraq War veteran and another Republican candidate from that state, portrayed the proposed mosque as a "martyr marker." Later, he described "the Christian underpinnings of our society and the Scriptural doctrine, which is the source for our morality, law, and culture."[31] As nativists in the 1850s and 1920s had disparaged Catholics in order to reaffirm a Protestant America, these politicians cast suspicion on Muslims in order to tout a Christian America.

The provocateurs who orchestrated this wildfire of fear, anger, and indignation were similar to those who had helped escalate the conflict with the Branch Davidians a decade before. While popular perceptions of the Branch Davidians were substantially different from those surrounding Cordoba House, the dynamics at work were not. In both cases, professional "experts," media reports, and political actors all drew support from one another to power an escalating cycle of fear built on existing anxieties and suspicions. The outrage voiced by the *Post,* the *Daily News,* and the *Examiner* about Park51 paralleled the investigations of the Australian *A Current Affair* and the *Waco Tribune-Herald* about Mount Carmel. The supposed "experts" of the SIOA were no more qualified to speak on Islam or Muslim cultures than the members of the Cult Awareness Network were to speak on cults; nevertheless, media representatives and government agents sought them out because these allegations affirmed their existing views. Seeking to maximize the perception of opposition, some provocateurs have fashioned multiple organizations to broadcast their message. For instance, Pamela Geller is executive director of SIOA, AFDI, and the more recent organization Stop the Islamization of Nations, while Robert Spencer directs Jihad Watch and is associate director of SIOA and AFDI. Meanwhile, various political candidates used their opposition to Cordoba House to help win local elections, echoing how the ATF may have planned their assault on the Branch Davidian Mount Tabor compound to curry political support while under the shadow of an earlier set of embarrassing failures. In both cases, the self-proclaimed "experts" used their media and government advising as evidence of their supposed credentials.

Both the Park51 controversy and the Mount Tabor assault relied on existing religious panic to successfully garner public support. While the concerns about the maltreatment of children certainly proved real enough, popular distrust of the Branch Davidians stemmed more directly from anxieties that developed in the 1970s around "cults." Similarly, the nation was understandably emotionally scarred following the 9/11 terrorist attacks. However, the claims that the community center represented a "victory mosque," a "den of terrorists," or a launch pad for the spread of sharia proved how baldly long-standing fears of Islam were being manipulated. Meanwhile, other comments reflected how adherents of non-Christian and non-Jewish religions could still be collectively dismissed as nonbelievers and mistaken for one another. For instance, Mark Williams of the Tea Party opined on his blog that Muslims "worship the terrorists' monkey god," apparently confusing Allah with the Hindu deity Hanuman.[32] Limbaugh made a similar mistake when he compared the Park51 proposal with building a Hindu shrine at Pearl Harbor's USS *Arizona* memorial, perhaps mistaking Japan's Buddhists for Hindus. Less a case of mistaken identity than religious malignity, musician Ted Nugent repeatedly referred to Islam as a "voodoo religion" in a *Washington Times* op-ed piece, concluding that "the mosque will attract extremists and radicals who will try to harm America."[33]

Although the dynamics at play in both the Park51 controversy and the Branch Davidian assault/siege paralleled one another, the comparison also demonstrates a double standard in American assessments of religion. In each case, government or political actors sought to align public representations in a manner that portrayed a religious community as a threat to the American social order, if not to many of its own members, while media outlets turned to professional provocateurs as so-called experts in their efforts to capitalize on a news spectacle. Yet while the public regarded the Branch Davidians as a *cult,* the Cordoba House project controversy impugned Islam as a *religion.* Preceding and throughout the fifty-one-day siege, commentators focused only on the group as a "cult," seldom if ever suggesting that Koresh and his community represented or reflected anything about Christianity overall. In contrast, many critics perpetuated Islamophobic stereotypes by declaring *all* Muslims responsible for the 9/11 tragedies. Such sentiments were on display among the signs held by some of the hundreds of protestors

"A demonstration opposing the proposed Islamic community center near ground zero in New York, Saturday, Sept. 11, 2010" (2010). Associated Press/David Goldman.

against Cordoba House organized by the SIOA on the eighth anniversary of the attacks in Manhattan, where they were met by a group calling for toleration.

Comparisons made at the time illustrated this dynamic. Gingrich said the Cordoba House proposal would be tantamount to Nazis putting "up a sign next to the Holocaust museum in Washington."[34] MSNBC contributor Pat Buchanan compared the center to a neo-Nazi march through Skokie, Illinois, where a number of Holocaust survivors live. Limbaugh suggested that Park51 would be the equivalent of the Ku Klux Klan establishing a memorial on the Gettysburg battlefield, apparently because their racial hatred would dishonor those fighting against slavery.[35] Each of these comparisons argues that every Muslim bears the same responsibility for the sentiments that drove the 9/11 terrorists as Nazi and Klan members have for their prejudices against Jews and blacks. The more appropriate comparison would be if all Christians and whites were held accountable for the historical violence of the Nazi party and the Ku Klux Klan and then disallowed from building churches anywhere near places at which Jews or blacks have suffered persecution.

The rhetorical efforts by many conservative candidates to generate fear about sharia law and the Park51 project in 2010 had its intended effect, even if many of the candidates' campaigns ended unsuccessfully. These heightened anxieties help explain why anti-Muslim sentiment swelled before the 2010 elections, despite previously showing evidence of being on the wane since 9/11. The FBI reported a surge of 50 percent in reported hate crimes against Muslims between 2009 and 2010, making the total higher than in any year since 2001.[36] This correlates with the increase in the percentage of Americans who believed President Obama to be a Muslim, as mentioned earlier.

The implications of this Islamophobic strategy are profound. Before 2010, controversies over mosque construction in New Jersey, Arizona, Georgia, and other states all originated with very local concerns regarding parking, traffic, zoning, and neighborhood design that Muslims negotiated with their neighbors. In contrast, national Islamophobic organizations like Pamela Geller and Robert Spencer's SIOA and AFDI have successfully galvanized political support in their efforts to portray mosque and Islamic center projects beyond Park51 as indicative of the anti-American aggressions essential to Islam.[37] It remains difficult to gauge the effect organizations such as SIOA and AFDI have in foment- ing the anger and violence actively targeted at Muslim Americans. None of these incidents can be traced directly to professional Islamophobic organizations, although their impact on Anders Behring Breivik was ap- parent: he cited many of these organizations' leaders in justifying his murder of seventy-seven fellow Norwegians for the sake of protecting the nation from Muslims.[38]

MANUFACTURING CRISIS

Terry Jones's Quran burning and Nakoula Basseley Nakoula's anti-Is- lamic video were low-budget operations that succeeded in co-opting the media to advance their causes. Both men sought to create spectacles that would be deemed newsworthy enough to describe in newspapers, broadcasts, and websites, so as to reach a global audience and provoke as severe a reaction as possible, prompting more spectacles and more news stories. While Jones and Nakoula were fairly transparent in their intent to prime and then stoke this engine of turmoil, more sophisticated and well-financed Islamophobes generally have done a better job at obfuscat- ing their intentions.

The ostentatiously mustachioed Jones serves as pastor of a diminu- tive Florida church attracting about fifty congregants. His Dove World Outreach Center—located at that time in Gainesville, Florida—attracted little attention until 2009, when he erected a sign declaring "Islam is of the devil." This proved a mild warm-up, and the next year the pastor threatened to burn the Quran on the anniversary of the 9/11 attacks. News reporters anxious to record the next twist to the tale descended on his church. As the story gained increasing traction in the national and international news media, prominent leaders weighed in trying to dissuade him, each effort offering another opportunity for news outlets to squeeze something out of the story for yet one more news cycle. Finally, after a personal plea from General David Petraeus, the chief US commander in Afghanistan, who warned about possible backlash against American service personnel there, Jones agreed to desist.[39]

However, Jones's change of heart was not permanent. Adding a dramatic flourish to his previous threat, Jones declared in 2011 that he would place the Quran on trial. He staged the elaborate affair within his meager means at his church, drawing a crowd of about thirty. Not unpredictably, the twelve members of Jones's church who served as jury (he acted as judge) found the Quran guilty and condemned it to the flames, the punishment preferred in an earlier vote on four options offered to Facebook users. When asked by a reporter about future such events, the pastor replied, "That is not our intention, to run around America burning Qurans."[40]

In significant contrast with the year before, the bulk of the national news media initially refused to cover the 2011 event. Recognizing its previous role in providing a megaphone for the otherwise non-noteworthy pastor, news outlets communicated little about the event immediately afterward, with only a few reporting on it. Muslim civil organizations like the Council on American-Islamic Relations (CAIR) and the Muslim Public Affairs Council (MPAC) also avoided any initial commentary in order to avoid drawing attention to Jones.[41] Although media resistance effectively robbed Jones of free promotion for his inflammatory event, the Internet offered access to his primary audience: Muslims. He streamed the Quran burning live on the Internet and then posted it on YouTube with a link to his new organization's Facebook page.[42] When some audiences abroad got wind of the event, a small proportion played into the provocation and protested, some violently. When a group of infuriated Afghans attacked and murdered foreigners in Mazar-i-Sharif, American news outlets decided they could not ignore that story and eventually—overcoming their own reluctance—reported on the initial burning event.

Jones had found a way to circumvent the media boycott that had removed him from the limelight. Since then, the pastor has tried to broaden his exposure with street protests against homosexuality, more Quran burnings, effigy burnings of presidents Barack Obama and Bill Clinton, and other baiting largely ignored by the now-cautious news media. Despite his turn to a broader field of issues, his church remains committed to its initial provocation, selling books, T-shirts, baseball caps, and coffee mugs emblazoned with the motto "Islam is of the Devil."

In the year after the Quran burning, an Egyptian-born American calling himself Nakoula Basseley Nakoula and just coming off a prison term for bank fraud hired actors, a studio, and a production crew to shoot a video with the title *Desert Warriors.* But once he recorded enough footage to meet his needs, he edited the material into a very different project. By dubbing different dialogue over parts of the existing soundtrack—including "Muhammad" for "George," the name of the purported protagonist—Nakoula changed the actors' lines without their knowledge. In 2012, he uploaded a crudely directed and woodenly acted fourteen-minute video to YouTube entitled *The Innocence of the Muslims,* describing it as a trailer for a forthcoming movie. The video repeated the tired allegations against Muhammad rehearsed over centuries by critical Christians and scandalized secularists. They showed a Muhammad who was listless, lustful, and loathing toward others.[43]

Reporters soon discovered that *The Innocence of the Muslims* was shot at no charge in the headquarters of Media for Christ, whose head participated in anti-Islam activities. Its funding came through the Egyptian Copt community, to which Nakoula belongs. He told crew members, however, that Jews had financed the film, suggesting one particularly cynical stratagem of his plan: to trade in on Muslim anti-Jewish and anti-Zionist sentiment in order to give the video even more conflagrant potential.[44] After the video led to riots, Nakoula self-identified as an Israeli Jew when speaking to the press and referred to Islam as a "cancer," which also seems to suggest that he sought to incite Muslims to violence.[45]

Both Jones and Nakoula probably sought to achieve the international level of attention achieved by a controversy such as that of the 2005 Danish cartoons satirizing Muhammad. That issue has continued its hold over the media and the popular imagination, with reporting still mischaracterizing Muslim dissent as based on a blanket rule forbidding the Prophet's visual depiction. In fact, most Muslims who have spoken out against the cartoons complain about the disparagement of the Prophet and, by association, of his religion and its followers, a sentiment voiced by Christians who have complained about artistic renditions of Christ that they judge as less than venerable. While Jones has positioned himself as a champion of free speech by provoking some Muslims to appear censorious, Nakoula attained his goals when his video prompted protests among some Muslims from Southeast Asia to North Africa, reaffirming many Americans' view of Muslims as overly sensitive and violently religious.

While this matter of free speech represents a particularly poignant issue in America today, other Islamophobic notions derive from much older sentiments. Both Jones and Nakoula have traded on ancient Christian slanders against Muslims dating at least as far back as the Middle Ages. The pastor's declarations of Islam as "satanic" repeats very old claims made by a Christian Church frustrated by Muslim success in converting former Christians while resisting being proselytized themselves. Meanwhile, Nakoula reiterated long-standing Christian allegations of Muhammad's sexual deviance. His video showed the Prophet as a bisexual, hedonistic, anti-Christian polygynist who fabricated the Quran and enabled pedophilia. These unfortunate representations demonstrate how provocateurs can adapt prejudicial sentiments that are historically resonant in a society to fit the issues of their day. By patching incendiary issues such as the freedom to criticize a religion or alleged sexual misconduct in the age of hyper-connectivity, they gain notoriety for themselves by inciting some Muslims to anger, which reaffirms the stereotype of a hostile Islam, helps them appear as victims of Muslim antagonism to freedom, and leads to sympathetic media and popular support.

SLANDER ON SOCIAL MEDIA

While the Islamophobia described in this chapter has clear parallels with past intolerance toward other American religious minorities, the digital age has introduced new avenues for the propagation of slander. The rapidity with which digital communication tools such as e-mails, Facebook posts, blogs, and videos posted on the Internet can communicate across the globe grants individual provocateurs unparalleled opportunities to throw painful rocks while remaining safe behind a wall of anonymity.

Viral e-mails and Facebook posts provide the most low-key avenue for slandering Muslims. Anyone can craft one, they are nearly impossible to trace to their author, and, for those with computers and Internet service, they cost nothing to produce. Most are outright untruths, while some take an actual event and twist it maliciously. Many of the e-mails claim authorship by someone in the know, such as a professional or family member with experience in the matter at hand. Somehow, this seems to lend the e-mail more credibility than if the author claimed the information as her or his own. Although it might be argued that viral e-mails and Facebook posts are just another form of gossip, the use of type, videos, and photographs makes them more convincing, playing as they do to an American trust of images and the printed word.

The urban legend–busting website Snopes.com offers a ready catalog of anti-Muslim and Islamophobic messages, listing 156 that involve Muslims in some way (notably, a large percentage mention Obama). These follow a variety of themes. Some warn that Muslims and Islam are inherently anti-American, including allegations that Muslim store employees have denied service to military personnel. Other e-mails suggest that Muslims have displaced the accepted social order—for example, that Whole Foods has replaced Israeli-made products with Muslim-approved ones, that meat used by Muslim butchers includes cows who died before being slaughtered, that a Fisher-Price talking doll repeats lines like "Satan is king" and "Islam is the light," and that Muslim population growth in the West soon "will overwhelm Christendom." Some messages charge that political correctness or government pressure inhibits Americans from recognizing the truth. One, for instance, complained that the news media refused to cover protests against the Park51 project (despite the attention of many major news outlets), while another argued that Obama's administration squashed a photograph of the president carrying an anti-American book (actually, a *New York Times* bestseller by prominent American journalist and *Time* editor Fareed Zakaria). The strategy of these e-mails is apparent: provide enough of them, get them circulating widely and repeat them often enough, and even initially doubtful viewers might eventually think, "Well, if there's this much evidence, some of it must be true."

In other cases, a single mention in social media appears to be enough to incite a response. Some Facebook postings have had consequences for Muslims that are more immediate than the slow yet insidious spread of malevolent e-mails. For example, in June 2012 more than fifty flag-waving protestors gathered in front of a gas station and convenience store in Bogalusa, Louisiana, just one day after the appearance of a malicious Facebook posting about a fictive event in an actual business.

> A local soldier walked into this Texaco outside Bogalusa, Louisiana and was told by the Muslim clerk, "We don't serve your kind here." This is getting out of hand. The feds will be giving Arab muslims [*sic*] special rights and privileges next week. More tax breaks to open businesses as well as funding. There are even areas in this country that the muslims [*sic*] have set up and are ruled by there [*sic*] own law with no fear of reprisal from our liberal government.[46]

This strategy is common: concoct a fictional event involving Muslims and associate it with the government's purported unwillingness to protect America from this menacing minority. Note that the author links the non-event to "Arab muslims," even though the clerk involved, Savi, was an Indian immigrant, showing again the racial stereotypes prevalent in anti-Muslim sentiment. Even days later, protestors encouraged arriving customers to take their business elsewhere, while Savi received threats—despite the failure of the National Guard or the local paper to discover anyone who complained of being turned away.[47]

MOVING FORWARD

Despite the increase in reported hate crimes against Muslim Americans and a rise in their neighbors' suspicions regarding them, the evidence overwhelmingly shows that Muslims are a more mainstreamed and acculturated religious minority than many. In separate polls of Muslims and Christians in the United States, the Pew organization found in 2011 that nearly equal percentages of the two groups identified with their religion before their nation. While Christians were more likely than Muslims to identify as Americans first, Muslims were more likely to identify religiously and nationally in equal measure. Meanwhile, the same percentage (31 percent) of Muslims and Christians found it difficult to live devoutly in a modern society.[48] This and other polls find most Muslim Americans well in line with Christian American perspectives. Notwithstanding fears of homegrown Muslim terrorism, the greatest threat of terrorism arises from right-wing militia and hate groups who target government officials, law enforcement, and racial, ethnic, and religious minorities. The Southern Poverty Law Center lists sixty attempted or foiled efforts at domestic terrorism by rightists since September 11, 2001, some connected to Christian extremism, as was Timothy McVeigh, the 1995 Oklahoma City bomber, and Eric Rudolph, the 1996 Atlanta Olympics bomber before then.[49]

Nevertheless, congressional hearings in 2011 and 2012 called by Republican representative Peter King of New York focused on Muslim radicalism without noting the tie between non-Muslim radicals and attempted violence. The rise in such political theater as well as the efforts by professional Islamophobes may explain why a higher percentage of Muslim Americans polled indicated experiences of discrimination in 2011—by both law enforcement and fellow citizens—than when a similar question was asked four years earlier.[50] Meanwhile, posters on blogs, callers on radio talk shows, and co-workers at water coolers parrot the dicta of professional Islamophobes such as "Not all Muslims are terrorists, but all terrorists are Muslims" despite the goodwill efforts of Muslim Americans to demonstrate their patriotism, invite their neighbors into their mosques and homes, and cooperate with government officials.

Although increasing numbers of Americans have become more sensitive to Islamophobia and anti-Muslim sentiment, the rhetoric that makes a binary of *American* and *Muslim* continues to damage people's lives and erode tolerance as surely as did the slander against Irish Catholics, Jews, Mormons, Native Americans, and Branch Davidians. Such was the case when, in 2013, a business executive was arrested for assaulting a Virginia cab driver he identified as Muslim. The businessman, asking whether the cabbie was Muslim after learning he was from Somalia, then declared in an invective-laced tirade that the driver was a terrorist before allegedly breaking his jaw. In a general pattern repeated against religious minorities throughout American history, in the mind of the slanderer, the cabbie's religious identity proved stereotypically monolithic, eclipsing any other association, such as the driver's naturalization as an American citizen. As part of a unique historical moment, the alleged assailant could not appreciate the irony that the driver, whose Muslim identity he equated with terrorism, had served in Iraq as an Army reservist in the putative war on terror.[51]

Conclusion

How We Can Do Better

Thomas Jefferson, when reflecting in his autobiography on the Virginia legislature's process of drafting a bill of rights, explained the importance of universal ideals over a more exclusive notion of religion.

> Where the preamble declares that coercion is a departure from the plan of the holy author of our religion, an amendment was proposed, by inserting the word "Jesus Christ," so that it should read "a departure from the plan of Jesus Christ, the holy author of our religion" the insertion was rejected by a great majority, in proof that they meant to comprehend, within the mantle of it's [*sic*] protection, the Jew and the Gentile, the Christian and Mahometan, the Hindoo, and infidel of every denomination.[1]

Although Jefferson and his legislative colleagues may have been aware that some Muslims lived in their state, they would not have likely known of any Hindus existing there. The words that they rejected and the language to which they agreed demonstrated an idealistic commitment to universal plurality (albeit one that was inherently theistic). Less than a year later, the drafters of the federal Constitution took Virginia's approach as their model for ensuring religious freedom in the First

Amendment in the Bill of Rights. Jefferson and most of the nation's other political founders rejected the religious partialities of the past, opting for pluralism and equality to ensure the freedom of conscience of all individuals. Whatever blind spots they had in their ideals—and grievous, self-serving ones there were in condoning slavery and tyrannizing Indians—they made their commitment to this clear. And so many religious communities historically have found safety in the United States when they suffered persecution elsewhere.

Since before the War of Independence established the United States, Americans have wrangled over the overall relationship of religion to the nation. They have debated the link between particular *religions* and the nation, and whether any one religion forms the essential foundation of the United States. And Americans have argued about what demands the nation and its religions can make of one another, and what bounds define the acceptable behavior of one to the other. Some members of minority religious groups who have crossed these often-shifting and commonly invisible lines have been condemned by majority society, ending up on the unwelcome margins of mainstream norms, if not ostracized as American heretics.

For so long, televisions, movie screens, magazine covers, and history books predominantly have featured white Christian males in their portrayals of the nation's past, with only a few figures like Sacagawea, Susan B. Anthony, Malcolm X, and Martin Luther King Jr. to diversify the historical honor parade of Christopher Columbus, George Washington, Thomas Jefferson, Abraham Lincoln, and John F. Kennedy, among others. Nevertheless, Islamic mosques, Mormon temples, Hindu temples, and Sikh *gurudwaras* have increasingly been popping up alongside mainstream Christian churches, even as many of the latter close for lack of congregants. As a teenager in the overwhelmingly white and Christian suburbs of New Jersey, I watched in fascination as immigrant Indian Hindus moved into my hometown of Parsippany and turned a small church into a temple at the same time as newly arrived Pakistanis in nearby Boonton transformed a Jewish synagogue into their Islamic center. While I, the child of German and Australian Catholic immigrants, barely stood out as such in my community, many of my new Indian American and Pakistani American classmates enjoyed no such luxury.

These changes have been occurring to varying degrees across the country, and for some European American Christians—raised in a particular order based on assumptions of race, ethnicity, and religion—the shifts are unsettling. Rather innocuously, some observe, "This isn't the America in which I grew up." More ominously, the nonpartisan Southern Poverty Law Center has noted that hate groups, motivated by a weakening economy and shrinking white majority, increased by 69 percent between 2000 and 2012. Most tellingly, the Patriot Movement— which had been on the decline for a decade—surged from 149 groups to 1,287, an increase of more than 700 percent, in the three years following 2008, when the economy sank and the nation elected a president so suspect that growing numbers of Americans believe he's Muslim.[2] Fortunately, as the previous chapters have demonstrated, the nation has some collective memory of the consequences of prejudiced responses to diversity—including the Puritan witch hunts, Native American genocide, and anti-Semitism—that have repeatedly helped motivate it to draw in response on the ideals established while the young nation first forged unity out of diversity.

One five-mile stretch of New Hampshire Avenue in Silver Spring, Maryland, demonstrates an instance of America's success in this regard. Along this short length of road, no fewer than eighteen communities have built their places of worship. These include examples of the former Protestant establishment, such as St. Stephen Lutheran Church, the Transfiguration Episcopal Church, and the Colesville Presbyterian Church. While Catholics primarily of European and African descent attend St. John the Baptist Catholic Community, Vietnamese Catholics pray beneath the pagoda roofs of Our Lady of Vietnam Parish. Meanwhile, the Korean Eun Sam Evangelical Church of Washington, the Iglesia Adventista del Septimo Dia, the Jehovah's Witnesses Witness

Transfiguration Episcopal Church, Silver Spring, Maryland (2013).

Iglesia Adventista del Septimo Dia (Seventh-day Adventist), Silver Spring, Maryland (2013).

*Muslim Community Center,
Silver Spring, Maryland
(2013).*

Hall, St. Andrew's Ukrainian Orthodox Cathedral, and St. Thomas Indian Orthodox Church represent other forms of Christianity. Finally,
the Cambodian Buddhist Temple and the Muslim Community Center
reflect the non-Christian religions that are increasingly at home in the
United States. While many Americans would view this multi-religious
parade as evidence of their nation's strength, some have recast the nativist reactions of the past, conspiratorially signaling to others that new
immigrants are dismantling the national character responsible for the
country's greatness. Although these impulses of intolerance have varied
historically, some common themes emerge. By self-consciously recognizing and addressing the prevalence of these themes in our society and
within ourselves, Americans have the best chance to not only recall instances of religious intolerance but understand the dynamics that have
made prejudice seem sensible so that we can do better in the future.

RECOGNIZING COMMON ANXIETIES
REGARDING RELIGIONS

Over the course of the history of the United States, various concerns about religious communities have repeatedly arisen, resulting in suspicion, if not antagonism, toward some or all religious traditions. These themes have taken different forms in different contexts, understood by their purveyors according to the perspectives of the day and adapted to fit the audience of the times. Many overlap and mutually reinforce one another.

Psychological coercion: Fear of forced submission to involuntary beliefs plays a strong role in many American anxieties regarding particular religions. Since the nation's founding, the Enlightenment and Protestant ideals of individualist free thinking and personal liberty have been highly valued. Religious groups with strong hierarchies such as the Catholic and Mormon churches have often been alleged to enforce an inescapable party line that denies individual reason. Much of the media frenzy over cults emerged from such anxieties, and that term, if it means nothing else, communicates the idea of "religious coercion." For most members of religious communities, participation represents a choice, for which they may have a strong predilection due to their upbringing. Such a choice inherently means accepting certain self-imposed restrictions (for example, tithing, attending services, periodic fasting) that, for many, offer certain opportunities if not freedoms.

Loss of physical privacy: Religious traditions with strong communitarian sensibilities—such as Catholic convents and utopian communities—often incite worries among outsiders, who cannot fathom why anyone would surrender their physical autonomy and who suspect that some members may be forced to participate against their will. The extreme value Americans place on the individual often overlooks the quotidian ways in which they physically submit themselves to communities at work, at home, and in sports (there is—as everyone knows who has ever been coached in a group sport—no "I" in "team"). However, these communal commitments appear "normal," while religious communities with practices less familiar to Americans have often been alleged to deny members their individual freedom.

Secrecy: Whether anxiety about Jesuitical machinations, Jewish conspiracies, the influence of the Mormons' Quorum of the Twelve Apostles, or the happenings in the Branch Davidians' communal home, claims of secret plans, languages, and organizations can trigger fears of an invisible malignant danger. Perhaps most insidiously, some claim that marginalized groups assume an air of normality and cooperation in order to lull fellow citizens into a false sense of amity even as they conspire against them. Claims of Islamophobes that most Muslims pretend to be moderate and patriotic under the doctrine of *taqiyya* (an allowance to hide one's identity when bodily threatened) is a particularly cynical argument that takes a community's acculturation as evidence of its opposite. The result is a self-justifying argument that discredits all counterevidence. Ultimately, maintaining secrets among a large community proves nigh impossible, so suspicions about secret machinations should be directed toward the rumor-mongers before doubting the community supposedly pulling strings in the shadows.

Oppressed women: Communities like the United States that have recognized how its women suffer inequalities and violence disproportionately to men often harshly judge societies with codes for women that diverge from their own. Such views commonly portray *those* women as passive victims who must submit to enforced male rule, while *our* women enjoy relative freedom. When it cannot be imagined that a woman might take a vow of celibacy, consent to marry an already-married man, or cover her head in public, such women suffer the conclusion that they are never active agents of their own conditions, but puppets of men. There remain many reasons to critically assess the gender distinctions and inequalities found within different communities. Yet poorly informed judgments of gender relations in other groups often allow individuals to overlook the unfair distinctions and pervasive inequalities in their own community. Ironically, efforts to invalidate what the majority sees as discriminatory practices frequently take away choices from the women they profess to champion and force them to fit the norms of the majority. While women's conditions and other human rights concerns are critically important, comparisons that contrast the gender ideals of our culture with the lived reality of another are inherently flawed.

Irrationality: The secularist impulse that informed the framers of the Constitution derives not only from the belief that government should neither intrude on religious freedoms nor establish a state-sanctioned church (as still exists in England) but also from an effort to safely constrain religious enthusiasm from too much influence in everyday public life. While the first style of secularism is formally enforced by law, the second style is informally enforced by social norms. The efforts of many Protestant churches and other religious communities to demonstrate a rational faith shows their understanding of religion's power to suspend reason and stoke emotion, and the negative impact this could have on the social order. Meanwhile, the use of words like "irrational," "fanatical," "fundamentalist," "zealous," and "extremist" as epithets flung at members of certain religions such as Quakers, Ghost Dancers, Mormons, and Muslims reflects many Americans' fears that these groups have threatened the stability of society. They also demonstrate how society uses such allegations as tools of control, seeking to shame individuals into behaving "normally." Often, such terms are empty of content, only signaling the observer's judgment that certain norms have been transgressed. Hence, the use of such adjectives should be assumed to speak more about the perceptions of the speaker than about the behavior of those purportedly described.

Social disorder: A related issue to irrationality is the perceived threat of particular religious communities to the "normal" social order. Puritans feared that Quakers' individualistic enthusiasm would undermine the community's moral discipline. Boston and Philadelphia Protestants fretted about excessive Irish Catholic drinking. European Americans worried that the Sioux Ghost Dance would derail their settlement and exploitation of the Black Hills. Many Americans suspected that the Mormon Church hierarchy's unification of religious and political power would undo the republic. Professional Islamophobes win supporters to their cause by concocting imaginary social threats such as "creeping sharia-ization." As each of the chapters has shown, while majority groups have fretted that specific religious communities will disrupt society, these anxieties invariably reflect broader changes to the social order, with the suspect religion serving as the chief symptom of the new conditions. Not infrequently, religions have come under criticism for offering women "too much freedom" and, thus, threatening society's foundation. Hence, New Englanders criticized Quakers for "inappropriately" allowing men and women to commingle in meetings, Boston's Protestants looked askance at mixed-gender Irish bars, and the federal government revoked the right of Utah women to vote after they elected candidates who supposedly oppressed them.

COMMON DYNAMICS OF INTOLERANCE

"Normal" people often justify marginalizing or victimizing religious minorities by using a set of rationalizations that have been repeated, in various and shifting forms, throughout the history of religious discrimination. Familiarity with these dynamics helps us avoid these common pitfalls of social engagement.

Religion is all that matters to them: At a physical distance, the individuals in any crowd of people appear visually difficult to distinguish from one another. Ultimately, we often characterize all the individuals in the group solely by their presence in that group. Similarly, in terms of social connection, although we may daily interact with members of groups to which we do not belong, without engaging them in the fullness of their humanity, we are likely to label and understand them solely as members of groups with which they associate, with which we do not, and about which popular society nurtures suspicion. In this situation, a yarmulke, a crucifix, or a hijab can become a marker of distinction and absolute difference if no common ground has been established between the wearer and the observer. For instance, a regular customer enters a store and sees the owner doing a prayer to images of Lakshmi and Ganesh discreetely placed near the storefront. Because she knows of no one else who venerates these deities, she may persistently and primarily see him as a Hindu after that, overlooking his other identities, such as a Boy Scout leader, Civil War reenactor, and volunteer ambulance worker. His particular devotion, therefore, may become a mark of absolute foreignness if the customer does not recognize the many social dimensions of his life.

This can occur on a level of broader, collective representation as well. When law enforcement officers use the term "person of interest," they are looking at that person through the lens of investigating her or his possible involvement in a crime. Their hobbies, friends, and accomplishments mean little if not pertinent to the matter at hand. Similarly, certain religious communities become "religions of interest." No matter what other identities individuals belonging to this community have (and most of us have multiple identities), mainstream society and the media often reduce them to their religious identity alone.

One reason that Muslim Americans may appear resistant to American norms is that the news and entertainment outlets almost always represent them *as* Muslims and Muslims alone. Seldom is a character who happens to be Muslim also given the identity of a lawyer, a suburbanite, a mother, a *Star Trek* fan, or a sports team booster. Muslim characters tend to appear because of their religious commitments alone and disappear when Islam no longer figures in the plot line.

Remaining under perennial suspicion: Mainstream society commonly assumes that certain religious communities have always been suspect, which then legitimates existing suspicion. Despite this circular reasoning, the type of intolerance faced by marginalized groups tends to change over time because the prejudices of mainstream society have more to do with the specific period of time in which they occurred than with any enduring qualities of the marginalized group. For instance, fears about the Mormon Church hierarchy and its potential influence on government have shifted over the decades. Whereas Joseph Smith faced a local fury fueled by Jacksonian populist ideals of individualism and the common man, Reed Smoot's congressional trials derived in no small part from the contemporary antagonism to monopolies. In contrast, Mitt

Romney's campaign excited secular concerns because of the influential role evangelicals played in the 2008 and 2012 elections, despite their silence during his father's 1968 effort.

There's a grain of truth in every stereotype: Stereotypes are generalizations about a group that are taken as true for every member of that group. As such, they cannot be true. Do we really believe that all women are worse drivers than men? Certainly the insurance companies who, in general, charge women less than men do not think so. Stereotypes do not gain credence because of some essential truth. Rather, they become popular because—no matter how baseless—they have been reiterated so frequently that this repetition itself appears to verify their truthfulness.

Their religion tells them to ignore/mistreat/hate us: As the examples of various Christian perspectives alone demonstrates, no universal agreement exists among a religion's members in regard to what is moral, who is right, how to read important texts, and why one should participate in that particular religion. Although stemming from the same Protestant branch, the Puritans and Society of Friends diverged significantly in their interpretations of the Bible. The history of the Seventh-day Adventists and their multiple splinter groups demonstrate how contrary perspectives within even small religious communities can be. Roman Catholicism, Sioux traditions, Judaism, Mormonism, and Islam have all proven to have highly diverse memberships and subcultures. We perhaps gain a more accurate portrait of a community when we speak about what Protestants, Catholics, Sioux, Jews, Mormons, and Muslims do instead of how their religions supposedly "behave": religions cannot act, only the people who associate with them can. And they seldom do so as a singular monolith.

Why can't they be normal?: While noticing unexpected difference— such as someone wearing a top hat in a fast food restaurant—might be understandable, the persistent and judgmental fixation on a minority group should give pause. Why do differences matter? In a great many instances, they matter because they offer an opportunity to negatively define the majority using a religious minority. For example, the Ku Klux Klan's fixation on Jews, Catholics, and blacks in the 1920s arguably served less to address any perceived threat and more as a means of negatively defining a white Protestant America at a time when it appeared vulnerable to non-Protestant immigration. In a more current instance, the false stereotypes of Muslims' religious and racial difference used by some reflect their efforts to define America according to a white European American Christian norm that is disappearing.

My people suffered prejudice in the past, it's their turn now, and in the future they'll become accepted when another group takes their place at the bottom of the ladder: This sentiment testifies to both an American recognition of historical prejudice and faith in eventual acculturation. Unfortunately, as the experiences of many Jewish and Muslim Americans—among others—testify, such faith proves misplaced. Despite the more than 300 years that Jewish communities have lived in the United States, incidents of Jewish hate crimes top the FBI's report of overall incidents.

Their foreign connections prove that they're not American: Nineteenth-century nativists suspected Irish Catholics of receiving money from Europe to undermine America's Protestant order. Twentieth-century anti-Semites alleged that an international Jewish order funneled money to newly arrived migrants, giving them an unfair business advantage. Twenty-first-century Islamophobes argue that Muslim prayers toward Mecca demonstrate their perpetual rootedness in the Middle East despite their US presence. All of these cases demonstrate a disregard to a simple fact of modern history: wide-scale migration has meant that immigrant communities commonly negotiate their twin rootedness in both the cultures of their origin and their destination. Given—among the myriad hyphenated ethnic identities among Americans—the celebrated pride of multiple-generation Irish and Italian Americans with the flags of their heritage lands flying in innumerable pubs, pizzerias, and other businesses, this would not appear to need repeating. However, the constancy of this allegation, albeit against different groups over time, reflects again how members of some groups assimilate into—and perhaps come to exemplify—a national norm, usually once they are perceived to fit ethnic, racial, and religious standards of Americanness.

RELIGION, NATION, AND THE UNITED STATES

Religion and nation: two of the most powerful motivators in modern history. If willingness to die in the promotion of a cause serves as one measure of the cause's importance, then evidence suggests that religion and nation have been two of the greatest. The Quaker missionaries' fatal persistence, the Jonestown mass suicide, the Branch Davidians' doomed resistance, and the 9/11 hijackers' terrible resolve all have confirmed the fears of some secularists that religion—however important in private—could ultimately threaten the nation if unrestrained in public.

But nationalism, too, can sustain and promote extreme behavior. While Americans have long disparaged as "fanatical" the suicidal or near-suicidal efforts of Japanese kamikazes, Vietcong guerillas, and Iranian revolutionaries, they have celebrated their compatriots who have engaged in missions with equally poor survival chances: Joseph Kennedy Jr.'s doomed flight, soldiers who throw themselves on hand grenades, Secret Service agents trained to take a bullet for the president.

Groups have sought to harness both nationalism and religion in ways that can as easily be destructive as they are constructive. Much depends on one's point of view. In no small part, black churches gave enormous impetus to Martin Luther King Jr.'s civil rights movement, which challenged and disrupted Jim Crow in the South. Most Americans applauded what they viewed as the fuller realization of the nation's founding ideals. Others considered the movement a threat to the nation's long-held white supremacist values. Yet others considered it a lesser threat compared to the separatist Nation of Islam movement that used religion to inspire inner-city blacks toward independence from white America.

Without a doubt, some individuals and groups have perpetuated injustices and even crimes through the motivation of their religion. A proper response to these clearly is not a naïve tolerance for whatever people do in the name of a religion. However, American history has demonstrated a sad parade of episodes of intolerance more often rooted in misunderstanding and anxiety than in actual social threat. The dizzying quickness with which digital reporting can communicate outrages, protests, and other events across the globe has shortened the time editors have to sort fact from rumor. The increasingly vast array of sources available to anyone with a connected computer makes discerning credible from self-serving sources increasingly difficult. And the expanding power of social media amplifies all of these issues as we progressively become targeted by what presents itself as "information" and which is shaped to appeal to what we already think we know. All of this can powerfully perpetuate and exaggerate chauvinisms that our society has bequeathed us without our knowledge. Just as the Ku Klux Klan utilized the new knowledge of mass marketing in the 1920s to forge a national organization built on bias and just as the Cult Awareness Network capitalized on the national news media scare regarding new religious movements during the 1980s and '90s, so professional Islamophobes today exploit digital avenues to prompt prejudice, provoke anger, and promote themselves with expanding success while profitably partnering with fundraisers, politicians, and media outlets.

The strategy of reducing complex issues of belief, practice, economics, politics, race, ethnicity, sexuality, and gender into a simplistic and singular portrait of a religion today threatens not only Muslims, but all religious communities. After all, what is to stop another set of organized provocateurs from applying the same strategy to any other religious group? Which community, after all, does not have some extremists who prefer confrontation over conversation, promote a vision of society at odds with the status quo, participate in practices that many Americans do not understand, or have faith in ideas that other Americans consider outlandish? Through greater insight into the varieties of religion, the dynamics of prejudice, and the complexities of national life, Americans can better avoid the biases, stereotypes, and provocations that betray their own ideals yet have too frequently appeared on the country's political and social landscape.

Notes

*For the reader's sake of ease, endnote citations are abbreviated except for periodicals and archival sources. Please consult the bibliography for the complete entry for all other sources.

FOREWORD

1. "Finley Peter Dunne Quotes," Brainy Quote, accessed September 18,2013, http://www.brainyquote.com/quotes/authors/f/finley_peter_dunne.html.

CHAPTER ONE: HERETICS! BLASPHEMERS! WITCHES!: QUAKERS IN COLONIAL AMERICA

1. Morgan 1965, 92.
2. Ibid., 92–93.
3. Boyarin 2004, 3–4.
4. Wood 2006, 31.
5. See Boyarin 2004.
6. Demos 2004, 10, 60.
7. Hamm 2003, 18, 23.
8. Demos 2004, 11.
9. Ibid., 10, 12–13, 80–81.
10. Ray 2010, 51.
11. Demos 2004, 309, 311–312; Demos 2008, 81-82.
12. Demos 2004, 10–12, 310.
13. Hamm 2003, 16–17, 21-22.
14. Bremer 2012, 88–89.
15. Butler 1990, 37–56.
16. Pestana 1991, 39–40.
17. Ryan 2009, 36–37, 45.
18. Worrall 1980, 18–19.
19. Ibid., 9–15.
20. Bremer 2006, 626–631.
21. Pestana 1991, 33–35.
22. Bremer 2012, 89–91.
23. Ryan 2009, 39, 42, 45.

CHAPTER TWO: UN-AMERICAN AND UN-CHRISTIAN: IRISH CATHOLICS

1. *The New-England Primer Improved,* 1823, 23–24.
2. Tumbleson 1998, 69–70, 74–76.
3. "*New England Primer* (1802)," Library of Congress, http://myloc.gov/Exhibitions/books-that-shaped-america/1800-1850/ExhibitObjects/New-England-Primer.aspx (accessed June 12, 2013).
4. Ray 1936, 102–103, 186–187, 257–258.
5. Bisson 1989, 31.
6. Tager 2001, 43–44.
7. Doyle 2006a, 182.
8. Franchot 1994, 100, 103, 107.
9. Doyle 2006a, 197–198.
10. Tumbleson 1998, 11, 13, 39, 78, 90.
11. Doyle 2006a, 198.
12. Ibid., 184, 191, 195–197.
13. Franchot 1994, 6, 9, 99–100.
14. Bisson 1989, 8, 12–14.
15. My gratitude to Edward T. O'Donnell for this insight.
16. Bisson 1989, 35–37, 60–63, 85.
17. Ibid., 35–37, 69–73.
18. Ibid., 56, 88–90, 95.
19. Franchot 1994, 106.
20. Ibid., 154–160.
21. Ibid., 100.
22. Ibid., 136–139.
23. *Trial of John R. Buzzell,* 1834, 17.
24. Franchot 1994, 140, 142.
25. Stevens 1835, 2–3.
26. Ray 1936, 269–270.
27. Feldberg 1980, 4, 5, 7, 35.
28. Ibid., 9.
29. Fessenden 2011, 71.
30. Feldberg 1980, 18–23.
31. Ibid., 18–23.
32. Ibid., 28–32.
33. Oates 1988, 104–105.

CHAPTER THREE: HEATHENS: THE SIOUX AND THE GHOST DANCE

1. Daunton and Halpern 1999, 4.
2. Jenkins 2004, 21–23; Wood 2006, 32.
3. Mandell 2010, 81–85.
4. Wood 2006, 33.
5. Breen 1999, 106.
6. Architect of the Capitol, "Explore Capitol Hill," http://www.aoc.gov/capitol-hill/other-statues/statue-freedom (accessed February 11, 2013).
7. Ellet 1840, 92–93.

8. Riggs 1869, 187–188.
9. Greenwood 1860, 80, 82, 431–432.
10. Witkin-New Holy 2000, 188, 201, 203–205; annotated notes by Raymond J. De-Mallie in Neihardt 2008, 49n9, 64n15.
11. Annotated notes by Raymond J. DeMallie in Neihardt 2008, 105n15, 182n6.
12. Powers 1977, 112–113.
13. Oberly 1888, xxix–xxx.
14. Custer 1999, 250–255.
15. Utter 1991, 15.
16. Coates 1985, 91.
17. Jones 1902, 375.
18. Utter 1991, 15; Miles 1892, 144.
19. Miles 1892, 148–149.
20. Walker 1991, 141.
21. Utter 1991, 16.
22. Neihardt 1984, 256–269.
23. Richardson 2010, 247–275.
24. Eastman 1916, 111–112.
25. Richardson 2010, 275, 294.
26. Ibid., 299.
27. Coates 1985, 94.
28. Prucha 2000, 185. Also personal communication with Raymond J. DeMallie, February 23, 2013.
29. DeMallie 1984, 32–34.
30. Ibid., 60.
31. Ibid., 47, 60–63.
32. Utter 1991, 27; Jenkins 2004, 35.
33. Kracht 1992, 468–469.
34. Jenkins 2004, 39.
35. I am indebted to Raymond J. DeMallie for this insight.
36. Powers 1977, 200–202.
37. Irwin 1997, 46–47.
38. Ibid., 44–46.
39. Forbes-Boyte 1999, 319.

CHAPTER FOUR: A RACE APART: JEWS IN THE EYES OF THE KU KLUX KLAN, HENRY FORD, AND THE GOVERNMENT

1. Cocoltchos 2004, 103–112.
2. Melching 1974, 176; Papers of the Ku Klux Klan, Library of Congress Manuscript Division.
3. Melching 1974, 178–182, 184; Papers of the Ku Klux Klan, Library of Congress Manuscript Division.
4. Dillingham 1911, 160, 177.
5. Ibid., 266, 271.
6. Cannato 2009, 195–202.
7. I am indebted to Annalise Glauz-Todrank for this insight.
8. Michael 2005, 58–65.
9. Frederickson 2002, 52–53, 59.

10. Thomas Jefferson, "Notes on the State of Virginia," University of Virginia Electronic Text Center, http://etext.virginia.edu/toc/modeng/public/JefVirg.html (accessed June 15, 2013).
11. Frederickson 2002, 74, 101, 110–111.
12. Tehranian 2000, 821–822, 837–838.
13. My appreciation to Jeremy Zwelling for this contribution.
14. Goldstein 2006, 19–21, 35, 126–127.
15. Pegram 2011, 185.
16. Lewis and Serbu 1999, 145.
17. Pegram 2011, 14–15.
18. Ibid., 8.
19. Papers of the Ku Klux Klan, Library of Congress Manuscript Division.
20. Romine and Romine 1924, 3–4, 8–9, 13–16.
21. Papers of the Ku Klux Klan, Library of Congress Manuscript Division.
22. Pegram 2011, 12.
23. Safianow 2004, 118.
24. Pegram 2011, 9.
25. Papers of the Ku Klux Klan, Library of Congress Manuscript Division.
26. Simmons 1921.
27. Evans 1923a.
28. Safianow 2004, 117–118.
29. Ibid., 122, 124.
30. Cocoltchose 2004, 108–109.
31. Evans 1926, 40–41, 60.
32. Karabel 2005, 87–88.
33. Messer-Kruse 1993, 4–5, 21–22.
34. Pegram 2011, 10.
35. Goldberg 1996, 34–38, 42–43.
36. Michael 2005, 139.
37. Dinnerstein 1994, 81.
38. Ford 1920, 5, 11–12, 15–17, 19, 39–40.
39. Ibid., 21–22, 36–37.
40. Ibid., 14, 33.
41. Ibid., 10, 12, 47.
42. Ibid., 9, 23, 24, 28, 30, 36, 48–49.
43. Dinnerstein 1994, 78–80.
44. Ford 1920, 47–49, 62–63.
45. Ibid., 13–14, 35, 60–61.
46. Ibid., 92, 94, 130–131.
47. Ibid., 6.
48. Ibid., 36, 39, 136.
49. Dinnerstein 1994, 81.
50. Hitler 1941, 930.
51. Goldstein 2006, 123–124.
52. *Anaheim Bulletin*, February 4, 1925, 1.
53. R. W. Ernest and Paul V. Hester, "*Plain Dealer* Admits and Repudiates Libel against Dr. Geissinger," *Orange County Plain Dealer*, May 8, 1925, 1.
54. "*Plain Dealer* Sold to Owners of *Bulletin*," *Orange County Plain Dealer*, May 8, 1925, 1.
55. Cocoltchos 2004, 116–117.

CHAPTER FIVE: FANATICS: SECULAR FEARS AND MORMON POLITICAL CANDIDATES FROM JOSEPH SMITH JR. TO MITT ROMNEY

1. Jeffrey Jones, "Americans See U.S. as Exceptional; 37% Doubt Obama Does," Gallup, December 22, 2010, http://www.gallup.com/poll/145358/Americans-Excep tional-Doubt-Obama.aspx (accessed May 3, 2013).
2. Hallwas 1990, 54; metaphors borrowed from Jesus's Sermon on the Mount, Matthew 5:14.
3. Bushman 1984, 55–58; Fluhman 2012, 54–55.
4. Bushman 1984, 108–111; Gutjahr 2012, 31–33; Fluhman 2012, 9–11.
5. Gutjahr 2012, 36–37.
6. Bowman 2012, 36-37.
7. Campbell 2004, 80; Fluhman 2012, 83–89.
8. Bushman and Bushman 2001, 1.
9. Wood 2000, 177–178.
10. Fluhman 2012, 99.
11. Wood 2000, 177, 187. My appreciation to David Walker for his insights into this issue.
12. Ibid., 185.
13. Ibid., 189–190.
14. Hallwas 1990, 53–54.
15. Ibid., 54.
16. Ibid., 55, 58.
17. Ibid., 60–61.
18. Fluhman 2012, 54–55.
19. Wood 2000, 189–190.
20. Flake 2004, 2–5.
21. Ibid., 7.
22. Jones et al. 2011, 26.
23. Flake 2004, 42–45, 91–92, 165; Paulos 2008, 211–213.
24. Song 2007, 151–154. Thanks to David Walker for sharing his knowledge on this issue.
25. "Converted Mormon on Smoot: Miss Stalker Declares Polygamy a Fundamental of Senator's Religion," *Washington Post,* December 11, 1903, 4.
26. "Mothers against Smoot: Officers of Their National Congress Send a Circular Letter to Senators," *Washington Post,* December 11, 1903, 4.
27. "A Talk With Reed Smoot," *Hartford Courant,* March 2, 1903, 10.
28. Bowman 2012, 157–158.
29. Cullom 1907, 574.
30. Bowman 2012, 157–158; Alexander 1996, 19.
31. "Reed Smoot for Senator: A Number of Excellent Reasons for His Election by the Republican Party," *Washington Post,* January 19, 1903, 6. The article was published originally in the *St. Louis Globe-Democrat.*
32. Alexander 1996, 26.
33. The source cites the quote's origin as Hinckley 1956, 202; "The Oath and Covenant of the Priesthood," Church of Jesus Christ of Latter-day Saints, http://www.lds.org/ldsorg/v/index.jsp?hideNav=1&locale=0&sourceId=37549207f7c20110VgnVCM 100000176f620a&vgnextoid=e1fa5f74db46c010VgnVCM1000004d82620aR CRD (accessed June 16, 2013).

34. Flake 2004, 5, 8.
35. "Romney Seeks Guidance on Political Role: Begins Fast, Promises Decision," *Chicago Daily Tribune,* February 10, 1962, 11.
36. Ralph McGill, "Romney for President?," *Hartford Courant,* January 25, 1962, 8.
37. Raymond R. Coffey, "Next Move by Unorthodox Romney Awaited," *Washington Post,* December 27, 1961, A4.
38. Bowman 2012, 224; Kranish and Helman 2012, 43–44; Romney 2010, 5.
39. King and King 2000, 9, 13.
40. "Polls Give Slight Edge To Romney," *Hartford Courant,* November 1, 1962, 39A; "George Romney and Segregated Voting," *Hartford Courant,* October 1, 1962, 14.
41. Daniel Allott, "Ted Kennedy's Anti-Mormon Moment," *American Spectator,* May 23, 2013, http://spectator.org/archives/2012/05/23/ted-kennedys-anti-mormon-moment (accessed March 23, 2013).
42. Richard A. Oppel Jr. and Erik Eckholm, "Prominent Pastor Calls Romney's Church a Cult," *New York Times,* October 7, 2011, http://www.nytimes.com/2011/10/08/us/politics/prominent-pastor-calls-romneys-church-a-cult.html?_r=0 (accessed March 23, 2013).
43. Eric Schroeck, "Why Is the Media Giving a Platform to Pastor with History of Inflammatory Rhetoric?" MediaMatters for America, December 9, 2010, http://mediamatters.org/blog/2010/12/09/why-is-the-media-giving-a-platform-to-pastor-wi/174214 (accessed March 23, 2013).
44. Amanda Winkler, "Mitt Romney Jabs at 'Anti-Mormon' Speakers," *Christian Post,* October 8, 2011, http://www.christianpost.com/news/mitt-romney-jabs-at-anti-mormon-speakers-57656/#ZCkcLkJIIYEVwYUz.99.
45. Associated Press, "Romney Dismisses Democrat's Remark about Polygamy," April 20, 2012, http://news.yahoo.com/romney-dismisses-democrats-remark-polygamy-225244804.html (accessed September 17, 2013).
46. Paul Stanley, "Voter Guide for Black Churches Compares Obama's Christianity to Romney's Mormonism," *Christian Post,* November 6, 2012, http://www.christianpost.com/news/voter-guide-for-black-churches-compares-obamas-christianity-to-romneys-mormonism-84481/#fHMR0LOXerLP6Szw.99 (accessed March 23, 2013); Greater Hampton Roads Christian Leadership Conference, http://greaterhamptonroadschristianleadershipconference.com/#welcome (accessed March 23, 2013).
47. J. Spencer Fluhman, "Why We Fear Mormons," *New York Times,* June 3, 2012, http://www.nytimes.com/2012/06/04/opinion/anti-mormonism-past-and-present.html (accessed April 6, 2013).
48. My appreciation to J. Spencer Fluhman for this insight.
49. David Gibson, "Why Mitt Romney Can't Be the Mormon JFK," Religion News Service, January 26, 2012, http://www.huffingtonpost.com/2012/01/25/mitt-romney-mormon-jfk_n_1232307.html?ref=religion (accessed March 26, 2012).
50. http://www.amazon.com/Mitt-Romney-Mormon-Church-ebook/dp/B00919UNCG/ref=sr_1_6?s=books&ie=UTF8&qid=1364016582&sr=1-6&keywords=mormons (accessed March 23, 2013).
51. Jones et al. 2011, 7, 33–34.
52. Pew Research Religion and Public Life Project, "Romney's Mormon Faith Likely a Factor in Primaries, Not in a General Election Religion and the 2012 Election," November 23, 2011, http://pewresearch.org/pubs/2136/mormon-mormonism-evangelical-christian-catholic-protestant-rligion-politics-presidential-primaries-race-mitt-romney-barack-obama-herman-cain (accessed April 22, 2012).
53. Jones et al. 2011, 34.
54. Flake 2004, 10–11.

55. Jeffrey M. Jones, "Atheists, Muslims See Most Bias as Presidential Candidates: Two-thirds Would Vote for Gay or Lesbian," Gallup, http://www.gallup.com/poll/155 285/atheists-muslims-bias-presidential-candidates.aspx (accessed March 23, 2012).
56. Repphun 2012, 57–69.

CHAPTER SIX: IT'S NOT A RELIGION, IT'S A CULT: THE BRANCH DAVIDIANS

1. Pitts 1995, 32.
2. Tabor and Gallagher 1995, 59–60.
3. Watts 1985.
4. Bromley and Silver 1995, 57.
5. Ellison and Bartkowski 1995, 126–131.
6. Bromley and Silver 1995, 61; Tabor and Gallagher 1995, 25.
7. Reavis 1995, 97.
8. Tabor and Gallagher 1995, 80–87.
9. Ibid., 80–93.
10. Gazecki 2003.
11. Wright 1995, 87–89.
12. Tabor and Gallagher 1995, 82–88, 105; Reavis 1995, 41–43, 176; Wright 1995, 87–88; Hall 1995, 215.
13. Tabor and Gallagher 1995, 101–103.
14. Ibid., 97; Ammerman 1993, 5; Sullivan 1993, 7–8.
15. Tabor and Gallagher 1995, 80–93.
16. United States Department of Justice 1993.
17. Ibid.
18. Ammerman 1993, 289.
19. United States Department of Justice 1993.
20. Ammerman 1993, 286, 289.
21. Ibid., 286.
22. Sam Howe Verhovek, "In Shadow of Texas Siege, Uncertainty for Innocents," *New York Times,* March 8, 1993, A1.
23. Michael Isikoff and Pierre Thomas, "Waco Siege Ends in Dozens of Deaths as Cult Site Burns after FBI Assault; Reno Says, 'I Made the Decision,'" *Washington Post,* April 20, 1993, A1.
24. Ammerman 1993, 290–291.
25. United States Department of Justice 1993.
26. Wessinger 2000, 110.
27. Ibid., 108–109.
28. Ibid., 105–112.
29. Gazecki 2003.
30. Ellison and Bartkowski 1995, 144.
31. Shupe and Darnell 2006, 180–184.

CHAPTER SEVEN: THE SUM OF ALL FEARS: ISLAMOPHOBIA AND ANTI-MUSLIM SENTIMENT TODAY

1. Marc Santora, "Woman Is Charged with Murder as a Hate Crime in a Fatal Subway Push," *New York Times,* December 29, 2012, http://www.nytimes.com/2012/12/30 .html (accessed March 24, 2013).

2. "Sikh Cab Driver Beaten in Alleged Hate Crime," Q13 FOX News Online, October 29, 2012, http://www.herald-mail.com/news/kcpq-federal-way-man-charged-with-hate-crime-after-alleged-taxi-driver-beating-20121029,0,1413667.story; Vera Chinese and Simone Weichselbaum, "Man Stabbed Outside Queens Mosque, Attacker Screamed Anti-Muslim Rant, Say Cops," *New York Daily News,* November 18, 2012, http://www.nydailynews.com/news/crime/man-stabbed-queens-mosque-article-1.1204122#ixzz2PmwFOjqt; Rocco Parascandola, "Queens Man, 70, Beaten by Pair after Being Asked If He Was Hindu or Muslim: Cops," *New York Daily News,* November 30, 2012, http://www.nydailynews.com/news/crime/queens-man-70-beaten-apparent-hate-attack-article-1.1210944#ixzz2PmvYyr7f; "Police Search for Man Who Threatened Fremont Mosque," KTVU, December 13, 2012, http://www.ktvu.com/news/news/local/police-search-man-who-threatened-fremont-mosque/nTWd2/; all accessed April 7, 2013.
3. Paul Fanlund, "In Wake of Wisconsin Temple Murders, Muslims Remain 'Enemy Du Jour,'" *Capital Times,* December 19, 2012, http://host.madison.com/news/local/writers/paul_fanlund/paul-fanlund-in-wake-of-wisconsin-temple-murders-muslims-remain/article_d13a6078-461e-11e2-88d5-0019bb2963f4.html (accessed June 18, 2013).
4. Nancy Krause, "Arrest Made in Mosque Vandalism," WPRI Providence, August 20, 2012, http://www.wpri.com/dpp/news/crime/north-smithfield-arrest-made-mosque-vandalism-robert-scalso; Alan Wang, "4 Teens Arrested for Hate Crimes against Mosque," KGO-TV San Francisco, August 8, 2012, http://abclocal.go.com/kgo/story?section=news/local/east_bay&id=8767266; Rebecca Trounson, "Islamic Group Asks for Investigation of Pig Legs at Mosque Site," *Los Angeles Times,* August 13, 2012, http://articles.latimes.com/2012/aug/13/local/la-me-mosque-20120813; "Pellet Rifle Shots Fired at Mosque near Chicago," *USA Today,* August 11, 2012, http://usatoday30.usatoday.com/news/nation/story/2012-08-11/mosque-illinois-shots/56989464/1; "Acid Thrown during Ramadan Prayers at Muslim School in Lombard," *Chicago Sun-Times,* August 13, 2012, http://www.suntimes.com/news/metro/14464894-418/acid-thrown-during-ramadan-prayers-at-muslim-school-in-lombard.html; "Surveillance Cameras Catch Vandals Shooting Mosque with Paintballs," KOKH-TV Oklahoma City, http://www.okcfox.com/newsroom/top_stories/videos/kokh_vid_6171.shtml; all accessed April 7, 2013.
5. Gottschalk and Greenberg 2007, 5.
6. Asbridge 2004, 16–22, 40–49, 84–89; Phillips 1995, 116–117.
7. Diouf 1998, 17–18, 54, 205.
8. Adams 1851, 219; Franklin 1837, 231–234.
9. Adams 1914, 426.
10. Ted Widmer, "People of the Book: The True History of the Koran in America," *Boston Globe,* September 12, 2010, http://www.boston.com/bostonglobe/ideas/articles/2010/09/12/the_true_history_of_the_koran_in_america/?comments=all&plckCurrentPage=2 (accessed April 6, 2013).
11. Fluhman 2012, 29–39.
12. See Gottschalk and Greenberg, 2007.
13. Associated Press, "Clinton Campaign Requests Resignation from Second Iowa Coordinator for Obama 'Muslim' E-Mail," December 9, 2007, http://www.foxnews.com/story/0,2933,316273,00.html (accessed April 7, 2013).
14. Ginger Gibson, "Newt Gingrich: Obama 'Quick to Apologize for Islam,'" *Politico,* March 1, 2012, http://www.politico.com/news/stories/0312/73528.html#ixzz1 qF InRy5G (accessed April 7, 2013).
15. Jackson 2011, 93–106.

16. Ibid., 103.

17. Bayoumi 2006, 268–270.

18. Ed Henry and Ed Hornick, "Rage Rising on the McCain Campaign Trail," CNN, October 11, 2008, http://www.cnn.com/2008/POLITICS/10/10/mccain.crowd/ (accessed April 7, 2013).

19. U.S. Religious Landscape Survey, Pew Forum on Religion & Public Life, http://religions.pewforum.org/portraits (accessed April 7, 2013).

20. Charles Kurzman, "American Attitudes Toward Islam and Muslims," unpublished chart, 2013.

21. Pew Research Center, "Growing Number of Americans Say Obama Is a Muslim," August 19, 2010, http://www.pewforum.org/uploadedFiles/Topics/Issues/Politics _and_Elections/growingnumber-full-report.pdf (accessed March 30, 2013); Public Policy Polling, "Democrats and Republicans Differ on Conspiracy Theory Beliefs," April 2, 2013, http://www.publicpolicypolling.com/pdf/2011/PPP_Release_Na tional_ConspiracyTheories_040213.pdf (accessed July 22, 2013).

22. Justin Elliott, "How the 'Ground Zero Mosque' Fear Mongering Began," *Salon,* August 16, 2010, http://www.salon.com/news/ground_zero_mosque/index.html ?story=/politics/war_room/2010/08/16/ground_zero_mosque_origins.

23. T. Topousis, "Panel Approves 'WTC' Mosque," *New York Post,* May 6, 2010, http:// www.nypost.com/p/news/local/manhattan/panel_approves_wtc_mosque_U46M kTSVJH3ZxqmNuuKmML (accessed May 15, 2012).

24. Pamela Geller, "Monster Mosque Pushes Ahead in Shadow of World Trade Center Islamic Death and Destruction," *Atlas Shrugs,* May 6, 2010, http://atlasshrugs2000 .typepad.com/atlas_shrugs/2010/05/monster-mosque-pushes-ahead-in-shadow-of -world-trade-center-islamic-death-and-destruction.html (accessed May 15, 2012).

25. Andrea Peyser, "Mosque Madness at Ground Zero," *New York Post,* May 13, 2010, http://www.nypost.com/p/news/national/mosque_madness_at_ground_zero _OQ34EB0MWS0lXuAnQau5uL (accessed May 4, 2013); Southern Poverty Law Center, "Anti-Muslim," http://www.splcenter.org/get-informed/intelligence-files /ideology/anti-muslim#.UYaBiytoQke (accessed May 4, 2013).

26. D. West, "A Mosque to Mock 9/11's Victims and Families," *Washington Examiner,* May 16, 2010, http://washingtonexaminer.com/article/32272 (accessed May 15, 2012).

27. Elliott, "How the 'Ground Zero Mosque' Fear Mongering Began."

28. Justin Berrier, "What Fox Has Wrought: Anti-Park51 Protests Full of Right-Wing Hate," MediaMatters, August 23, 2010, http://mediamatters.org/research/2010 /08/23/what-fox-has-wrought-anti-park51-protests-full/169666 (accessed March 29, 2013).

29. Glenn Beck, "Pelosi Wants to Investigate Ground Zero Mosque Opponents," Glenn Beck, August 18, 2010, http://www.glennbeck.com/content/articles/article /198/44403/ (accessed May 15, 2011).

30. Rush Limbaugh, "Why This Mosque on This Spot?," transcript, Rush Limbaugh, August 17, 2010, http://www.rushlimbaugh.com/home/daily/site_081710/content /01125111.guest.html (accessed May 15, 2012).

31. Anderson Cooper and Renee Ellmers, transcript, *Anderson Cooper 360 Degrees,* September 24, 2010, http://transcripts.cnn.com/TRANSCRIPTS/1009/24/acd.02 .html (accessed March 30, 2013); "Pantano Wades into Sharia Firestorm at CPAC," Pantano for U.S. Congress, February 9, 2012, http://www.pantanoforcongress.com /posts/pantano-wades-into-sharia-firestorm-at-cpac (accessed July 22, 2013).

32. J. D. Goodman, "Strangers: A Problem That Won't Go Away," *New York Times,* April 20, 2010, http://cityroom.blogs.nytimes.com/2010/05/20/strangers-a-prob

lem-that-wont-go-away/?scp=2&sq=%22Mark%20Williams%22%20and%20 Muslim&st=cse (accessed May 15, 2012).

33. Berrier, "What Fox Has Wrought."

34. Andy Barr, "Newt Gingrich Compares Mosque to Nazis," *Politico,* August 16, 2010, http://www.politico.com/news/stories/0810/41112.html (accessed March 30, 2013).

35. Rush Limbaugh, "The Terrorists Win: NYC Panel Votes 9-0 for Ground Zero Mosque," Rush Limbaugh, August 3, 2010, http://www.rushlimbaugh.com/daily /2010/08/03/the_terrorists_win_nyc_panel_votes_9_0_for_ground_zero_mosque (accessed March 30, 2013).

36. Southern Poverty Law Center, "FBI: Dramatic Spike in Hate Crimes Targeting Muslims," *Intelligence Report* 145 (Spring 2012), http://www.splcenter.org/get -informed/intelligence-report/browse-all-issues/2012/spring/fbi-dramatic-spike-in -hate-crimes-targetin (accessed May 15, 2011).

37. Foley 2010, 11–16, 51.

38. Scott Shane, "Killings in Norway Spotlight Anti-Muslim Thought in U.S.," *New York Times,* July 24, 2011, http://www.nytimes.com/2011/07/25/us/25debate.html ?pagewanted=all&_r=0 (accessed June 18, 2013).

39. Tom A. Peter, "UN Staff Killed by Afghan Mob Enraged over Florida Quran Burning," *Christian Science Monitor,* April 1, 2011, http://www.csmonitor.com/World /Asia-South-Central/2011/0401/UN-staff-killed-by-Afghan-mob-enraged-over -Florida-Quran-burning (accessed March 31, 2012).

40. Adelle M. Banks, "Florida Pastor Oversees Quran Burning," *USA Today,* March 21, 2011, http://usatoday30.usatoday.com/news/religion/2011-03-21-quran-burning -florida_N.htm (accessed March 31, 2013).

41. "Karzai Criticized for Feeding Quran Burning Firestorm," *Politico,* http://www .politico.com/blogs/onmedia/0411/Karzai_criticized_for_feeding_Quran_burn ing_firestorm.html (accessed March 31, 2013).

42. Paul Harris and Paul Gallagher, "Terry Jones Defiant Despite Murders in Afghanistan over Qur'an Burning," *Guardian,* April 2, 2011, http://www.guardian.co.uk /world/2011/apr/02/pastor-terry-jones-burning-koran (accessed March 31, 2013).

43. Serge F. Kovaleski and Brooks Barnes, "From Man Who Insulted Muhammad, No Regret," *New York Times,* November 25, 2012, http://www.nytimes.com/2012/11/26 /us/from-the-man-who-insulted-islam-no-retreat.html?pagewanted=3&_r=2&hp &pagewanted=all&; Peter Bradshaw, "*Innocence of Muslims:* A Dark Demonstration of the Power of Film," *Guardian,* September 17, 2012, http://www.guardian .co.uk/film/filmblog/2012/sep/17/innocence-of-muslims-demonstration-film; both accessed July 8, 2013.

44. Kovaleski and Barnes, "From Man Who Insulted Muhammad"; Bradshaw, "*Innocence of Muslims.*"

45. Russell Goldman and David Wright, "Who Is Sam Bacile? Anti-Islam Filmmaker's Bio Doesn't Add Up," ABC News, September 12, 2012, http://abcnews.go.com /US/sam-bacile-anti-islam-filmmakers-bio-add/story?id=17222103 (accessed April 8, 2013).

46. "Bogalusa Whisper," June 15, 2012, http://www.snopes.com/politics/military/boga lusa.asp (accessed March 31, 2013).

47. Richard Meek, "Facebook Protest Affects Business, *Daily News,* June 13, 2012, http:// www.gobogalusa.com/news/article_a9ef82a6-b559-11e1-a277-0019bb2963f4 .html (accessed March 31, 2013).

48. Pew Research Center, "Muslim Americans: No Signs of Growth in Alienation or Support for Extremism," August 7, 2011, 36, 46, 51.

49. Southern Poverty Law Center Intelligence Project, "Terror from the Right: Plots, Conspiracies and Racist Rampages since Oklahoma City," 2012.

50. Pew Research Center, "Muslim Americans," 46.

51. "Exclusive Cellphone Video of Alleged Cab Assault," *Washington Post,* May 1, 2013, http://www.washingtonpost.com/video/thefold/exclusive-cellphone-video-of-alleged-cab-assault/2013/04/30/31a4a8c2-b1dd-11e2-baf7-5bc2a9dc6f44_video .html (accessed May 5, 2013).

CONCLUSION: HOW WE CAN DO BETTER

1. Jefferson 1914, 71.

2. Mark Potok, "The 'Patriot' Movement Explodes," *Intelligence Report* 145 (Spring 2012), http://www.splcenter.org/get-informed/intelligence-report/browse-all-issu es /2012/spring/the-year-in-hate-and-extremism (accessed March 29, 2013).

Select Bibliography

The listings below include:

Branch Davidians
Church of Jesus Christ of Latter-day Saints
Friends, the Society of Friends, and Colonial America
Jews and Judaism
Muslims and Islam
Religion and History in General
Roman Catholics and Catholicism
Sioux, Native Americans, and Westward Expansion

BRANCH DAVIDIANS

Ammerman, N. T. 1993. "Report to the Justice and Treasury Departments Regarding Law Enforcement Interaction with the Branch Davidians in Waco, Texas." In "Recommendations of Experts for Improvements in Federal Law Enforcement After Waco," United States Department of Justice, September 3.

Bromley, David G., and Edward D. Silver. 1995. "The Davidian Tradition: From Patronal Clan to Prophetic Movement." In *Armageddon in Waco: Critical Perspectives on the Branch Davidian Conflict,* edited by Stuart A. Wright, 43–72. Chicago: University of Chicago Press.

Ellison, Christopher G., and John P. Bartkowski. 1995. "'Babies Were Being Beaten': Exploring Child Abuse Allegations at Ranch Apocalypse." In *Armageddon in Waco: Critical Perspectives on the Branch Davidian Conflict,* edited by Stuart A. Wright, 111–149. Chicago: University of Chicago Press.

Gazecki, William. 2003. *Waco: The Rules of Engagement.* New York: New Yorker Films Artwork.

Hall, J. R. 1995. "Public Narratives and the Apocalyptic Sect: From Jonestown to Mt. Carmel." In *Armageddon in Waco: Critical Perspectives on the Branch Davidian Conflict,* edited by Stuart A. Wright, 205–235. Chicago: University of Chicago Press.

Pitts, William L. Jr. 1996. "Davidians and Branch Davidians: 1929–1987." In *Armageddon in Waco: Critical Perspectives on the Branch Davidian Conflict,* edited by Stuart A. Wright, 20–42. Chicago: University of Chicago Press.

Reavis, D. J. 1995. *The Ashes of Waco: An Investigation.* Syracuse, NY: Syracuse University Press.

Shupe, Anson, and Susan E. Darnell. 2006. *Agents of Discord: The Cult Awareness Network, Deprogramming, and Bad Science.* New Brunswick, NJ: Transaction.

Shupe, Anson, and J. K. Hadden. 1995. "Cops, News Copy, and Public Opinion: Legitimacy and the Social Construction of Evil in Waco." In *Armageddon in Waco: Critical Perspectives on the Branch Davidian Conflict,* edited by Stuart A. Wright, 177–202. Chicago: University of Chicago Press.

Sullivan, L. E. 1993. "Recommendations Concerning Incidents Such as the Branch Davidian Standoff in Waco, Texas between February 28, 1993 and April 19, 1993." In "Recommendations of Experts for Improvements in Federal Law Enforcement After Waco," United States Department of Justice, September 2.

Tabor, J. D., and E. V. Gallagher. 1995. *Why Waco? Cults and the Battle for Religious Freedom in America.* Berkeley: University of California Press.

United States Department of Justice. 1993. "Report to the Deputy Attorney General on the Events at Waco, Texas: February 28 to April 19, 1993." October 8. Accessed November 14, 2012, at http:// Wessinger, Catherine. 2000. *How the Millennium Comes Violently: From Jonestown to Heaven's Gate.* New York: Seven Bridges Press.

Wright, Stuart A. 1995. "Construction and Escalation of a Cult Threat: Dissecting Moral Panic and Official Reaction to the Branch Davidians." In *Armageddon in Waco: Critical Perspectives on the Branch Davidian Conflict,* edited by Stuart A. Wright, 75–94. Chicago: University of Chicago Press.

CHURCH OF JESUS CHRIST OF LATTER-DAY SAINTS

Alexander, Thomas G. 1996. *Mormonism in Transition: A History of the Latter-day Saints, 1890–1903.* Urbana: University of Illinois Press.

Bowman, Matthew. 2012. *The Mormon People: The Making of an American Faith.* New York: Random House.

Bushman, Richard L. 1984. *Joseph Smith and the Beginnings of Mormonism.* Urbana: University of Illinois Press.

Bushman, Claudia Lauper, and Richard Lyman Bushman. 2001. *Building the Kingdom: A History of Mormons in America.* New York: Oxford University Press.

Campbell, Craig S. 2004. *Images of the New Jerusalem: Latter Day Saint Faction Interpretations of Independence, Missouri.* Knoxville: University of Tennessee Press.

Cullom, Shelby M. 1907. "The Reed Smoot Decision." *North American Review* 184 (611): 572–576.

Flake, Kathleen. 2004. *The Politics of American Religious Identity: The Seating of Senator Reed Smoot, Mormon Apostle.* Chapel Hill: University of North Carolina Press.

Fluhman, J. Spencer. 2012. *"A Peculiar People": Anti-Mormonism and the Making of Religion in Nineteenth-Century America.* Chapel Hill: University of North Carolina Press.

Gutjahr, Paul C. 2012. *The Book of Mormon: A Biography.* Princeton, NJ: Princeton University Press.

Hallwas, John E. 1990. "Mormon Nauvoo from a Non-Mormon Perspective." *Journal of Mormon History* 16:53–69.

Hinckley, Bryant S. 1956. *The Faith of Our Pioneer Fathers.* Salt Lake City: Deseret Book Company.

King, Robert R., and Kay Atkinson King. 2000. "Mormons in Congress, 1851–2000." *Journal of Mormon History* 26 (2): 1–50.

Kranish, Michael, and Scott Helman. 2012. *The Real Romney.* New York: Harper Books.

Paulos, Michael Harold. 2008. "Under the Gun at the Smoot Hearings: Joseph F. Smith's Testimony." *Journal of Mormon History* 34 (4): 181–225.

Repphun, Eric. 2012. "Mormon Science Fiction: Interstellar Exodus and Perfection." In *Handbook of New Religions and Cultural Production,* edited by Carole M. Cusack and Alex Norman, 39–70. Leiden: Brill.

Romney, Mitt. 2010. *No Apology: The Case for American Greatness.* New York: St. Martin's Press.

Shipps, Jan. 1985. *Mormonism: The Story of a New Religious Tradition.* Urbana: University of Illinois Press.

Wood, Timothy L. 2000. "The Prophet and the Presidency: Mormonism and Politics in Joseph Smith's 1844 Presidential Campaign." *Journal of the Illinois State Historical Society* 93 (2): 167–193.

FRIENDS, THE SOCIETY OF FRIENDS, AND COLONIAL AMERICA

Bremer, Francis J. 2006. *Puritans and Puritanism in Europe and America.* Vol. 1. Santa Barbara, CA: ABC-CLIO.

———, ed. 2012. *First Founders: American Puritans and Puritanism in an Atlantic World.* Lebanon: University of New Hampshire Press.

Demos, John Putnam. 2004. *Entertaining Satan: Witchcraft and the Culture of Early New England.* Updated edition. New York: Oxford University Press.

———. 2008. *The Enemy Within: 2,000 Years of Witch-Burning in the Western World.* New York: Viking.

Hamm, Thomas D. 2003. *The Quakers in America.* New York: Columbia University Press.

Morgan, Edmund S. 1965. *Puritan Political Ideas: 1558–1794.* Indianapolis: Hackett.

Pestana, Carla Gardina. 1991. *Quakers and Baptists in Colonial Massachusetts.* New York: Cambridge University Press.

Purkiss, Diane. 1996. *The Witch in History: Early Modern and Twentieth-Century Representations.* New York: Routledge.

Ray, Benjamin C. 2010. "'The Salem Witch Mania': Recent Scholarship and American History Textbooks." *Journal of the American Academy of Religion* 78 (1): 40–64.

Ryan, James Emmett. 2009. *Imaginary Friends: Representing Quakers in American Culture, 1650–1950.* Madison: University of Wisconsin Press.

Wood, Timothy L. 2006. *Agents of Wrath, Sowers of Discord: Authority and Dissent in Puritan Massachusetts, 1630–1655.* New York: Routledge.

Worrall, Arthur J. 1980. *Quakers in the Colonial Northeast.* Hanover, NH: University Press of New England.

JEWS AND JUDAISM

Burrows, George W. c. 1923. *The Big 3 in One.* No place: no publisher.

Campbell, Sam H. 1923. "The Jewish Problem in the United States." Atlanta: Knights of the Ku Klux Klan.

Cannato, Vincent J. 2009. *American Passage: The History of Ellis Island.* New York: HarperCollins.

Clason, George S., ed. 1924. *Catholic, Jew, Ku Klux Klan: What They Believe, Where They Conflict.* Chicago: Nutshell Publishing Company.

Cocoltchos, Christopher N. 2004. "The Invisible Empire and the Search for the Orderly Community: The Ku Klux Klan in Anaheim, California." In *The Invisible Empire in the West: Toward a New Historical Appraisal of the Ku Klux Klan of the 1920s,* edited by Shawn Lay, 97–120. Chicago: University of Illinois Press.

Department of Realms. 1923. "Klan Building: An Outline of Proven Klan Methods for Successfully Applying the Art of Klancraft in Building and Operating Local Klans." Atlanta: Knights of the Ku Klux Klan.

Dever, Lem A. 1925. *Masks Off! Confessions of an Imperial Klansman.* 2nd ed. No place: no publisher.

Dillingham, William Paul. 1911. "Reports of the Immigration Commission: Statements and Recommendations Submitted by Societies and Organizations Interested in the Subject of Immigration." Washington, DC: Government Printing Office.

Dinnerstein, Leonard. 1994. *Antisemitism in America.* New York: Oxford University Press.

Evans, H. W. 1923a. "The Attitudes of the Knights of the Ku Klux Klan toward the Jew." Atlanta: Knights of the Ku Klux Klan.

———. 1923b. "The Menace of Modern Immigration." Atlanta: Knights of the Ku Klux Klan.

———. 1926. "The Klan's Fight for Americanism." *North American Review* 223 (830): 33–63.

Ford, Henry. 1920. *The International Jew: The World's Foremost Problem.* Dearborn, MI: Dearborn Publishing Company.

Frederickson, George M. 2002. *Racism: A Short History.* Princeton, NJ: Princeton University Press.

Goldberg, David J. 1996. "Unmasking the Ku Klux Klan: The Northern Movement against the KKK, 1920–1925." *Journal of American Ethnic History* 15 (4): 32–48.

Goldstein, Eric L. 2006. *The Price of Whiteness: Jews, Race, and American Identity.* Princeton, NJ: Princeton University Press.

Hitler, Adolf. 1941. *Mein Kampf.* New York: Reynal and Hitchcock.

Karabel, Jerome. 2005. *The Chosen: The Hidden History of Admission and Exclusion at Harvard, Yale, and Princeton.* New York: Mariner.

Ku Klux Klan. 1921. *Constitution and Laws of the Knights of the Ku Klux Klan (Incorporated).* Atlanta: no publisher.

———. 1922. "America for Americans." Atlanta: no publisher.

———. 1923. *Papers Read at the Meeting of Grand Dragons, Knights of the Ku Klux Klan at their First-Annual Meeting.* Atlanta: Knights of the Ku Klux Klan.

Lewis, Michael, and Jacqueline Serbu. 1999. "Kommemorating the Ku Klux Klan." *Sociological Quarterly* 40 (1): 139–158.

López, Ian Haney. 2006. *White by Law: The Legal Construction of Race.* Revised edition. New York: New York University Press.

Melching, Richard. 1974. "The Activities of the Ku Klux Klan in Anaheim, California 1923–1925." *Southern California Quarterly* 56 (2): 175–196.

Messer-Kruse, Timothy. 1993. "The Campus Klan of the University of Wisconsin: Tacit and Active Support for the Ku Klux Klan in a Culture of Intolerance." *Wisconsin Magazine of History* 77 (1): 2–38.

Michael, Robert. 2005. *A Concise History of American Antisemitism.* Lanham, MD: Rowman & Littlefield.

Pegram, Thomas R. 2011. *One Hundred Percent American: The Rebirth and Decline of the Ku Klux Klan in the 1920s.* Lanham, MD: Rowman & Littlefield.

Romine, W. B., and W. B. Romine. 1924. *A Story of the Original Ku Klux Klan.* Pulaski, TN: Pulaski Citizen.

Safianow, Allen. 2004. "'You Can't Burn History': Getting Right with the Klan in Noblesville, Indiana." *Indiana Magazine of History* 100 (2): 109–154.

Simmons, William Joseph. 1921. "The Ku Klux Klan: Yesterday, Today and Forever." Atlanta: no publisher.

Tehranian, John. 2000. "Performing Whiteness: Naturalization Litigation and the Construction of Racial Identity in America." *Yale Law Journal* 109 (4): 817–848.

White, Alma. 1925. *The Ku Klux Klan in Prophecy.* Zarephath, NJ: Good Citizen.

————. 1926. *Klansmen: Guardians of Liberty.* Zarephath, NJ: Good Citizen.

Women of the Ku Klux Klan. 1934. *Constitution and Laws of the Women of the Ku Klux Klan.* No place: no publisher.

MUSLIMS AND ISLAM

Adams, John. 1851. *The Works of John Adams, Second President of the United States.* Volume 6. Boston: Charles C. Little and James Brown.

Adams, John Quincy. 1914. *1801–1810.* Vol. 3 of *Writings of John Quincy Adams.* Edited by Worthington Chauncey Ford. New York: Macmillan.

Ali-Karamali, Sumbul. 2008. *The Muslim Next Door: The Qur'an, the Media, and That Veil Thing.* Ashland, OR: White Cloud.

Allison, Robert J. 1995. *The Crescent Obscured: The United States and the Muslim World, 1776–1815.* Chicago: University of Chicago Press.

Asbridge, Thomas. 2004. *The First Crusade: A New History.* New York: Oxford University Press.

Bakalian, Anny, and Medhi Bozorgmehr. 2009. *Backlash 9/11: Middle Eastern and Muslim Americans Respond.* Berkeley: University of California Press.

Bayoumi, Moustafa. 2006. "Racing Religion." *CR: The New Centennial Review* 6 (2): 267–293.

Diouf, Sylviane. 1998. *Servants of Allah: African Muslims Enslaved in the Americas.* New York: New York University Press.

Esposito, John L., and Ibrahim Kalin, eds. 2011. *Islamophobia: The Challenge of Pluralism in the 21st Century.* New York: Oxford University Press.

Esposito, John L., and Dalia Mogahed. 2007. *Who Speaks For Islam?: What a Billion Muslims Really Think.* New York: Gallup.

Foley, Kathleen E. 2010. "'Not In Our Neighborhood': Managing Opposition to Mosque Construction." Institute for Social Policy and Understanding, October.

Franklin, Benjamin. 1837. "On the Slave Trade." In *The Works of Benjamin Franklin: Consisting of Essays, Humorous, Moral, and Literary with His Life, Written by Himself,* 231–234. Halifax: H. Pohlman.

Gottschalk, Peter, and Gabriel Greenberg. 2007. *Islamophobia: Making Muslims the Enemy.* Latham, MD: Rowman & Littlefield.

Jackson, Sherman. 2011. "Muslims, Islam(s), Race, and American Islamophobia." In *Islamophobia: The Challenge of Pluralism in the 21st Century,* edited by John L. Esposito and Ibrahim Kalin, 93–106. New York: Oxford University Press.

Lean, Nathan. 2012. *The Islamophobia Industry: How the Right Manufactures Fear of Muslims.* London: Pluto Press.

Morey, Peter, and Amina Yaqin. 2011. *Framing Muslims: Stereotyping and Representation after 9/11.* Cambridge, MA: Harvard University Press.

Peek, Lori A. 2010. *Behind the Backlash: Muslim Americans after 9/11.* Philadelphia: Temple University Press.

Phillips, Jonathan. 1995. "The Latin East, 1098–1291." In *The Oxford Illustrated History of the Crusades,* edited by Jonathan Riley-Smith. New York: Oxford University Press.

Qureshi, Emran, and Michael A. Sells, eds. 2003. *The New Crusades: Constructing the Muslim Enemy.* New York: Columbia University Press.

Sayyid, S., and AbdoolKarim Vakil, eds. 2010. *Thinking through Islamophobia: Global Perspectives.* New York: Columbia University Press.

Shryock, Andrew, ed. 2010. *Islamophobia/Islamophilia: Beyond the Politics of Enemy and Friend.* Bloomington: Indiana University Press.

RELIGION AND HISTORY IN GENERAL

Asad, Talal. 2003. *Formations of the Secular: Christianity: Islam, Modernity.* Stanford, CA: Stanford University Press.

Butler, Jon. 1990. *Awash in a Sea of Faith: Christianizing the American People.* Cambridge, MA: Harvard University Press.

Chidester, David. 1991. *Salvation and Suicide: An Interpretation of Jim Jones, the Peoples Temple, and Jonestown.* Bloomington: Indiana University Press.

Dinnerstein, Leonard, Roger L. Nichols, and David M. Reimers. 1996. *Natives and Strangers: A Multicultural History of Americans.* New York: Oxford University Press.

Hutson, James H. 1998. *Religion and the Founding of the American Republic.* Washington, DC: Library of Congress.

Jefferson, Thomas. 1914. *Autobiography of Thomas Jefferson, 1743–1790: Together with a Summary of the Chief Events in Jefferson's Life.* Introduction and notes by Paul Leicester Ford. New York: G. P. Putnam's Sons.

Jones, Robert P., Daniel Cox, William A. Galston, and E. J. Dionne Jr. 2011. *What It Means To Be American: Attitudes in an Increasingly Diverse America Ten Years after 9/11.* Governance Studies Program, Brookings Institution and Public Religion Research Institute.

Porterfield, Amanda. 2006. *The Protestant Experience in America.* Westport, CT: Greenwood Press.

Song, Sarah. 2007. *Justice, Gender, and the Politics of Multiculturalism.* New York: Cambridge University Press.

Watts, Pauline Moffitt. 1985. "Prophecy and Discovery: On the Spiritual Origins of Christopher Columbus's 'Enterprise of the Indies,'" *American Historical Review* 90 (February): 73–102.

ROMAN CATHOLICS AND CATHOLICISM

Bisson, Wilfred J. 1989. *Countdown to Violence: The Charlestown Riot of 1834.* New York: Garland.

Boardman, H. A. (1841) 1977. "Is There Any Ground to Apprehend the Extensive and Dangerous Prevalence of Romanism in the United States?" In *Anti-Catholicism in America, 1841–1851: Three Sermons,* ed., iii–vi, 1–69. New York: Arno Press.

Boyarin, Daniel. 2004. *Border Lines: The Partition of Judeo-Christianity.* Philadelphia: University of Pennsylvania Press.

Doyle, David Noel. 2006a. "The Irish in North America, 1776–1845." In *Making the Irish American: History and Heritage of the Irish in the United States,* edited by J. J. Lee and Marion R. Casey, 171–212. New York: New York University Press.

———. 2006b. "The Remaking of Irish America, 1845–1880." In *Making the Irish American: History and Heritage of the Irish in the United States,* edited by J. J. Lee and Marion R. Casey, 213–252. New York: New York University Press.

Duncan, Jason K. 2005. *Citizens or Papists? The Politics of Anti-Catholicism in New York, 1685–1821.* New York: Fordham University Press.

Feldberg, Michael. 1975. *The Philadelphia Riots of 1844: A Study of Ethnic Conflict.* Westport, CT: Greenwood Press.

———. 1980. *The Turbulent Era: Riot and Disorder in Jacksonian America.* New York: Oxford University Press.

Fessenden, Tracy. 2011. *Culture and Redemption: Religion, the Secular, and American Literature.* Princeton, NJ: Princeton University Press.

Franchot, Jenny. 1994. *Roads to Rome: The Antebellum Protestant Encounter with Catholicism.* Berkeley: University of California Press.

Hopkins, John Henry. (1846) 1977. "An Humble but Earnest Address to the Bishops, Clergy, and Laity of the Protestant Episcopal Church in the United States, on the Tolerating among Our Ministry of the Doctrines of the Church of Rome." In *Anti-Catholicism in America, 1841–1851: Three Sermons,* ed., 3–23. New York: Arno Press.

Knobel, Dale T. 2003. "'Celtic Exodus': The Famine Irish, Ethnic Stereotypes, and the Cultivation of American Racial Nationalism." In *Fleeing the Famine: North America and the Irish Refugees, 1845–1851,* edited by Margaret M. Mulrooney, 79–95. Westport, CT: Praeger.

Murray, Nicholas. (1851) 1977. "The Decline of Popery and Its Causes." In *Anti-Catholicism in America, 1841–1851: Three Sermons,* ed., 333–370. New York: Arno Press.

The New-England Primer Improved: Or, an Easy and Pleasant Guide to the Art of Reading. To Which is Added, the Shorter Catechism, as Composed and Agreed upon by the Reverend Assembly of Divines at Westminster. 1823. Amherst: Charles Wells.

The New-England Primer Improved for the More Easy Attaining the True Reading of English. To Which Is Added the Assemblies of Divines and Mr. Cotton's Catechism. (1777) 1883. Albany: Joel Munsell's Sons.

Oates, Mary J. 1988. "'Lowell': An Account of Convent Life in Lowell, Massachusetts, 1852–1890." *New England Quarterly* 61 (1): 101–118.

Ray, Mary Augustina. 1936. *American Opinion of Roman Catholicism in the Eighteenth Century.* New York: Columbia University Press.

Stevens, Abel. 1835. "An Alarm to American Patriots: A Sermon on the Political Tendencies of Popery, Considered in Respect to the Institutions of the United States, Delivered in the Church Street Church, Boston, November 27, 1834. Being the Day of Thanksgiving." 2nd edition. Boston: David H. Ela.

Storrs, Richard Salter. 1901. "The Puritan Scheme of National Growth." In *The New England Society Orations: Addresses Sermons [sic] and Poems Delivered Before the New England Society in the City of New York, 1820–1885,* edited by Cephas Brainerd and Eveline Warner Brainerd, Vol. 2, 326–369. New York: Century.

Tager, Jack. 2001. *Boston Riots: Three Centuries of Social Violence.* Boston: Northeastern University Press.

Trial of John R. Buzzell, the Leader of the Convent Rioters, for Arson and Burglary. 1834. Boston: Lemuel Gulliver.

Tumbleson, Raymond D. 1998. *Catholicism in the English Protestant Imagination: Nationalism, Religion, and Literature, 1660–1745.* Cambridge: Cambridge University Press.

SIOUX, NATIVE AMERICANS, AND WESTWARD EXPANSION

Breen, Louise A. 1999. "Praying with the Enemy: Daniel Gookin, King Philip's War and the Dangers of Intercultural Mediatorship." In *Empire and Others: British Encounters with Indigenous Peoples, 1600–1850,* edited by Martin Daunton and Rick Halpern, 101–122. Philadelphia: University of Pennsylvania Press.

Coates, Lawrence G. 1985. "The Mormons and the Ghost Dance." *Dialogue: A Journal of Mormon Thought* 18 (4): 89–111.

Custer, G. A. 1999. "My Life on the Plains." In *Documents of American Prejudice: An Anthology of Writings on Race from Thomas Jefferson to David Duke,* edited by S. T. Joshi, 250–255. New York: Basic Books.

Daunton, Martin, and Rick Halpern. 1999. "Introduction: British Identities, Indigenous Peoples and the Empire." In *Empire and Others: British Encounters with Indigenous Peoples, 1600–1850,* edited by Martin Daunton and Rick Halpern, 1–18. Philadelphia: University of Pennsylvania Press.

DeMallie, Raymond J. 1982. "The Lakota Ghost Dance: An Ethnohistorical Account." *Pacific Historical Review* 51 (4): 385–405.

———. 1984. "Introduction." In *The Sixth Grandfather: Black Elk's Teachings Given to John G. Neihardt,* edited by Raymond J. DeMallie, 1–74. Lincoln: University of Nebraska Press.

Eastman, Charles A. 1916. *From the Deep Woods to Civilization: Chapters in the Autobiography of an Indian.* Boston: Little, Brown.

Ellet, E. F. 1840. *Rambles about the Country.* Boston: Thomas H. Webb and Company.

Forbes-Boyte, Kari. 1999. "*Fools Crow versus Gullett:* A Critical Analysis of the American Indian Religious Freedom Act." *Antipode* 31 (3): 304–323.

Greenwood, A. B. 1860. *Report on the Commissioner of Indian Affairs, Accompanying the Report of the Secretary of the Interior, for the Year 1859.* Washington, DC: George W. Bowman.

Irwin, Lee. 1997. "Freedom, Law, and Prophecy: A Brief History of Native American Religious Resistance." *American Indian Quarterly* 21 (1): 35–55.

Jenkins, Philip. 2004. *Dream Catchers: How Mainstream America Discovered Native Spirituality.* New York: Oxford University Press.

Jones, W. A. 1902. *Annual Reports of the Secretary of the Interior for the Fiscal Year Ended June 30, 1901. Indian Affairs. Part 1. Report of the Commissioner, and Appendixes.* Washington, DC: Government Printing Office.

Kracht, Benjamin R. 1992. "The Kiowa Ghost Dance, 1894–1916: An Unheralded Revitalization Movement." *Ethnohistory* 39 (4): 452–477.

Mandell, Daniel R. 2010. *King Philip's War: Colonial Expansion, Native Resistance, and the End of Indian Sovereignty.* Baltimore: Johns Hopkins University Press.

Miles, Nelson A. 1892. "Report of Major General Miles." In *Annual Report of the Secretary of War for the Year 1891,* Vol. 1, 132–155. Washington, DC: Government Printing Office.

Mooney, James. (1896) 1991. *The Ghost Dance Religion and the Sioux Outbreak of 1890.* Lincoln: University of Nebraska Press.

Neihardt, John G. 1984. *The Sixth Grandfather: Black Elk's Teachings Given to John G. Neihardt.* Edited by Raymond J. DeMallie. Lincoln: University of Nebraska Press.

———. 2008. *Black Elk Speaks: Being the Life Story of a Holy Man of the Oglala Sioux.* Premier edition. Annotated by Raymond J. DeMallie. Albany: State University of New York Press.

Oberly, John H. 1888. *Fifty-Seventh Annual Report of the Commissioner of Indian Affairs to the Secretary of the Interior.* Washington, DC: Government Printing Office.

Powers, William K. 1977. *Oglala Religion.* Lincoln: University of Nebraska Press.

Prucha, Francis Paul. 2000. *Documents of United States Indian Policy.* 3rd edition. Lincoln: University of Nebraska Press.

Richardson, Heather Cox. 2010. *Wounded Knee: Party Politics and the Road to an American Massacre.* New York: Basic Books.

Riggs, Stephen R. 1869. *Tah-Koo Wah-Kan or, The Gospel Among the Dakotas.* Boston: Congregational Sabbath-School and Publishing Society.

Steltenkamp, Michael F. 1993. *Black Elk: Holy Man of the Oglala.* Norman: University of Oklahoma Press.

Utter, Jack. 1991. *Wounded Knee and the Ghost Dance Tragedy.* Memorial edition. Lake Ann, MI: National Woodlands Publishing Company.

Walker, James R. 1991. *Lakota Belief and Ritual*. Edited by Raymond J. DeMallie and
    Elaine A. Jahner. Lincoln: University of Nebraska Press.
Witkin-New Holy, Alexandra. 2000. "Black Elk and the Spiritual Significance of *Paha
    Sapa* (the Black Hills)." In *The Black Elk Reader*, edited by Clyde Holler, 188–205.
    Syracuse, NY: Syracuse University Press.

Index